Talent Development for
# English
# Language
# Learners
Identifying and Developing Potential

# Talent Development for
# English
# Language
# Learners

## Identifying and Developing Potential

Edited by
**Michael S. Matthews, Ph.D.,**
**& Jaime A. Castellano, Ed.D.**

PRUFROCK PRESS INC.
WACO, TEXAS

Library of Congress Cataloging-in-Publication Data

Talent development for English language learners : identifying and developing potential / Edited by
Michael S. Matthews, Ph.D. ; and Jaime A. Castellano, Ed.D.
    pages cm
  ISBN 978-1-61821-105-7 (pbk.)
  1. English language--Ability testing--Evaluation. 2. Literacy--Ability testing--Evaluation 3.
Language acquisition--Ability testing--Evaluation. 4. Communicative competence. 5. English lan-
guage--Study and teaching--Foreign speakers--Evaluation. 6. Education, Bilingual. I. Matthews,
Michael S., 1968- editor of compilation. II. Castellano, Jaime A. editor of compilation.
  P118.7.T25 2013
  428.0076--dc23
                                    2013023317

Prufrock Press Inc.
P.O. Box 8813
Waco, TX 76714-8813
Phone: (800) 998-2208
Fax: (800) 240-0333
http://www.prufrock.com

# Table of Contents

# Acknowledgments

Many people have contributed to the development of this volume. In addition to acknowledging the strong contributions by the authors of each chapter, we would like to acknowledge the many scholars and classroom teachers on whose work and experience we have based our recommendations. Collaborative effort that draws from and builds upon prior learning is how we all—whether teacher, scholar, administrator, or student—advance the development of talents and interests in ourselves and in others.

Paul Matthews was the mover and shaker behind the initial proposal for this book, but had to step aside when his job responsibilities changed. Fortunately, he was able to contribute an excellent chapter on service learning. Vicki Krugman also contributed to the initial proposal for the book, and she went on to contribute a chapter (with Linda Iza) despite taking her retirement during the early stages of the project.

Jaime Castellano, whom I have known since we presented together in a shared session at the National Association for Gifted Children's annual convention in Atlanta in 2000, has been an invaluable contributor as my co-editor. Thank you Jaime for lending your considerable expertise to this book! It has been a pleasure working on it with you.

Last, but certainly not least, we also would like to acknowledge our editor, Bethany Johnsen, and Prufrock Press in general, for their helpfulness throughout the process and for their willingness to work with us in reaching the book's final form. We hope that the reader finds our perspective useful, and that our suggestions may help more high-ability learners to achieve the potential they carry within.

# Introduction

"We must recognize that beneath the superficial classifications of sex and race the same potentialities exist, recurring generation after generation, only to perish because society has no place for them."
—Margaret Mead

Recent and projected demographic trends point toward an increasingly diverse future for U.S. schools and our society at large. Whether individuals arrive in the U.S. as documented or undocumented, or for temporary or permanent residence, immigration has become a key force in shaping the U.S. population. How we respond to these changes will have immediate repercussions for society in the present moment, and it also will influence both the short- and long-term future of the United States.

Changing demographics bring numerous challenges, but they also present multiple opportunities. We believe that improving education for all students will lead not only to positive long-term outcomes in terms of economic productivity and effective citizenship, but also to a more satisfied populace who understand and are able to meet their own needs for personal growth and for professional and life satisfaction.

Students who are classified as English language learners (ELLs) are one of several populations who traditionally have been underrepresented in programming for academically advanced learners. There is a substantial overlap between poverty and ELL status, and although poverty has larger effects on educational performance and outcomes than almost any other single factor, English language ability also is a key to students' ability to succeed in the United States. Unfortunately, many people who are fluent in only one language (as most U.S. residents are) tend to view proficiency in their majority language as synonymous with intelligence; those who are not yet proficient in English must not be very smart, right? Of course this is a fallacy, but unfortunately these widespread fallacious beliefs often prevent bright learners who are not proficient in English from receiving an education at the advanced level they are capable of mastering.

Although targeted English language instruction can be very effective, evidence suggests that it is more effective when students also have regular interactions with native speakers of English. Because of this, and perhaps also because it is more cost-effective, schools often strive to move ELLs as rapidly as possible into mainstream classrooms for content area instruction. Thus, many students who still are learning English find themselves placed in inclusion settings rather than with a teacher specifically trained in English language acquisition. This too can lead to a loss of potential achievement if the inclusion teacher is not aware of the additional educational needs and learning characteristics of these learners.

Simple solutions to these complex problems do not exist. However, we intend that this book may offer some small steps in the right direction by informing teachers, parents, and school administrators about some of the salient issues related to fostering high achievement among ELLs in inclusive classroom settings.

# Chapter 1

# Advanced Academics, Inclusive Education, and English Language Learners

*Michael S. Matthews*

What do we mean by *academically advanced learners*? How can we determine whether a child's ability is advanced in comparison with others of his or her age or experience? How are our perceptions of a person's academic potential shaped by our observations of the individual's English language ability? Why is it important to provide students with an appropriate academic setting? These questions and many more are relevant to our understanding of how best to educate students whose first language is not English. This opening chapter offers an overview of the terms and ideas that will help you, the reader, to understand the nuanced and multifaceted issues surrounding these important questions.

## Defining the Important Terms

The phrase *academically advanced* suggests that we are talking about students who are ahead of their classmates in one or more academic areas. This is becoming a preferred usage in some settings for several important reasons. Advanced academics is broader than the term *gifted*, which generally indicates those students formally identified under state or local rules who need advanced educational services due to their academic and intellectual differences from the general student population. These rules or definitions can vary widely across schools, and in fact, some states provide no formal definition of giftedness to guide the schools in this area. Additionally, the term gifted carries some negative connotations that are not present to the same degree in the term academically advanced. These negative connotations include the idea that a student "has" or "does not have" ability, when in fact ability falls along a continuum; the idea that "giftedness" is some innate quality that stands alone, rather than being comprised of a combination of ability, perseverance, and hard work; and the idea that students classified as "not gifted" somehow cannot benefit from the enriching educational experiences that schools sometimes offer only to children identified formally to receive gifted programming.

An advanced academics perspective implies that educational services are needed at some times but not at others, whereas giftedness implies a permanent condition regardless of current need. It certainly makes sense that student needs should be met at any given time, but it also seems clear that individual instructional needs will change over time. The peer group plays an important role in establishing need, because the girl who is an advanced learner in one setting actually may be an average learner in another setting with different peers. As a consequence, she would benefit from advanced academic services in the first setting, but she would have her needs met fully by the general curriculum in the second setting.

For all of these reasons, we have chosen to use the term advanced academics rather than gifted in this book whenever possible. We still occasionally will refer to gifted students to indicate those learners formally identified as such under a local- or state-mandated definition of giftedness. For additional background about gifted education, we encourage the reader to consult any of the numerous references we provide (e.g., Harris, Plucker, Rapp, & Martinez, 2009; Mandelman, Tan, Aljughaiman, & Grigorenko, 2010).

The term *English language learner* or ELL is currently preferred for those students who do not speak English as their first or home language, but who are learning English because they attend schools in the United States where English is the primary language of instruction. The federally mandated phrase for labeling these individuals, *LEP* or *limited English proficient*, is frowned upon in many circles because it implicitly considers the lack of English language as a deficit rather than simply a difference that is largely due to factors outside of the student's control; obviously we can't choose our parents. The related terms *ESL*, or *English as a second language*, and *ESOL*, or *English for speakers of other languages*, should be reserved to describe programming that is provided for ELL students, rather than as a description for the students themselves. Schools may have several different classifications within the larger category of ELL, and these may reflect important differences such as the student's oral versus written proficiency, the elapsed time since their most recent English proficiency assessment, or other related details (Matthews & Kirsch, 2011).

The term *inclusion* describes a particular approach to educational programming. The term initially referred to the practice of placing students eligible for special education into the regular education classroom. This can happen for part of the day (*partial inclusion*), with additional support in the classroom and specialized support services outside of the classroom. Partial inclusion turns out to be in many cases more practical than the theoretical ideal of *full inclusion*, which involves placing all students with special needs in the regular classroom for the entire school day; in full inclusion, any needed individualized services are fully integrated into the regular classroom setting, and students with special needs always learn alongside students without disabilities. In a related approach known as *mainstreaming*, students with disabilities are placed in the regular education classroom for specific subjects based on their individual skills and needs. Inclusion is widely used for children with mild or high-incidence disabilities such as dyslexia, and for those with physical (rather than cognitive) disabilities, but it does not work as well for students who have behavior disorders that affect others around them in a negative manner. Mainstreaming is widely used in nonacademic classes such as physical education, art, and music, among others.

Inclusion also has a broader meaning than students with disabilities, in the sense of providing access to academic learning for students from all backgrounds. In international settings, for example, groups of interest may include girls, members of religious or cultural minority groups within a given society, poor children, and other groups traditionally marginalized from receiving equitable access to education.

In this book, we use *inclusive settings* to refer to the education of students whose first or home language is not English within classroom settings that are comprised predominantly of students who are native English speakers. Although researchers have not yet come to a consensus about what instructional models are most effective for ELLs, larger political and social forces have stepped in to dictate the practice of inclusion for these learners as well as for many students with disabilities. What do teachers in such settings need to know when they are faced with a classroom that contains large numbers of native English speakers along with a relatively small number of students who still may be struggling to learn English as their second or even third language?

# Language and Education in the U.S.

We know that relatively few people in the U.S. are bilingual or multilingual compared to the populations in many other European, Asian, or African countries. We know that our world (foreign) language education system has had relatively little success in producing citizens with native or even near-native fluency in a second language, and that students who speak a language other than English face a variety of pressures that native English speakers do not encounter (Hurd, 2008; Shaunessy & Alvarez McHatton, 2008). We know that people who had little access to formal education in their country of origin comprise the bulk of some immigrant populations, whereas other immigrants were highly educated in their home country but their credentials are not recognized in the U.S. (Yoon & Gentry, 2009).

We know that teachers in U.S. schools are predominantly White, female, and middle class. Additionally, in response to political pressures many states have dismantled or greatly weakened schools' ability to deliver effective bilingual education; bilingual programming has been replaced with services designed to move students rapidly toward a very basic level of English proficiency, often in a very short time frame of only 1–3 years. At the end of this process, students are judged to be proficient in English and are placed into inclusive or mainstreamed classrooms for the remainder of their public education, often with little attention to their subsequent achievement (de Jong, 2004).

Likely as a result of all of these factors, the natural inclination of many people in the contemporary U.S. is to equate intelligence (i.e., potential for learning or general ability) with the capacity to communicate in one specific language (English). It should immediately be obvious that this is a fallacious belief. Unfortunately, it has led to widespread undereducation of many students whose needs likely would have been met in the schools had they been native speakers of English. Due to the widespread adoption of the practice of inclusion, it is up to the general education teacher to recognize and meet the needs of a very broad range of students within a single classroom.

Policy guiding the education of high-ability and academically gifted learners is fragmented and inconsistent. Because there is no federal mandate for gifted education, states may choose to define gifted children in whatever manner they wish. Many states provide only a very general framework for this purpose, purposefully leaving the details to be worked out at the local level. This has the advantage of being responsive to local need, but it also has the disadvantage that few local districts have extensive expertise in what research says about what effective identification and programming look like in practice.

Academic programming available to advanced learners often can be spotty as well. At the elementary level, enrichment is often the only programming offered, even though the effectiveness of various forms of acceleration (Colangelo, Assouline, & Gross, 2004) is well established. By high school, Advanced Placement (AP) or International Baccalaureate (IB) programming often is the de facto choice for high-ability learners. Although effective in terms of academics alone, these programs do not systematically address the affective needs of high-ability learners. For students who already have learned English as a second language, IB programming may be the most valuable option because of its internationally focused perspective and the opportunity it presents for students to begin learning an additional world language. These attributes match well with the strengths of students who have grown up being bilingual and bicultural. Indeed, one valuable lesson that transfers from gifted education into advanced academics is the need to focus on students' strengths, rather than solely on the remediation of weaknesses. Both are important, but it is their strengths that ultimately will allow students of all backgrounds to become successful adults.

## Finding High-Ability English Learners

In an inclusion setting, how does high academic ability manifest itself? What should we be looking for to find students learning English who also are capable of benefitting from advanced or more rigorous instruction in the academic content areas of language arts, mathematics, science, and social studies? Once we have found one or more such students, how can we meet their needs without neglecting other learners who may be struggling to reach basic proficiency in the content area?

This is a tricky question, as evidenced by the extensive literature that examines the identification of students for gifted programming. Identifying high ability among native English speakers, a group for whom language-based IQ tests are fairly effective, remains contentious. What do we do when faced with the added complexity of a student who may not be able to express his or her full understanding in English? Fortunately there are a few other angles from which to approach this problem.

The best predictor of academic achievement (i.e., grades) is prior performance on similar tasks. Hence, college admissions rely on high school GPA in addition to standardized testing and letters of recommendation to make admissions decisions. Grades may not be as strong of a predictor for students learning English because a still-developing English proficiency may artificially depress grades, but student performance on extended projects or their ability to convey an understanding in unique or different ways may predict an aptitude for learning in the content area. Strong interest in a subject area may also be a good predictor of the student's ability to benefit from advanced learning opportunities. Although their relationship is complex and not necessarily direct, motivation and ability are interrelated and both likely predict future academic success.

One specific advantage of the practice of inclusion with ELLs is that language acquisition is an extremely social process, and the ability to interact with native speakers of a language leads to deeper and more effective learning. If students learning English are only allowed to interact with other students learning English, they may not learn the new language as well or as rapidly. This offers an interesting contrast to the tenets of gifted education, which suggest that high-ability learners feel constrained when they are forced to work with students of average ability. This is because students identified as gifted often need fewer repetitions to learn new content, so they become bored or unmotivated when material is repeated for other learners; they may be more motivated by grades, causing them to do work in place of work by other group members who are not as concerned about grades; and they may have mastered specific content before it is taught in class.

Some of these concerns of students with gifts and talents, such as the drawbacks of group work, can be addressed by careful consideration to rubrics and other instructional design efforts. Other aspects can be ameliorated through the use of preassessments followed by appropriately differentiated instruction. All of these practices traditionally advocated in gifted education are likely also to be appropriate for advanced academics and for students who are ELLs, but there are additional practices that are specifically beneficial to this latter group of students. Students striving to master academic English are likely to encounter specific barriers that may be in spoken form—such as colloquialisms, speed of delivery, or regional accents—or barriers due to the language itself—such as homophones, words with multiple meanings that depend on their context, or the high level of vocabulary in fields such as science (this also can be challenging for native English speakers, due to the complexity and presence of root words drawn from other languages!).

One of the most widely recommended models for instructing ELLs is known as *sheltered instruction*. Stated briefly, sheltered instruction focuses on the role of language in communication, rather than focusing primarily on grammar. It emphasizes working in mixed-language-ability groups and with hands-on and authentic learning activities, using academic and content-specific vocabulary and developing questioning skills, teaching metacognitive strategies, and incorporating students' background knowledge into instructional activities. The reader may recognize many of these strategies as also belonging to gifted education pedagogy. This should not be too much of a surprise, as both gifted education and second language acquisition are grounded in the individual differences approach (Ardasheva, Tong, & Tretter, 2012) within the broader fields of education and psychology that they inhabit.

## Two Approaches to English Instruction

U.S. schools generally have followed one of two broad approaches to instruction in English for students who are not native English speakers. These are structured English immersion (SEI) and bilingual education. Political rather than educational concerns clearly have been the driving force behind states' decisions about which instructional approach to adopt.

A key difference in these approaches lies in whether or not the student's native language is used in instruction. Instruction in the SEI approach involves efforts to maximize students' exposure to English, and SEI focuses on the use of second language acquisition strategies in the absence of exposure to or formal instruction in the native language. Some evidence for the effectiveness of structured English immersion is drawn from the successful results of French language programs in Canada, although there are clearly differences in the relative status of French in Canada as compared to the status of Spanish or other world languages in the U.S.

Instruction in the SEI approach is characterized by direct instruction in English grammar and usage, with content learning relegated to a secondary role, by grouping of students based on English proficiency levels, and by its relatively short duration, sometimes as little as a single year.

Bilingual programs, in contrast, are based in the idea that academic learning in the student's native language fosters the development of both content knowledge and, with exposure, English proficiency. Thus, bilingual education programs have a shared emphasis on providing academic instruction in the native language, and often they also focus on developing an understanding and appreciation of the cultural heritage that accompanies the non-English language. Other related programs, such as dual-immersion schools (which strive to teach native English speakers a second language, while also instructing native speakers of that language in English), also fall under the rubric of bilingual education. Bilingual education tends to be provided over a greater span of time than SEI, often lasting 3–6 years before students exit the program and adequate second language proficiency is assumed.

## What's Next?

Although this background provides a starting point for many productive discussions, identifying students for advanced programming or suggesting specific activities to do in the classroom are not the central goal of this book. Rather we strive to broaden the reader's perceptions, both in terms of what characteristics to look for in your own practice while seeking to meet the needs of these students, and what opportunities you can provide or point toward that may prove helpful in the development of their talents and interests. To foster discussion, we have developed three case studies (see below) that some chapter authors have built upon to provide examples of what the strategies they discuss might look like in practice. In future chapters the case study examples are presented as sidebars for ease of reading.

# Case Studies

## *Herminda*

Herminda is a first-grader in Ms. Anthem's class. Herminda's family emigrated from Guadalajara, Mexico, 7 years ago, and she and her two younger sisters were all born in the U.S. She lives in a predominantly Latino trailer-park enclave and is taking part in an after-school tutoring program there for 4 days a week this year. Herminda did not attend Pre-K, but entered school as a kindergartner last year speaking only Spanish; however, over the last year, she has learned to read in both English and Spanish. At the beginning of the year, she tested at "Level 5-Bridging" on the WIDA English language proficiency performance descriptors and is not being pulled out for English to Speakers of Other Languages (ESOL) support. She proudly told Ms. Anthem that she helps interpret for her parents, who don't speak English, at the store and the doctor's office, and that she is teaching her sisters some English. Ms. Anthem has noticed that Herminda spends a lot of her free time reading as well as writing stories about her family and friends, using advanced vocabulary and linguistically complex structures, and that she has a strong memory for new words. She especially likes to read about animals.

## *Joaquin*

Joaquin is a seventh-grader whose family moved from El Salvador last year. Before moving, Joaquin was enrolled in sixth grade in San Salvador, and a counselor who knows Spanish says he has excellent conversational and academic skills in that language. Although he is somewhat shy when interacting with teachers and peers, and is sometimes slow at completing assignments because he wants them to be "just right," Joaquin was able to pass his classes with accommodations last year and did especially well in his math class. His reading and listening skills in English tested at "Level 4-Expanding" and his writing and speaking skills at "Level 3-Developing" at the start of this school year; however, apart from one segment of ESOL per day with Ms. Arrieta, all of his courses are mainstreamed. During free time, Joaquin is especially interested in reading books on how things work, and his teachers have noticed that he also draws a lot, with precision and detail.

### *Minh*

Minh and his parents arrived from Vietnam during the summer before this school year started so that his parents could attend graduate school in the U.S. Although he is 16, Minh is being placed in the ninth grade because the school thought it would give him more time to learn English. However, he has completed 10th grade in Vietnam at the Lê Hồng Phong High School for the Gifted, specializing in literature, history, and geography. Although he can read and write in Vietnamese and French, and had some private English tutoring prior to coming to the U.S, he tested at the Beginning level of proficiency in English for reading, writing, listening, and speaking. At his high school, which follows block scheduling, he is being placed into four classes: ESOL I with Mr. Berm; Geometry with Ms. Shelby; Advanced World History with Coach T.; and Physical Education with Coach Doster.

## Structure and Organization of the Book

Now that you have been introduced briefly to some background on the relevant terms and issues, you may wish to look ahead to those chapters that discuss specific issues you find of interest. The remaining eight chapters of this book are organized into sections that broadly address what we know (chapters 1–3), what we can do (chapters 4–6), and taking a broader view (chapters 6–8). Specific chapters address talent development, language development, and writing skills (2); gifted education in cross-cultural perspective (3); moving from deficit-based to strength-based perspectives (4); motivational strategies for students with gifts and talents who are learning English (5); building collaborative partnerships in schools and communities (6); using service learning to build effective policies and procedures (7); and working within the system to build effective policies and procedures (8). In a ninth and final chapter, we sum up the major points of the book and offer our thoughts for the future.

# References

Ardasheva, Y., Tong, S., & Tretter, T. (2012). Validating the English Language Learner Motivation Scale (ELLMS): Pre-college to measure language learning motivational orientations among young ELLs. *Learning and Individual Differences, 22,* 473–483.

Colangelo, N., Assouline, S. G., & Gross, M. U. M. (2004). *A nation deceived: How schools hold back America's brightest students* (Vol. 1). Iowa City: The University of Iowa, The Connie Belin & Jacqueline N. Blank International Center for Gifted Education and Talent Development.

de Jong, E. J. (2004). After exit: Academic achievement patterns of former English Language Learners. *Education Policy Analysis Archives, 12*(50), 1–20. Retrieved from http://epaa.asu.edu/ojs/article/view/205/331

Harris, B., Plucker, J. A., Rapp, K. E., & Martinez, R. S. (2009). Identifying gifted and talented English language learners: A case study. *Journal for the Education of the Gifted, 32,* 368–393.

Hurd, C. A. (2008). Cinco de Mayo, normative Whiteness, and the marginalization of Mexican-descent students. *Anthropology & Education Quarterly, 39,* 293–313. doi:10.1111/j.1548-1492.2008.00023.

Mandelman, S. D., Tan, M., Aljughaiman, A. M., & Grigorenko, E. L. (2010). Intellectual giftedness: Economic, political, cultural, and psychological considerations. *Learning and Individual Differences, 20,* 287–297. doi:10.1016/j.lindif.2010.04.014

Matthews, M. S., & Kirsch, L. (2011). Evaluating gifted identification practice: Aptitude testing and linguistically diverse learners.

*Journal of Applied School Psychology, 27,* 155–180. doi:10.1080/153
77903.2011.565281

Shaunessy, E., & Alvarez McHatton, P. (2008). Language at the
fault lines. *Cultural Studies↔Critical Methodologies, 8,* 325–336.
doi:10.1177/1532708607310803

Yoon, S. Y., & Gentry, M. (2009). Racial and ethnic representation
in gifted programs: Current status of and implications for gifted
Asian American students. *Gifted Child Quarterly, 53,* 121–136. doi:
10.1177/0016986208330564

# Talent Development, Language Development, and Writing Skills

*Jaime A. Castellano & Robert Robertson*

In a school-based context, talent presents itself in multiple ways. Liam is a seventh-grade student on the Navajo Indian Reservation who struggles with the traditionally language-rich and verbally intensive core curriculum in English/language arts, science, and social studies. In math, however, he has demonstrated an aptitude that places him years above grade level. Math comes easily for Liam and it is clearly a talent he possesses.

Jasmine is a scholar athlete, excelling in the classroom and as the point guard of the girls middle school championship basketball team. She is a natural leader as well, having served as a student council officer and volunteering for various school and community sponsored events. Because she is a member of the Navajo tribe, historically recognized as a matriarchal society, identifying and developing her multiple talents opens a pathway to endless opportunities.

In both cases, these learners' talents were recognized and nurtured by caring adults who supported their unique abilities and offered them opportunities to flourish, allowing them to be successful and to feel good about themselves and encouraging them to capitalize on their talents. Development of natural ability, genius, gifts, or aptitude involves the inclusion of significant others whose primary roles are to motivate, counsel, nurture, and guide. This chapter focuses primarily on the academic domain through the lens of gifted education. Within this focus, we address what schools have to offer students to actualize and/or maximize their individual talents, particularly in writing.

## How Do Talent Development and Language Development Intersect?

It is possible for schools to build programming that connects the often disparate program areas of talent development and English for speakers of other languages. Connecting Worlds/Mundos Unidos is an innovative two-way, dual-language immersion gifted and talented magnet program at El Paso ISD in El Paso, TX. The program integrates second language acquisition and gifted and talented strategies and curriculum with goals of achieving high academic excellence and dual-language proficiency in English and Spanish. Students participating in the program develop an awareness of language and its function. Language development in both the first and second language takes place on a daily basis through the implementation of a challenging curriculum enriched with depth and complexity. As students develop or acquire their language through content, they unconsciously and automatically construct the knowledge that is inherent in the context within which each of these languages functions. Students in this program construct their work within two phonological systems, sort out two spelling patterns, and learn to apply the appropriate phonics system for each of the language frameworks (Green, Spivey, Ferris, Bernal, & Izquerido, 2011).

The ability to switch from one language to another—in speaking, reading, and writing—at an accelerated rate, through a cognitively challenging curriculum, reflects gifted behavior. Students build a solid foundation in their primary language through strong concept development and apply this to their emerging language. The use of two languages heightens learning for students. They learn new content and become able to communicate and process information in both languages (Green et al., 2011).

# Developing a Second Language

## *Overview of Language Development*

Language acquisition is the process by which humans acquire the capacity to perceive and comprehend language, as well as to produce and use words to communicate. Research in language development, and specifically in second language acquisition, defines it as a fluid, often creative, and affective process that is inherent in our human make-up and is best developed through "contextual, meaningful processes, practices, and activities that target language use guided by highly qualified and highly effective teachers" (Collier, 1995, p. 23). Language learning, or development, is the result of direct instruction in the rules of language. In language learning, students have conscious knowledge of language. In a typical American classroom, the development of language is most often reserved for the reading, literacy, and English/language arts program areas. However, in recent years language development has become a target of instruction in virtually all content areas, and this is true internationally as well as in the U.S.

According to Whitehurst (1997), the literacy environment of the home accounts for between one eighth and one fifth (12%–18%) of the variation in a child's language ability/development. Hart and Risley (1995) also pointed out that the level of verbal communication, recorded as utterances from parent(s) to child, plays a dramatic role in the language development of the child. Thus, interaction is vital to the language learning process. The language growth and development of school-aged children is manifested in multiple ways—verbally, in writing, through performance-based project learning, and across different genres with different audiences. Can teachers influence the development of language in the students they serve? The unequivocal response is yes, they can. Of course, the greatest amount of progress results when both schools and parent(s) work together.

## The Developmental Trajectory of Second Language Acquisition

ELLs begin learning English in much the same way as they do their first language—by developing oral language skills. Pronunciation is the first thing that young ELLs master. Studies of immigrants who learn a second language upon arrival in a new country show that only the youngest children (up to about age 7 at the age of arrival) achieve native-like or near-native-like pronunciations in their new language (Myers-Scotton, 2006). Morphology and syntax—the patterns of word formations and sentence structure—develop later, as does vocabulary acquisition.

Just as young monolingual English speakers begin to learn their language by listening and repeating what they hear, so do ELLs. The phases of oral language development are well documented and are considered fundamental in building academic language later in the learning process. The first phase of oral language development is often dubbed the silent period, although this is bit of a misnomer, as many ELLs will repeat everything they hear right from the beginning. During this phase, ELLs listen attentively to the speech patterns and vocabulary of English as they process their new language. They may have up to 500 words in their receptive vocabulary but may not yet speak, or they may be repeating everything they hear with little to no understanding of what any of it means. In the second phase, ELLs begin to produce simple one- to two-word phrases and simple sentences that are easily memorized. Their vocabulary grows to around 1,000 words, and they begin to understand more and more of what is being said around them. By phase three of oral language development, ELLs are becoming more confident with their language skills. They are able to speak in full simple sentences and can hold simple conversations with their teacher and classmates. Their vocabulary is now at around 3,000 words. It is at this phase that ELLs can begin to complete basic academic work in school while receiving support from the teacher. The fourth phase of oral language development pushes ELLs into English fluency. They rapidly build their vocabulary and begin to sound more native in their speech. Basic conversational skills are mastered, and their vocabulary is now at more than 6,000 words (Haynes, 2005).

As ELLs move through these phases, they are actively constructing principles for the regularities that they hear in the speech of those around them (Genessee, 1997). Like native English-speaking children, they are making sense of the rules as they learn them. Often they make the same mistakes as English speakers, such as overgeneralizing language rules (e.g., putting regular past tense endings on verbs that are irregular—*goed* instead of went, or *teached* instead of taught—or applying the plural -s to all nouns whether regular or irregular—*foots* for feet).

Building this linguistic and grammatical competency happens at different rates for different individual ELLs, but their progress can be affected by the language rules that they transfer over from their first language. Both positive and negative transfer can occur depending on their depth of knowledge in their first language. For example, native speakers of Spanish often have no problem with the regular plural -s ending of nouns in English because the same rule exists in Spanish. This is an example of positive transfer because it helps the ELL with English. However, they will often struggle with pronouncing words that begin with *sp*, such as *Spanish*, *space*, and *speaker*, by adding an aspirated *eh-* in front of them. *Spanish* becomes *eh-Spanish*, *space* becomes *eh-space*, and *speaker* becomes *eh-speaker*. This is a negative transfer example because it impedes their ability to pronounce these specific English words correctly.

The older the ELL, the more likely it is for both positive and negative transfer from their first language to occur. Younger ELLs often have not had time to internalize their first language to the same extent as older ELLs, and therefore transfer is less likely to occur. Only when both English and the ELLs' first language are developed equally do we find balanced bilingualism.

## *Benefits of Bilingualism*

Balanced bilingualism is defined as a person being functionally bilingual in two languages, meaning that he or she can speak, read, and write both languages with equal proficiency. This type of bilingualism is relatively rare. Most bilinguals have a dominant language, one that they are more comfortable in than the other. For example, many bilinguals grow up in homes where the home language is different from that of the mainstream American society. In the U.S., English is the language of our schools and the one in which individuals have to function in society, while their home language is limited to family members and perhaps neighbors and friends. The depth and knowledge of the home language often becomes limited to the environment in which it is spoken, and English, with time, can become more dominant because it is the language in which they are being educated and the one that they will use in the workplace every day. Unless a conscious effort is made to educate students equally in both their home language as well as English, one language will inevitably become more dominant.

Regardless of how proficient a bilingual person is in his or her two languages, just being bilingual has advantages. Recently researchers have been interested in the study of metalinguistic knowledge, and many conclude that bilingual children may excel in having the mental flexibility associated with this type of knowledge (Myers-Scotton, 2006). Metalinguistic awareness, the understanding of how one's language functions, leads to metalinguistic knowledge. The more a student knows about his first language and how it works, the more he can transfer that knowledge over to other languages he is learning. Studies on bilinguals to measure this transfer have shown that bilinguals demonstrate more "mental agility" than do monolinguals, and their performance is superior in the area of symbolic recognition (Ben-Zeev, 1977; Cromdal, 1999; Galambos & Hakuta, 1988; Peal & Wallace, 1962; Ricciardelli, 1992). Children with a high degree of bilingual language proficiency also are capable of entering into creative processes in divergent and convergent thinking more fully than their monolingual peers (Kessler & Quinn, 1987).

### *The Interface of Creativity and Bilingualism*

The most frequently cited characteristics of creative individuals are precisely the same characteristics evident in successful bilingual individuals (see Table 2.1). In an unpublished manuscript, Castellano (2005) delineated the relationship between creativity and bilingualism.

The intersection between creativity and bilingualism allows for both talent development and language development to occur simultaneously. Creative individuals are risk takers, much like monolingual individuals who are learning a new language, taking risks in written and verbal form. Intrinsically, those moving toward bilingualism feel a need to be precise in their use of the new vocabulary and grammar rules, and they persevere in getting the language "right" in the appropriate context. With continued practice and support, creativity invites curiosity and inquisitiveness, as in the use of slang, idioms, and colloquialisms in verbal discourse and in writing.

The interface between creativity and bilingualism is also expressed through emotion, or affect, and reflects what one is thinking or feeling about events in school or personal life. In the classroom, teachers can support the simultaneous development of bilingualism and biliteracy just as we have seen in the Mundos Unidos/Connecting Worlds dual-language program in El Paso ISD. In the sections to follow, we will strategically focus in the area of writing, a literacy skill that promotes overall language skill, talent, and potential.

# The Importance of Communication, Collaboration, and Collegiality

### *Role of the Home, School, and Community in Fostering Talent Development*

The home, school, and community play an integral part in how a student progresses in his or her talent area. To make meaningful connections beyond the classroom, students should apply their talents

# Table 2.1

*Common Characteristics of Creative and Bilingual Individuals*

| Characteristics of Creative Individuals | Connections to Successful Bilingual Individuals |
|---|---|
| Risk-Taking | Learning a new second language<br>Open to new experiences<br>Ventures forth to a new country |
| Intrinsic Motivation | Needed to persevere<br>Challenge of precise vocabulary and grammar |
| Perseverance | Getting the language right<br>Appropriate context |
| Curiosity and Inquisitiveness | Supports fluent bilingualism<br>Wants to learn more (slang, idioms) |
| Openness | Emotions; depth |

across multiple contexts to demonstrate what they know and are able to do.

Teachers should participate in professional development opportunities designed to enrich and/or accelerate learning through appropriate pacing, complexity, and depth. Teachers also should serve as models for students by applying and modeling advanced knowledge and understanding of how language and talent are developed simultaneously. Schools and districts that offer a continuum of choices that includes gifted education, honors programs, advanced placement, and IB programs provide a platform that allows students to develop their talents through practice on a daily basis.

The role of the family and community is then to showcase student work and accomplishments through print media, social networking, and by serving as sponsors, such as by paying the expenses associated with participating in local, state, and national competitions. This type of collaboration of people and resources, and programs and services, provides fertile ground for students to actualize their potential and to demonstrate how the development of language and talent interact.

## *Collaborative Strategies*

It is generally recognized by today's educational and instructional leaders in the field of gifted education that in order to develop the talent of the students we serve, we must follow a collaborative and collegial approach rooted in clear communication. Developing a "plan of action" is essential, and such a plan should include the setting of personal goals and the outlining of resources and responsibilities for promoting talent growth and development. In addition to collaboration across levels of the educational infrastructure (see Figure 2.1), effective collaboration among parents, teachers, and community services also is vital. Collaborative efforts at both of these levels allow for collegial interactions that keep the best interests of the students in mind. This process requires the explicit assignment of responsibilities across these varied stakeholders. In addition, the students themselves must play an active role in developing the plan of action, regardless of what theory is considered or what model is implemented.

Feldhusen (1996) advocated the following six strategies to aid teachers and others who are in a position to facilitate and promote talent development.

1. Be alert to signs of talent. Point out strengths to the students and parents, and test to verify possible emerging talent.
2. Structure learning activities that will give students the opportunity to demonstrate their talent potential.
3. Use praise to recognize and reinforce signs of talent.
4. Help students who have talent in a particular area to set learning goals in that area.
5. Locate resources in the school and community that can foster the student's talent.
6. Enlist parents in developing and nurturing their children's talents by providing resources and experiences and by encouraging goal-setting behavior.

The ultimate goal of talent recognition and development is to help students understand their own talent strengths and potential, to know

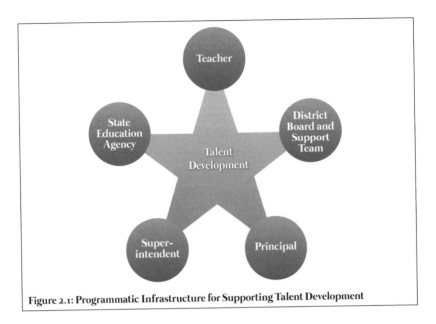

**Figure 2.1: Programmatic Infrastructure for Supporting Talent Development**

how to pursue and engage in talent development activities, and to commit themselves to the development of their talents.

# Developing Talent: Social and Emotional Considerations

As we continue to discuss how talent development is manifested in gifted education programs, with a focus on the academic domain, we would be remiss if we did not, at least briefly, share some research and comment on the simultaneous social and emotional growth and development of talented students. How students learn to handle failure is one important area in which development is crucial to students' long-term academic success.

## *Learning to Handle Failure*

Neihart (2008) wrote that setbacks and defeat are easier to work through if we understand that they are inevitable and prepare for them. Failure is part of our life experience. Keeping students focused on the progress they are making is an important aspect of the mindset of successful learners (see discussion in Chapter 5), and it will establish a foundation from which they can launch an even bigger success. In defeat, we can set the stage for future victories.

Neihart (2008) went on to identify four things we can do to help manage students' disappointments when success proves more elusive than they expected:

1. Remind them that the higher they reach, the more frequently they will experience defeat, disappointment, and rejection. It is part of the process, so expect it.
2. When setbacks occur, go easy on students and give them time. People need time to recover emotionally when they've been defeated.
3. Keep them focused on the big picture. Recovery from disappointment is easier when we remember that the goal (of talent development) is growth and learning.
4. Avoid equating their self-worth with their achievements. They are not their accomplishments.

We also can help students persevere through setbacks by anticipating the obstacles they might encounter and discussing ahead of time how they can respond when these obstacles occur. Different learners will require different types of support, as the following example illustrates.

## *Acceleration for Promoting Talent*

The talent development perspective of gifted education should be the same regardless of the specific program model implemented—the focus is on what is in the best interest of the students served. One highly recognized and accepted strategy that accounts for the academic talent of students is that of content acceleration, often in the form of grade skipping (see also Chapter 5). Acceleration can help meet students' social and emotional needs by providing them with a peer group with whom they can discuss shared interests.

In 2010, the National Work Group on Acceleration, of which I (Castellano) had the privilege to be a member, reported that high-ability students need more academic challenge and more opportunities to develop their talent. Content acceleration provides them with these opportunities. The research support for acceleration that has accumulated over many decades is robust and consistent, and it allows us to conclude confidently that carefully planned acceleration designs are successful in developing the talents of our nation's youth. As a former teacher serving gifted students, an assistant principal and principal supervising such programs, a gifted education program director at the district level, a recognized expert with the state department of education, and now as a sitting superintendent, I have found accelerating students based on their individual talents to be a successful practice and I believe it should be a routine consideration for students who warrant the opportunity.

## *A Personal Narrative*

My (Castellano's) own gifted daughter, Gisell, breezed through high school and graduated in the top 5% of her 2012 graduating class of almost 500 students. She achieved multiple honors and earned an academic scholarship as a Florida Bright Futures Scholar. She is academically talented but has questioned whether she has the ability to do well at the University of Florida, where she would like to major in business administration. My wife and I have been very supportive of her and have routinely encouraged her to do her best, emphasizing that the goal is to successfully complete one semester at a time. We have also encouraged her to seek out new friends and to identify a club or service to join in order to receive social and emotional support. So far, so good; she is adjusting well to her new environment.

Her twin brother, Gabriel, has received similar accolades but decided to stay local and attend Palm Beach State College, where he has been recognized as a President's Scholar and will be part of the Honors College. Unlike Gisell, he is an extrovert, confident, and looking forward to college life. His independence leads me to believe he will adjust quickly and do well. My point here is that the support we provided the twins in anticipation of this new challenge in their lives was, in part, differentiated, taking into account their personalities, strengths, and perceptions they have about themselves and their future. As a parent of gifted and talented children, my hope is that they receive this same differentiated support from their respective institutions of higher education.

# Supporting Biliteracy in the Culturally Responsive Classroom

Successful classrooms and schools are defined by a commitment to a common purpose—the increased academic achievement of all students. Fostering shared beliefs and a sense of community and cooperation promotes continuity among staff and allows them to focus on developing the talent and potential of the students they serve.

## *Four Instructional Strategies to Promote Achievement*

There is general consensus among researchers and scholars in the field of instructional leadership regarding the cement that binds this commitment to talent development in culturally responsive classrooms. This view holds that successful classrooms are defined by four categories of instructional strategies that directly impact student achievement, and thus, individual skill and ability.

The first category addresses the monitoring of progress, balancing individual work with group work, reinforcing effort, and celebrating success. In promoting talent and language development in two languages, teachers must provide the explicit feedback necessary for continuous improvement. The second category speaks to identifying individual goals; for ELLs, this may mean that in the area of writing they will be able to use the mechanics of written language in different genres. For the teacher, this means providing students with clear evaluations of their progress and allowing them time to reflect on their own growth, evaluating themselves in order to compare their own perceptions with those of their teacher.

Category three requires that teachers use engaging, motivating, focused, and culturally responsive instruction in order to help students understand and assimilate content knowledge. The fourth and last category expects that teachers will help students review, practice, and apply content through problem-solving tasks requiring critical thinking, inquiry-based tasks, and decision-making opportunities; of course, these are the same practices that facilitate skill, talent, and potential. When these four research-based practices are effectively applied, the result is not only increased student achievement, but also the development of individual student talent. For ELLs acquiring a new language, these expectations are essential to their success.

## Coaching Tool for Classrooms Supporting Gifted Education

The Coaching Tool for Classrooms Supporting Gifted Education (Table 2.2) was created by a collaborative working group of gifted education experts representing state, district, and school administrators, classroom teachers, and university faculty, and was supported through Project Bright Horizon, funded by the Jacob K. Javits Gifted and Talented Education Grant program through the United States Department of Education and awarded to the Washington Elementary School District located in Phoenix, AZ. It is intended to be a representative reflection of current evidence-based exemplary and promising practices with respect to providing classroom services for culturally and linguistically diverse gifted student populations. It provides a framework for advocating, developing, and maximizing the talent and potential of a unique demographic of students as they demonstrate what they know and are able to do through verbal and written discourse.

The tool is designed to assist classroom teachers to become more effective educators of their culturally and linguistically diverse gifted students—and to help administrators to become more effective instructional leaders in supporting diverse gifted and talented programs on their campuses. To use this coaching tool, a colleague

## Table 2.2

*Coaching Tool for Classrooms Supporting Gifted Education*

"How to create and effectively support an inclusive, culturally-rich gifted education classroom environment that meaningfully respects and honors the diversity of all learners"

This *Coaching Tool for Classrooms Supporting Gifted Education* was created by a collaborative working group of gifted education experts representing state, district, and school administrators, classroom teachers, and university faculty, and was supported through the Washington Elementary School District's Project Bright Horizon Jacob K. Javits Gifted & Talented Education Grant program, and Project REGALOS Title III gifted education grant program. It is intended to be a representative reflection of current evidenced-based exemplary and promising practices with respect to providing classroom services for culturally and linguistically diverse gifted student populations.

Building and district administrators, site coordinators and program coaches may utilize this tool to support their diverse gifted education programs. It may also be used to assist classroom teachers to effectively reflect upon, and inform, their own classroom practices. The primary goal of this tool is to foster and support a culture of high expectations and program standards for diverse gifted education classrooms and to achieve the following outcomes:

| Outcomes for Administrators: | Outcomes for Teachers: | Outcomes for Students and Families: |
| --- | --- | --- |
| • Enable administrators to become more effective instructional leaders to support diverse gifted education programs on their campus<br>• Ensure classrooms are responsive to the unique needs of diverse gifted learners | • Ensure classrooms are responsive to the unique needs of diverse gifted learners<br>• Guide and inform teachers on how to effectively provide curriculum and instruction, and implement assessment practices in a classroom of diverse gifted learners | • Ensure a positive classroom environment that values and honors each student's unique learning style and cultural and linguistic background, and provides opportunities to grow academically, cognitively, socially, and emotionally according to their abilities and talents |

**This tool was not designed or intended for use as a formal program assessment,** but rather as a coaching tool to assist classroom teachers to become more effective educators of their culturally and linguistically diverse gifted learners—and to help administrators to become more effective instructional leaders in supporting diverse gifted education programs on their campuses.

**Table 2.2 Continued.**

*For more information, please contact:*

**Peter C. Laing**
*Project Director*

**Project Bright Horizon**
*Jacob K. Javits Gifted & Talented Education Grant Program*
Washington Elementary School District
4650 West Sweetwater
Glendale, Arizona 85304
Phone: (602) 347-2644
Fax: (602) 346-2683
Email: plaing@wesd.k12.az.us

*Coaching Tool for Classrooms Supporting Gifted Education* Development Team:

**Dr. Jaime Castellano,** Consultant—*Project Bright Horizon, Washington Elementary School District*
**Peter C. Laing,** Project Director—*Project Bright Horizon, Washington Elementary School District*
**Andree Charlson,** Principal—*Washington Elementary School District*
**Barbara Post,** Administrator for Gifted Services—*Washington Elementary School District*
**Jeff Hipskind,** Director of Gifted Education—*Arizona Department of Education*
**Laura Anderson,** Director of Gifted Education—*Paradise Valley Unified School District*
**Dr. Dina Brulles,** Director of Gifted Education—*Glendale Elementary School District*
**Kim Landsdowne,** Director of Gifted Education—*Scottsdale Unified School District*
**Sue Goltz,** Principal—*Madison Elementary School District*
**Heidi Cocco,** Teacher of the Gifted—*Paradise Valley Unified School District*

| Physical Environment | 3: Clear and Convincing Evidence | 2: Somewhat Evident | 1: Not Evident |
|---|---|---|---|
| Flexible organization of classroom space and furniture to create an inviting atmosphere and positive environment that accommodates diverse teaching and learning styles | 3 | 2 | 1 |
| Extensive visuals supporting specific, relevant academic and affective learning and language acquisition objectives (i.e., relevant bulletin boards having a multicultural focus) | 3 | 2 | 1 |
| Learning and language objectives are written in comprehensible student language and clearly displayed in the classroom | 3 | 2 | 1 |
| Student products representative of current language acquisition and content area standards and objectives, and that reflect the use of critical thinking processes, are prominently displayed | 3 | 2 | 1 |
| Integrated use of technology and multimedia resources to authentically facilitate student instruction and enhance learning | 3 | 2 | 1 |

## Table 2.2 Continued.

| Physical Environment | | | 3: Clear and Convincing Evidence | 2: Somewhat Evident | 1: Not Evident |
|---|---|---|---|---|---|
| 3 | 2 | 1 | A literature corner incorporating a variety of interesting, culturally diverse reading materials and resources, addressing a wide range of reading levels and abilities | | |
| 3 | 2 | 1 | A supply center readily accessible to children that incorporates a broad range of diverse user-friendly materials and resources to encourage, engage, and support creative thinking activities | | |

| Classroom Interactions | 3: Clear and Convincing Evidence | 2: Somewhat Evident | 1: Not Evident |
|---|---|---|---|
| **Student to Student** | **Teacher to Student** | **Student to Content** | |

| Student to Student | | | | Teacher to Student | | | | Student to Content | | |
|---|---|---|---|---|---|---|---|---|---|---|
| 3 | 2 | 1 | Mutual respect of cultural and linguistic diversity of peers | 3 | 2 | 1 | Respectful of the cultural and linguistic diversity of all students | 3 | 2 | 1 | Quality student products of appropriate complexity, depth and breadth |
| 3 | 2 | 1 | Respectful of the diverse ability levels of peers | 3 | 2 | 1 | Clear, high expectations of performance and positive reinforcement | 3 | 2 | 1 | Active participation, allows for experimental, hands-on, discovery learning |
| 3 | 2 | 1 | Supportive, positive reinforcement | 3 | 2 | 1 | Encourages divergent, critical and creative thinking | 3 | 2 | 1 | Engages students at the higher levels of Bloom's taxonomy |
| 3 | 2 | 1 | Active cooperative learning groups | 3 | 2 | 1 | Shared inquiry, Socratic and higher-level questioning techniques | 3 | 2 | 1 | Allows for acceleration where appropriate |
| 3 | 2 | 1 | Flexible grouping strategies | 3 | 2 | 1 | Use of guided and informal group discussions | 3 | 2 | 1 | Provides opportunities for independent study, research, and extended learning |
| 3 | 2 | 1 | Active listening to build upon and refine ideas and concepts | 3 | 2 | 1 | Effective use of accountable talk | 3 | 2 | 1 | Use of effective time-management strategies |

**Table 2.2 Continued.**

| Classroom Interactions | 3: Clear and Convincing Evidence | 2: Somewhat Evident | 1: Not Evident |
| --- | --- | --- | --- |
| **Student to Student** | **Teacher to Student** | **Student to Content** | |
| 3 2 1 — Frequent opportunities for academic linguistic interaction, to build and accelerate CALP (*Cognitive Academic Language Proficiency*) | 3 2 1 — Guides and facilitates instruction, allowing for student exploration, discovery, and growth | 3 2 1 — Appropriate use of graphic organizers | |
| 3 2 1 — Opportunities to demonstrate and build leadership and character | 3 2 1 — Engages and informs parents regarding the academic growth of their child | 3 2 1 — Utilizes effective note-taking strategies to independently facilitate their own learning | |
| **Student Metacognition** | | | |
| 3 2 1 — Active sharing, describing, and feedback regarding thinking strategies individual students use to solve problems | 3 2 1 — Models task-specific effective reflective thinking processes and strategies (planning, reflecting, and evaluating) | 3 2 1 — Encourages ongoing self-reflection, evaluation, and feedback on how their thinking strategies impact learning | |

| Curriculum Instruction | 3: Clear and Convincing Evidence | 2: Somewhat Evident | 1: Not Evident |
| --- | --- | --- | --- |
| 3 2 1 | Students are able to see themselves reflected in the curriculum materials used in the classroom | | |
| 3 2 1 | Instructional methods of delivering the curriculum actively integrates strategies that provide for the accelerated development of CALP (*Cognitive Academic Language Proficiency*) | | |
| 3 2 1 | Differentiated according to individual ability and need, allowing for growth, increased depth and breadth and acceleration as appropriate | | |
| 3 2 1 | Incorporates objectives for affective and personal development and growth and exploring heritage culture | | |
| 3 2 1 | Designed to reflect higher levels of Bloom's taxonomy | | |

# Table 2.2 Continued.

| Curriculum Instruction | 3: Clear and Convincing Evidence | 2: Somewhat Evident | 1: Not Evident |
|---|---|---|---|
| Instructional strategies that promote critical and creative thinking, to include flexible grouping, higher level questioning, compacting, tiered assignments, scaffolding, interdisciplinary thematic units, and open-ended projects | 3 | 2 | 1 |

| Assessment Practices | 3: Clear and Convincing Evidence | 2: Somewhat Evident | 1: Not Evident |
|---|---|---|---|
| Performance-based assessment options are available and appropriately utilized | 3 | 2 | 1 |
| Appropriately considers the cultural, ethnic, linguistic, and socioeconomic diversity of the students assessed | 3 | 2 | 1 |
| Assessment practices and options are transparent, with clearly stated teaching objectives and aligned outcomes, and students are aware of the specific expectations and criteria for assessment | 3 | 2 | 1 |
| Students are evaluated and assessed on content knowledge only—*not* on level of language proficiency | 3 | 2 | 1 |
| Flexible and adaptable to diverse learning styles of students, and incorporates both structured (observations, conferences, interviews) and unstructured assessment practices (journals, portfolios, storytelling, games, groups, technology), and allows for self-assessment, peer assessment, and student developed rubrics for assessment | 3 | 2 | 1 |
| Effectively assesses higher-order thinking, critical and creative thinking, and problem solving | 3 | 2 | 1 |
| Assessment data are used to authentically inform instructional practices | 3 | 2 | 1 |
| Effectively builds upon and gauges prior knowledge through the use of frequent preassessment | 3 | 2 | 1 |
| Students are assessed using grade-level standards | 3 | 2 | 1 |
| Assessment practices are used to accommodate and strengthen student's CALP (*Cognitive Academic Language Proficiency*) level | 3 | 2 | 1 |
| Divergent solutions, when substantiated by students, are accepted and supported | 3 | 2 | 1 |
| Parents, as practicable, are informed of assessment results in their heritage language | 3 | 2 | 1 |

*Adapted from:* Coaching Tool for Classrooms Supporting Gifted Education Development Team & Montgomery, W. (2001) Creating Culturally Responsive, Inclusive Classrooms. *Teaching Exceptional Children, 33*(4), 4–9 (teacher, supervisor, or administrator) spends time in a given class-room with the specific intentions of making evidence-based obser-vations in one or two of the four domains (physical environment, classroom interactions, curriculum and instruction, and assessment practices). During an informal postconference, the colleagues engage in reflective discussions specific to the domains observed. The empha-sis is on communication, collaboration, and collegiality.

The coaching tool also helps teachers to effectively reflect upon, and inform, their own classroom practices. Reflection is a powerful strategy in our efforts to promote the talent potential of our most able students from diverse backgrounds. The basic tenet for developing the talent of students is the same. That is, this coaching tool serves as a "how to" in creating and effectively supporting an inclusive, cul-turally rich classroom environment that meaningfully respects and honors the diversity of all learners and that promotes a climate for talent development, including talent in the writing area. The quality or talent of ELLs in the area of writing not only reflects their indi-vidual ability, but also is a general characteristic of gifted behavior: Academically gifted students show advanced potential and achieve-ment in language skills in written form, in comparison to their same age, same-grade classmates.

## Developing the Writing Skills of English Language Learners

ELLs need a focused approach to writing instruction that looks markedly different from that designed for mainstream English speak-ers. According to Robertson (2010), the focus for ELLs needs to be on the following:

- Sentence types versus sentence structures
- Conventions, rather than all six traits that instruction empha-sizes for native speakers of English:
  - ideas
  - organization
  - voice

- ○ word choice
- ○ sentence fluency
- ○ conventions
- varied vocabulary (synonyms) versus basic vocabulary (as long as it is spelled correctly)

The sections that follow explain each of these different areas of focus in effective writing instruction for ELLs.

## Focus: Sentence Types versus Sentence Structures

*Sentence types* refers to declarative, negative, and interrogative sentences. These focus attention on the grammatical structure of English and clearly show the unique conjugation of English verbs using the auxiliary "do." As ELLs learn the verb tenses of English, they often struggle with negative and interrogative constructions due to the fact that the auxiliary verb "do" forms both of these syntactic structures. Most other languages simply add a negative marker to the main verb to make it negative and invert the subject and verb to create interrogatives. ELLs will often transfer this syntactic knowledge from their first language over to English unless they are explicitly taught the unique syntactic structure of English. Here are examples of each sentence type with a common ELL transfer structure from their first language underneath.

> **Declarative:** The boy eats lunch every day.
> The boy eat lunch every day.
> **Negative:** The boy does *not* eat lunch every day.
> The boy *no* eat lunch every day.
> **Interrogative:** Does the boy eat lunch every day?
> Eat boy lunch every day?

Understanding these sentence types helps ELLs frame out the structure of English as they learn the conjugation of English verbs. It gives them a foundation from which to build the more complex sentence structures that they will encounter later. If teachers begin by teaching sentence structures (compound, complex, compound-complex) to ELLs before teaching them the underlying syntax and grammar of English, they are not providing students with the linguistic foundation on which they can build. This is a common mistake made by teachers with little or no background in teaching limited English proficient students. For native English speaking students, the English sentence types—declarative, negative, and interrogative syntax—are innate. Native speakers of English know no other way to form these structures, so they do not need to be taught them explicitly as ELLs do.

Language and grammar texts that are written for K–12 mainstream English speakers generally outline verb tenses and the four sentence structures of the English language—simple, compound, complex, and compound-complex. Examples of each are listed here.

> **Simple:** The boy eats breakfast at school.
> **Compound:** The boy eats breakfast at school, but he eats lunch at home.
> **Complex:** After the boy eats lunch, he goes back to school.
> **Compound-complex:** Even though the boys eats breakfast at school, he does not always like the lunches his mother serves, but he still prefers to eat dinner at home in the evenings. (Nordquist, 2013)

The simple sentence offers a structure in which the relationship is focused on the subject and verb. This basic grammar rule is important for understanding the more complex structures that require a higher level of language sophistication to be able to manipulate and master.

Can ELLs learn to become proficient at all of these sentence structures? Of course they can, but they get there a lot faster if they understand the foundational sentence types of English. The story of Ning (see Sidebar 2.1) illustrates this quite well. By consciously using the instructional strategies described previously, and by monitoring the effectiveness of the school and classroom environments using the coaching tool, many more learners will be able to achieve high degrees of English proficiency, as Ning did. Providing these learners with appropriate strategies and resources will enable them to reach and to keep pace with their high-ability and gifted peers who are monolingual speakers of English.

---

# Sidebar 2.1: Ning

Ning immigrated to the United States from Vietnam at the age of 9. As part of the Hmong minority of Vietnam, he came from a home where formal education had been almost non-existent. He entered school in late August speaking no English, although he was eager to learn. His drive to communicate in a new language led him to use every new word he learned as he tried to talk with his classmates and teacher. Within a month, he was communicating effectively in broken English and we began to work on simple sentences and the three basic sentence types. By Christmas, he had nearly mastered the syntax of all three sentence types. By the end of the school year, Ning sounded like any other American boy his age. He had no accent, could communicate fluently and was able to read and write almost at grade level. He was what today we would call a gifted ELL.

Ning went on to fourth grade able to hold his own academically with his peers with minimal ELL support. He was able to be exited from ELL services later that spring after producing an almost perfect essay utilizing compound and complex sentences. Ning's example shows clearly how appropriate instruction that accounts for the specific instructional needs of high-ability students learning English as a second language can produce tremendous gains in a very short period of time.

---

## *Focus: Instruction on the Conventions Versus on All of the Six Traits*

Although writing time must be focused on form and structure, conventions are the most important area on which instruction for ELLs should concentrate. Conventions include such aspects as achieving subject/verb agreement, punctuating sentences effectively, and spelling words correctly. Without this fundamental knowledge, the more advanced aspects of language use, such as voice and sentence fluency, are far more difficult to achieve. For ELLs, the conventions form the building blocks of accurate writing.

Gifted and high-ability ELLs often can show quick mastery of the conventions and can then move directly into working on the other more advanced traits along with their native English-speaking peers. They may even show excellent writing skills with regard to other traits such as voice and fluency. However, teachers often can observe the linguistic gaps that ELLs have by paying close attention to their use of writing conventions. Of course, both ELLs and non-ELLs who are academically talented may need review lessons on subject/verb agreement and the basics of punctuation and syntax, depending on where they may be falling short.

### *Focus: Varied Vocabulary Versus Basic Vocabulary*

The writing of ELL students often is characterized by repetitious use of basic vocabulary words like "the boy" or "the girl." As these students advance in their understanding of English, so too should their vocabulary. The average native English speaker has anywhere from 10,000 to 20,000 words in his or her vocabulary. The Oxford English Dictionary cites 616,500 entries for English; compare this with 185,000 words for German, 130,000 words for Russian, and roughly 100,000 words for French (Lederer, 1991). In short, the English language has a very rich vocabulary in comparison to other languages. Therefore, ELLs need to be encouraged to expand their English vocabulary by using synonyms of commonly used words. One way to encourage this is through the use of synonym walls in classrooms to show all of the words that can mean the same or be substituted for words like "the boy." These might include, for example, words like "he," "him," "my cousin," etc. As their vocabulary expands, ELLs' writing becomes richer and more descriptive. This expansion is vital, as ELLs will need to keep up with increasing academic writing demands as they progress through school.

With gifted ELLs, vocabulary can build rapidly. They often experiment in their writing with new words that they are learning. These may be spelled phonetically or misspelled entirely, but they give teachers a strong clue that these students are pushing themselves beyond the basics and trying to articulate in their writing a more complex vocabulary. They need to be encouraged to continue this practice and not be penalized for misspelling these more complex words.

Peregoy and Boyle (1997) offered a number of strategies that also promote the writing talent of ELLs. For each of the strategies described below, they recommend at what grade level the practice should begin (see Table 2.3). Culturally and linguistically diverse (ELL) students who demonstrate rapidly developing skill and talent in writing can be introduced to writing strategies recommended for a higher grade, thus differentiating for their individual needs.

- **Author's Circle**: An opportunity for writers to share their papers/work in a small group. The purpose is to get specific feedback from their classmates. Not only does this process provide feedback for the author, but it also encourages writers to assume the role of critical and supportive reader.
- **Buddy Journals**: A written conversation between two students. They involve students in meaningful, self-selected dialogues about issues that concern them.
- **Clustering**: Assists writers in developing vocabulary and preparing for writing. To create a cluster, a student places a key word/theme in the center of a circle and then quickly writes all of the other things that come to mind.
- **Concept Books**: Excellent for beginning writers, concept books focus on and illustrate one concept or idea. Students are then asked to create their own concept book. These books build vocabulary, provide opportunities for productive language use, and create opportunities for successful participation in classroom activities.
- **Dialogue Journals**: Students can continue to write about the same topics and ideas as in personal journals except that now,

# Table 2.3

### Grade Levels at which Writing Strategies may be used with LEP/ELL/ESOL Students

| Strategy | K | 1 | 2 | 3 | 4 | 5 | 6 | 7 | 8 |
|---|---|---|---|---|---|---|---|---|---|
| Author's Circle | | | | • | • | • | • | • | • |
| Buddy Journal | | • | • | • | • | • | • | • | |
| Clustering | • | • | • | • | • | • | • | • | |
| Concept Books | • | • | • | • | | | | | |
| Dialogue Journals | • | • | • | • | • | • | • | • | • |
| Editing Groups | | | | • | • | • | • | • | • |
| I Remember | | | • | • | • | • | • | • | • |
| Life Murals | • | • | • | • | • | • | • | • | • |
| Mapping | | | • | • | • | • | • | • | • |
| Partner Stories | | • | • | • | • | • | • | | • |
| Patterned Poems | • | • | • | • | • | • | | | |
| Peek-A-Boo Books | • | • | | | | | | | |
| Response Groups | | | • | • | • | • | • | • | • |
| Sentence Combining | | | | | • | • | • | • | • |
| Sentence Models | | | | | | • | • | • | • |
| Sentence Shortening | | | | | | • | • | • | • |
| Show & Not Tell | | | • | • | • | • | • | • | • |

*Note.* Adapted from *Reading, writing, and learning in ESL*, by S. F. Peregoy and O. F. Boyle, 1997, p. 213, New York, NY: Longman. Copyright 1997 by Longman Publishing Group.

the teacher will respond to the writing on a regular basis. The purpose of interactive journals is to develop fluency and authentic conversation on paper.

- **Editing Groups**: Forming cooperative editing groups not only promotes better writing, but also provides numerous opportunities for oral discussion within which a great deal of "comprehensible input" is generated, promoting overall language development.
- **I Remember**: The "I remember" activity ties well into literature study because published authors often make use of

their own personal and family memories as the basis for their writing. All students bring rich personal experiences into the classroom. If they are given the opportunity to voice these experiences orally and in writing, you will find they will always have valid topics to write about and plenty to say.

- **Life Murals**: Another activity that provides a scaffold for ELL students is creating life murals. Using murals, students create drawings depicting significant events, people, and places in their lives and then write about them.
- **Mapping**: A map is a visual/spatial representation of a composition or story and can assist students with shaping stories they are writing.
- **Partner Stories**: One activity that promotes second language development between partners is the use of wordless books. Partners use wordless books to tell stories through their pictures only and thus offer a unique opportunity for them to interact with a book. Partners may try labeling pictures and developing a written story.
- **Patterned Poems**: These are sentence-level scaffolds that make use of repeated phrases, refrains, and sometimes rhymes. The predictable patterns allow beginning writers to become immediately involved in a literacy event.
- **Peek-A-Boo Books**: These stories allow young children to be actively involved in a nonthreatening writing activity. In this strategy, the student generates a sentence that the teacher dictates. The student then copies the sentence.
- **Response Groups**: The purpose of response groups is to give writers a chance to try out their writing on a supportive audience, usually of 3–5 people. The intent is to obtain honest constructive feedback. Students will need explicit instruction in how to respond effectively and sensitively.
- **Sentence Combining**: This simply teaches students to combine shorter sentences into longer ones while retaining the meaning. Practice assists students in producing more mature writing.

- **Sentence Shortening**: The opposite of sentence combining, sentence shortening assists students with changing wordy sentences into more concise sentences.
- **Show & Not Tell**: A sentence that tells simply makes a flat generalization. Sentences that show, a concept that is easy to teach to intermediate writers, give specific information to the reader. They make actions specific by illustrating with words in multisensory detail exactly what happened.

## Summary and Conclusion

There is an abundance of research and practice available to classroom teachers regarding how to develop the writing ability of their ELLs. For those ELLs identified as gifted, talented, or high ability, the acquisition of language in verbal and written form occurs at a more accelerated rate. Success in writing will be fostered when teachers and students develop a healthy emotional rapport. Furthermore, creative and intellectual processes such as writing may merge through opportunities that allow for metacognitive reflection, or the ability to understand and verbalize how one thinks. This is especially important for ELLs who have demonstrated talent in writing, as the world in which they live is defined by two languages, two cultures, and a continuum of variables such as talents, norms, and rules (Granada, 2003). By building on student strengths in writing and collaborating across programs and curricula, ELLs are put in a position where they can be successful while being supported and nurtured; all of these ingredients are vital to developing their unique talents and potential.

## Resources

Castellano, J. (2008). Critical issues and best practices in promoting equity and excellence for gifted Hispanic/Latino students. *Gifted Education Communicator, 39*(4), 24 –31.

Feldhusen, J. F. (2001). *Talent development in gifted education.* ERIC EC Digest #E610.

Gagné, F. (1993). Constructs and models pertaining to exceptional human abilities. In K. A. Heller, F. J. Mönks, & H. Pasow (Eds.), *International handbook of research and development of giftedness and talent* (pp. 69–87). New York, NY: Pergamon Press.

Gardner, H. (1983*). Frames of mind: The theory of multiple intelligences.* New York, NY: Basic Books.

Heller, F. J. Mönks, & H. Passow (Eds.), *International handbook of research and development of giftedness and talent* (pp. 69–87). New York, NY: Pergamon Press.

Izquierdo, E. (2001). *Literacy development in two-way dual language education* (Leadership Vol. 2). Glenview, IL: Scott Foresman.

Sternberg, R. J. (1991). Giftedness according to the triarchic theory of human intelligence. In N. Colangelo & G. A. Davis (Eds.), *Handbook of gifted education* (pp. 45–54). Boston, MA: Allyn & Bacon.

# References

Ben-Zeev, S. (1977). The influence of bilingualism on cognitive strategy and cognitive development. *Child Development, 48,* 1009–1018.

Castellano, J. (2005). *The relationship between creativity and bilingualism.* Unpublished manuscript.

Coaching Tool for Classrooms Supporting Gifted Education Development Team, & Montgomery, W. (2001). Creating culturally responsive, inclusive classrooms. *Teaching Exceptional Children, 33*(4), 4–9.

Collier, V. P. (1995). *Promoting academic success for ESL students: Understanding second language acquisition for school.* Jersey City, NJ: NJTESOL-BE.

Cromdal, J. (1999). Childhood bilingualism and metalinguistic skills: Analysis and control in young Swedish-English bilinguals. *Applied Psycholinguistics, 20,* 1–20.

Feldhusen, J. F. (1996). How to identify and develop special talents. *Educational Leadership, 53*(5), 66–69.

Galambos, S., & Hakuta, K. (1988). Subject-specific and task-specific characteristics of metalinguistic awareness in bilingual children. *Applied Psycholinguistics, 9,* 141–162.

Genessee, F. (1997). *Educating second language children.* Cambridge, UK: Cambridge University Press.

Granada, J. (2003). Casting a wider net: Linking bilingual and gifted education. In J. A. Castellano (Ed.), *Special populations in gifted education: Working with diverse gifted learners* (pp. 1–16). Boston, MA: Allyn & Bacon.

Green, F., Spivey, S. P., Ferris, L., Bernal, E. M., & Izquierdo, E. (2011). Our diversity, our treasure: Connecting Worlds/Mundos Unidos gifted and talented dual language immersion program. In J. A. Castellano & A. D. Frazier (Eds.), *Special populations in gifted education: Understanding our most able students from diverse backgrounds* (pp. 287–303). Waco, TX: Prufrock Press.

Hart, B., & Risley, R. (1995). *Meaningful differences in the everyday experience of young American children.* Baltimore, MD: Brooks.

Haynes, J. (2005). *Stages of second language acquisition.* Retrieved from http://www.everythingesl.net/inservices/language_stages.php

Kessler, C., & Quinn, M. E. (1987). Language minority children's linguistic and cognitive creativity. *Journal of Multilingual and Multicultural Development, 8*(1 & 2), 173–186.

Lederer, R. (1991). *The miracle of language.* New York, NY: Pocket Books.

Myers-Scotton, C. (2006). *Multiple voices: An introduction to bilingualism.* Malden, MA: Blackwell.

National Work Group on Acceleration. (2010). Guidelines for developing an academic acceleration policy. *Journal of Advanced Academics, 21,* 180–203.

Neihart, M. (2008). Preparing for high achievement: Managing distractions and setbacks. *Gifted Education Communicator, 39*(4), 9.

Nordquist, R. (2013). *Exercises in identifying sentences by structure: Identifying simple, compound, complex, and compound-complex sentences.* Retrieved from http://grammar.about.com/od/sentence-combining/a/Exercise-In-Identifying-Sentences-By-Structure. htm

Peal, E., & Wallace, L. (1962). The relation of bilingualism and intelligence. *Psychological Monographs, 76*, 1–23.

Peregoy, S. F., & Boyle, O. F. (1997). *Reading, writing, & learning in ESL.* New York, NY: Longman.

Ricciardelli, L. A. (1992). Creativity and bilingualism. *Journal of Creative Behavior, 26*, 242–254.

Robertson, R. (2010, December). *Teaching writing to English language learners.* Paper presented at the Arizona Department of Education's Office of English Language Acquisition Services (OELAS) Conference, Litchfield Park, AZ.

Whitehurst, G. J. (1997). Language processes in context: Language learning in children reared in poverty. In L. B. Adamson & M.A. Romski (Eds.), *Research on communication and language disorders: Contributions to theories of language development* (pp. 233–266). Baltimore, MD: Brooks.

# Chapter 3

# Cross-Cultural Perspectives on Gifted Education

*Bryn Harris*

This chapter provides an overview of the current state of U.S. schools in terms of their demographics, teacher preparation when working with children and families from diverse cultural backgrounds, and best practices for teaching and intervening with these students. In addition, the chapter explores gifted education programming and practices in other countries. This content is imperative for school professionals, because they must understand the cultures of origin of students and their families in order to provide optimal learning environments that will maximize student potential.

## Current Demographics

The demographics of the U.S. population are rapidly changing, especially among school-aged children. The U.S. population has more than doubled since 1950, to 308.7 million in the 2010 Census, with greatly increased racial and ethnic diversity (Shrestha & Heisler, 2011). In the decade between 2000 and 2010, 15 states saw their non-Hispanic White populations decline (these states were California,

Illinois, Iowa, Kansas, Louisiana, Maryland, Massachusetts, Michigan, Mississippi, New Jersey, New York, Ohio, Pennsylvania, and Rhode Island). During this same time period, Black populations declined in just two states (Alaska and Hawaii), while Hispanic and Asian populations grew in every state. In the same decade, the Hispanic population grew by 43%, the Asian population by 43%, and the Black population by 12.3%; however, the non-Hispanic White population grew by only 4.9%. Among all foreign-born U.S. residents in 2009, 53% were born in Latin America, 27% in Asia, 13% in Europe, and 7% in other regions of the world (Center for Public Education, 2012).

One of the greatest challenges educators face is the shifting demographic landscape of today's student population. If current immigration trends continue, data from the 2010 Census forecast that culturally and linguistically diverse populations will be the majority by 2023 (Frey, 2011). Using 2005 figures, the Population Reference Bureau estimated that about 45% of children younger than 5 were minorities, implying that more diverse students will enter U.S. schools than ever before. More specifically, with regard to ELLs, in the period between 1997–1998 and 2008–2009, enrollment in public schools increased by 51%, from 3.5 million to 5.3 million (National Clearinghouse for English Language Acquisition, 2011). In fact, the most rapidly growing student group in this country is the ELL population (Kindler, 2002), and in particular first-generation (i.e., U.S.-born) children of Spanish-speaking immigrant parents (Fry & González, 2008).

These statistics highlight many important points for school professionals in the U.S. First, educators need to be aware of and prepared for these demographic changes. Secondly, school districts need to review data, policies, and practices to ensure that children of diverse cultural backgrounds are receiving educational services that best meet their needs. Lastly, in regard to gifted education practices, educators using traditional U.S. approaches and supports will need to be aware that these traditional practices may or may not be culturally relevant to culturally diverse families. Greater understanding and awareness of cultural differences and similarities will be needed to promote effective gifted education programs in the United States.

# Teacher Preparation When Working With Diverse Students

Although the demographics of students in schools are rapidly changing, there have not been corresponding changes within the teaching force. The racial composition of teachers remains largely White; numerous reports have identified the severe underrepresentation of teachers of color. Furthermore, limited focus is directed to preparing teachers for the radical demographic transformation in the United States (Ford, Moore, & Milner, 2005). More than ever, it is important for teachers to become adequately prepared to meet the needs of their culturally and linguistically diverse students.

In a recent study, more than one in three teachers reported very little or no training regarding strategies to assist ELL students (Frankenberg & Siegel-Hawley, 2008). In recent years preservice teacher education programs have devoted their efforts to improving multicultural competencies. However, this emphasis still tends to be minimal, varies by program, and includes extremely limited evaluation of both promises and challenges. Furthermore, the types of in-service trainings that occur within the teaching profession depend highly on geographic location and school district type, which suggests that the effectiveness of this training may vary widely across settings (Frankenberg & Siegel-Hawley, 2008). Thus, teachers, especially those who have not received formal training in recent years, are less likely to be prepared to work with diverse populations. The potential impact of limited or ineffective teacher preparation on diverse students within their classrooms is large.

One of the biggest influences this can have is on identifying and retaining diverse students in gifted education programs, because these depend on the teacher's practices and likelihood of recognizing or nominating students for these programs. Teachers must have knowledge, understanding, and awareness of the culture of their students to promote appropriate recognition of their talents (Ford, Moore, & Milner, 2005). Many teacher biases have been reported in the literature, including linguistic bias, communication style bias, and cognitive style bias (Briggs, Reis, & Sullivan, 2008), indicating that there are many ways in which teachers may unintentionally reduce the probability that diverse students receive access to gifted or advanced academic programming. Ford, Moore, & Milner (2005) stated, "Teachers must delve into what it means to have a culture, and how culture emerges in their own as well as their students' judgments and decisions in a particular learning context" (p.X). Classroom teachers should practice systemic, routine ways of looking at each child holistically and ecologically for cultural differences that may impact their educational and social contexts, as well as for looking for high-ability learners at potential and at promise. Although many teachers in the U.S. are aware of gifted programming laws, policies, and practices for their own districts, states, and national organizations, this knowledge may not be as comprehensive as needed when working with diverse children and their families. Cultural differences in prior experiences with educational and mental health systems, in attitudes toward ability and disability, in awareness of gifted programming in the United States, and with regard to advocacy and the role of parents and teachers may influence underrepresentation of various cultural groups in gifted programming.

# Underrepresentation of Diverse Cultural Groups in Gifted Education

The underrepresentation of diverse populations in gifted education has been acknowledged for decades; despite this, the representation of these students in gifted programs generally has remained very low. Reports such as *Mind the (Other) Gap! The Growing Excellence Gap in K–12 Education* by Plucker, Burroughs, and Song (2010) and the *2010–2011 State of the States in Gifted Education* by the National Association for Gifted Children and the Council of State Directors for Programs of the Gifted (2011) have highlighted the underrepresentation of specific populations as well as the need for more systematic monitoring efforts. Currently, because states collect different types of data on these populations (or do not collect data on gifted learners at all!), it can be incredibly difficult to aggregate data regarding practices that are effective and those that may not be. Thus, obtaining current and accurate data regarding the underrepresentation of diverse cultural groups in gifted education is challenging.

Past research gives us some insight into this phenomenon. Plummer (1995) estimated that culturally and linguistically diverse students are "underrepresented by 30% to 70% in national gifted programs and overrepresented by 40% to 50% in special education programs" (p. 289). A 1997 study using data from the National Educational Longitudinal Study (NELS) found that some ethnic groups are significantly less likely than their White counterparts to be involved in gifted programming (Resnick & Goodman, 1997). The study found that 17.6% of Asian students, 6.7% of Hispanic students, and 2.1% of Native American students were involved in gifted programming, compared with 9% of White students (Resnick & Goodman, 1997). In addition, although the rate at which some ethnic groups (e.g., American Indian/Alaskan Native) are identified for gifted programming has increased, there has not been a corresponding rise for Hispanic students over the past three decades (Donovan & Cross, 2002).

Even though some cultural and language ability groups are underrepresented in gifted programming, the benefits of gifted programming have been well documented for all students. Support for gifted programming increased in the 1980s and 1990s in part due to the release of *A Nation at Risk* (National Commission on Excellence in Education, 1983). The authors of this report emphasized the need for gifted programming in all school districts, stating, "We must demand the best effort and performance from all students, whether they are gifted or less able, affluent or disadvantaged, whether destined for college, the farm, or industry" (National Commission on Excellence in Education, 1983, p. 24). Similarly, during the past two decades the Jacob Javits grants from the U.S. Department of Education have aimed at reducing inequality in gifted programming and developing more equitable referral and identification procedures for underrepresented groups. Although the potential of these initiatives is high, in most districts, little change in the presence of diverse students, particularly ethnically and linguistically diverse ones, has occurred in gifted programming.

So far I have not defined important terms such as *culture;* instead I have offered an overview of the current situation and of some of the salient issues. In the following sections of this chapter, I provide an overview of cultural influences that are relevant to gifted education programming and I offer some specific strategies for working with students from diverse cultural backgrounds.

## *Cultural Variations Within Gifted Education Programming*

**Defining culture.** Terms such as *intelligence* and *giftedness* are difficult to define, and so is culture. The term culture incorporates abstract and concrete components that are highly complex (Ford, Moore, & Milner, 2005). One definition frames culture as those "patterns or traditions, beliefs, values, norms, and meanings that are shared in varying degrees by interacting members of a community" (Ting-Toomey, 1999, p.10). Another way to view culture is as a set of meanings or information that is nongenetically transmitted from person to person or within a population and that continues across generations. All cultural material is socially transmitted, and in general, the ideas, behaviors, and traditions passed on from generation to generation within a culture are resistant to change over time. There are many other definitions and philosophies regarding culture that are outside of the purview of this article. For a more thorough understanding of culture within gifted education, please refer to Ford, Moore, and Milner (2005).

**Cultural challenges within gifted education.** Some scholars have proposed that ignorance of different traditions, beliefs, values, and norms (i.e., culture) may contribute to unintentional clashes among people or groups (Ford, Harris, Tyson, & Frazier, 2002). Such clashes may have unintentional ramifications for educational attainment, home-school collaboration, and other educational factors. Historically, many people believed that immigrants had cultural deficits (as opposed to differences), and that assimilation was the only option for entering U.S. society as a productive citizen. Immigrants were viewed as inferior because they did not share or possess the beliefs and values that people in the United States generally acknowledged and respected. In the past, attempts to acculturate immigrants have included practices such as restriction of use of their native language and placing students in groups or tracks in public schools based on immigrant status (Briggs & Reis, 2003). Over the last few decades, efforts have been made to improve the immigrant experience and to value cultural beliefs and contributions in the classroom; however, there remains substantial room for progress in this regard.

The cultural differences that students bring into the classroom should be valued and encouraged, yet some of these differences might be reducing access for learners who could benefit from gifted programming. Educators may hold different expectations of gifted behaviors than the students do, thus making students ineligible for advanced academic programming despite their high ability. In the next section of this chapter, I offer an overview of some immigrant cultural groups and the role of gifted education in their respective countries. It is important to note that this list of cultural groups is limited; I have focused on the country of origin, but it is important to note that there are many other varied and overlapping categories of learner (e.g., by poverty level, gender, etc.) that should also be considered. Lastly, the reader should not assume from these groupings that all children and families from a particular country share beliefs and understanding about gifted education. Educators should work with each child and family on an individual basis and learn about their own unique values, beliefs, and experiences with gifted education and with education in general.

**Selection process for inclusion.** There has been extremely limited information about gifted education and programming in other countries despite numerous recommendations to pursue this research (Milner, 2000). Furthermore, the types of countries that are researched might not be of the most value or impact to teachers in the United States. This is because the research conducted on these countries does not match the immigration trends within the United States. Thus, the immigrant children and families that U.S. educators are most likely to encounter are only rarely described in the U.S. gifted education literature.

Table 3.1 lists the most common countries of origin for the U.S. immigrant population, whose gifted education practices are described in the following sections of this chapter. These countries were determined by analyzing rates of immigration as cited by the U.S. Department of Homeland Security (Hoefer, Rytina, & Baker, 2012; Monger & Yankay, 2012). Two main groups were selected, those immigrants who were granted legal permanent residency status and those who are unauthorized immigrants. Thus, all people who obtained legal permanent residency status and those who were unauthorized immigrants living in the U.S. during 2011 were counted; the most common countries of origin for these persons were selected for inclusion. Thus, I selected Mexico, China, India, the Philippines, the Dominican Republic, El Salvador, Guatemala, and Honduras to be included in this analysis. I attempted to collect information on three main areas, although some countries were more limited in scope than others due to insufficient data. The main areas that will be described for each country are the legal requirements for gifted education, the conceptualization of giftedness, and gifted programming.

## *Background by Country*

**Mexico.** Particular attention should be given to the Mexican population in the United States. Mexico was the leading country for unauthorized immigrants living in the United States in 2011. There were 6.8 million unauthorized immigrants from Mexico living in the United States during 2011, representing 59% of the unauthorized population. As of 2008, 12.7 million Mexican immigrants lived in the U.S., which is 17 times the number in 1970. People from Mexico constitute the largest population of immigrants in the United States from a single country, with about 11% of people born in Mexico currently living in the United States.

Mexican populations are younger on average than both other immigrant populations and the U.S.-born population (Pew Hispanic Center, 2009). Because their greatest growth is occurring in young populations, the Mexican American population will have a direct impact on the U.S. school system in many ways and will continue to

## Table 3.1

### Information on Countries Included in Analysis

| Country | Type of Residency | Percentage* | Source |
|---|---|---|---|
| Mexico | Legal Permanent | 14 | (Monger & Yankay, 2012) |
| China | Legal Permanent | 8.2 | (Monger & Yankay, 2012) |
| India | Legal Permanent | 6.5 | (Monger & Yankay, 2012) |
| Phillipines | Legal Permanent | 5.4 | (Monger & Yankay, 2012) |
| Dominican Rebublic | Legal Permanent | 4.3 | (Monger & Yankay, 2012) |
| Mexico | Unauthorized | 59 | (Hoefer et al., 2012) |
| El Salvador | Unauthorized | 6 | (Hoefer et al., 2012) |
| Guatemala | Unauthorized | 5 | (Hoefer et al., 2012) |
| Honduras | Unauthorized | 3 | (Hoefer et al., 2012) |
| China | Unauthorized | 2 | (Hoefer et al., 2012) |

*Percentage refers to the percentage of the total legal permanent resident population or the total unauthorized population as of 2011.

do so for the foreseeable future. Although school staff should be culturally and linguistically responsive to all students, particular attention is warranted for the Mexican population due to its current size and projected growth.

**Legal requirements for gifted education in Mexico.** Gifted education and programming are relatively recent additions to educational programming in Mexico. The beginnings of gifted education were rooted in private schools and special programs and organizations that arose in the 1980s. Thus, for much of its history, middle and upper class socioeconomic groups were more likely to access these programs. During the 1980s and 1990s, various programs were established as stand-alone offerings in the public schools, although there was limited consistency and evaluation of these programs nationally. In the 2000s, the Secretariat of Public Education (SEP), responsible for public education in Mexico, established a few programs across the country geared at providing enrichment for gifted students. These programs were not supported throughout the entire country and were used mainly for research and evaluation purposes. Furthermore, they occurred in more urban areas with populations that tended to be in middle or upper class socioeconomic groups. The SEP became more purposeful regarding creating gifted education programming for the entire country and providing teacher training for these populations in the mid-2000s. The first law regarding gifted education, Article 41, has had the most impact on the education of high-ability learners; it was enacted in 2008 and enforced beginning in June of 2010. It states that special education is directed toward individuals with disabilities (permanent or transitory) as well as for those with "gifted skills" (or "aptitudes sobresalientes"; Harris & Sanchez-Lizardi, 2012).

Gifted services in Mexico have a short history, especially within public schools. Depending on when parents immigrated to the United States, they may or may not have been exposed to these educational initiatives and requirements. Furthermore, the fact that gifted programming existed first in private school settings might have facilitated an unjust view of gifted education, particularly because most immigrants from Mexico in the U.S. have come from lower income backgrounds and therefore would have been more likely to attend public schooling (Pew Hispanic Center, 2009). Educational attainment among the general population in Mexico is relatively low, with only about two thirds of students completing the basic level of education (9 years); the average educational attainment among the Mexican population aged 15 or older is just 7.9 years (Santibañez, Vernez, & Razquin, 2005), so many immigrant parents from Mexico would have had relatively little exposure to education before coming to the U.S.

**The conceptualization of giftedness in Mexico.** The conceptualization of giftedness in Mexico is different than the United States federal definition. The Intervention Model (Secretaría de Educación Pública, 2006), which is the SEP's plan for gifted education programming, reports that high-ability learners are those who stand out, qualitatively or quantitatively, in the social and educational environment in one or more of the following areas: science-technology, social-humanistic, artistic, and in physical activities such as sports. These students have above average natural abilities in one or more of the following areas: intellectual, creative, socioemotional, artistic, and psychomotor. Readers should note that this conceptualization has many similarities to the U.S. Government's Marland Report definition (Marland, 1972). Having above-average intelligence is an important factor, but it is not enough to be considered gifted. In addition to the student's above-average cognitive ability, other factors must also be present, such as having personal characteristics like motivation, interest, and a positive self-concept, and having quality environmental factors related to family, community, and education. The child must have ability, personal characteristics, and environmental factors that contribute to giftedness, because it is thought that the lack of any one of those factors cannot be compensated by the others. Thus within the Intervention Model it is understood that giftedness and talent can only develop through the successful interchange of individual and social factors, and that the social context conditions human behavior and therefore is incredibly important for future success (Harris & Sanchez-Lizardi, 2012).

**Gifted programming in Mexico.** Although there are guidelines for gifted services in Mexico provided by the SEP, the implementation of these services varies widely. For example, the SEP guidelines recommend using multiple practices that teachers in the United States may be familiar with (i.e., Renzulli's Enrichment Triad Model). The SEP encourages educators to provide gifted programming in the general education classroom through differentiated instruction. The suggested models also encourage the use of curricular enrichment opportunities that capitalize on existing resources in the school, classroom, and community. There is a strong emphasis on social skill development and acquiring prosocial skills; for this reason it is advantageous for programming in Mexico to be offered in an inclusive environment with a diverse array of students. Pull-out or self-contained gifted programs are not discussed in the SEP recommended practices for gifted programming. Therefore, parents from Mexico may not desire this type of gifted program (which is relatively common in U.S. schools), as it may separate their child from some peer groups and therefore limit the child's opportunities for social development (Harris & Sanchez-Lizardi, 2012). Additionally, parent organizations such as the PTA are conspicuously absent from the public education landscape in Mexico, where the government and the teacher's union are the primary stakeholders (Santibañez et al., 2005); thus, parents' experience with and expectations for parental involvement in the schools may differ.

It is important to note that there are no academic studies of specific gifted education programs in Mexico. Therefore, how the SEP requirements for gifted services are being implemented is not fully known. In rural areas, it is likely that students and educators have minimal services and knowledge regarding gifted programming. Therefore, where a child has lived in Mexico and what type of school he or she attended will be a strong factor in his or her access and opportunity to participate in gifted education (Harris & Sanchez-Lizardi, 2012).

## *China*

**Legal requirements for gifted education in China.** The People's Republic of China began promoting gifted education within the public school system in 1978 after the formation of a special national planning group. Since this time, elementary, middle (which includes high school in China), and university programs have been developed for high-ability students (Yewchuk, 1992). Many experimental programs were developed in the 1980s, although over time these programs have diminished at the university level. Gifted programs within the elementary and middle school level have increased over the past few decades and recently a gifted preschool experimental program was created (Phillipson et al., 2009). I was unable to find any information regarding the Chinese legal mandates regarding gifted education.

**The conceptualization of giftedness in China.** Chinese educators are trained to search and find qualities of giftedness within all of their students. They look for students who may fit any of these characteristics: high achievers, highly motivated, good memory (especially metamemory), quick thinking, and high intelligence. However, intelligence alone is not considered a sufficient determinant of giftedness. The definition also includes much more emphasis on environment and perseverance over heredity (Phillipson et al., 2009; Yewchuk, 1992) than is common in U.S. definitions. Thus, a child who perseveres on tasks and spends a substantial amount of time studying may demonstrate gifted abilities. More recently, researchers in China have begun to explore creativity as a potential aspect of giftedness. Other recent research has pointed to nonintellectual factors relating to giftedness. For example, one study found that the self-concept of gifted students in China was lower than that of a control group of nongifted individuals (Shi, Li, & Zhang, 2008). Based on this line of research, researchers are currently looking at the mental health of children in gifted programs in China (Phillipson et al., 2009).

**Gifted programming in China.** China funds gifted education through public institutions. These programs exist through a system of "key" schools that receive different funding—often more funding—than traditional public schools. These stand-alone "key" schools often specialize in certain areas (i.e., foreign languages), and students must apply and be admitted through a highly selective process (Yewchuk, 1992). In terms of the programming that occurs within these schools, China utilizes many of the techniques that professionals in the United States may be familiar with. For example, acceleration, enrichment, afterschool programs, and grade skipping are popular practices (Phillipson et al., 2009).

## India

**Legal requirements for gifted education in India.** According to the Indian Constitution Article 21A, primary school is free to all children ages 6–14. Although legally this is the case, there continue to be large segments of the population that are eligible to receive education yet are not receiving it (Weinberg, 1997). The National Policy on Education of 1986 was the first policy in India to specifically mention gifted and talented or high-ability learners. This policy focuses on providing children with opportunities regardless of their demographic and social background. The policy states that children with special talents should be provided with opportunities to learn at a faster pace and should be provided with good, quality education (Government of India, 1986). Based on this policy, residential schools, called Jawahar Navodaya Vidyalaya (JNV), were created with the aim of providing a similar education for learners in rural and urban areas and for those unable to pay for education. Thus, a social justice focus is apparent within this policy. There are currently 595 of these schools, one in each Indian district (Navodaya Vidyalaya Samiti, 2012).

The Navodaya Vidyalaya Samiti (NVS) is the federal agency that oversees the JNV schools. They utilize a system to ensure the inclusion of rural students, Adivasi students (ancestry from indigenous tribes), Dalit students (also referred to as scheduled castes and previously referred to as untouchables), female students, and students with disabilities. A total of 75% of the seats are reserved for rural children. Allocations are further divided such that a minimum of 33% of the seats are reserved for girls; a minimum of 15% of the seats are reserved for Dalit; a minimum of 7.5% of the seats are reserved for Adivasi; and a minimum of 3% of the seats are reserved for students who are twice-exceptional (Wright, 2008; Navodaya Vidyalaya Samiti, 2008).

**The conceptualization of giftedness in India.** Many researchers describe the Indian education system as being qualitatively different from the system used during the ancient period and from that following the British colonization. In ancient texts, excellence is believed to be the combination of knowledge, positive attitudes, and deep and meditative thinking. During the colonial period, this definition was challenged partially because there was no testable way to assess for giftedness. Increasing emphasis was placed on Western concepts of giftedness, and advanced academic achievement was considered the most definitive aspect of giftedness. Today, advanced academic achievement continues as the main (and some say the only) criterion for giftedness. An emphasis on Western values of giftedness and programming remains in India. Furthermore, this definition of giftedness varies greatly in India depending on the social class of people. For example, one measure of giftedness found in middle to upper class groups is admittance and attendance to top-ranked schools of higher education in other countries (Raina & Srivastava, 2000).

**Gifted programming in India.** Most classrooms in India offer one-size-fits-all classroom pedagogies that may not be appropriate for the needs of high-ability children. Some researchers have found that within regular classroom settings, teachers are unprepared to nurture talent or potential and thus these classrooms provide a discouraging environment for high-ability children (Yasmeen, Raghupathi, Nehru, & Chatterjee, 1999). Thus, many professionals in India advocate for gifted children attending the JNV schools that are specifically designed for the needs of high-ability children.

Within JNV schools, there is a holistic model in which students are exposed to academic development as well as character formation, development of social responsibility, and viewing the individual as part of a society (National Academy for Gifted and Talented Youth, 2005; Wright, 2008). These schools are coeducational, residential schools where people of all backgrounds are encouraged to learn and develop their full potential together. The JNV philosophy of education is as follows:

(i) To provide good quality modern education including a strong component of culture, inculcation of values, awareness of the environment, adventure activities, and physical education to the talented children predominantly from rural areas.

(ii) To ensure that students attain a reasonable level of competency in three languages.

(iii) To promote national integration through migration of students from Hindi to non-Hindi speaking States and vice versa.

(iv) To serve in each district as focal point for improvement of quality of school in general through sharing of experiences and facilities. (Navodaya Vidyalaya Samiti, 2012, para. 2)

In terms of educational programming strategies, the emphasis is on enrichment. The curriculum follows the mandated curriculum provided by the department of education of India and is not accelerated. It is common for the JNV schools to include enrichment opportunities such as multimedia and web technology, physical education, music and dance, and entrepreneurship (National Academy for Gifted and Talented Youth, 2005).

## The Philippines

**Legal requirements for gifted education in the Philippines.** Article XIV, Sec. 11 of the 1987 Constitution stated for the first time that it is the "responsibility of the State to provide scholarships, grant-in-aids, and other forms of incentives to deserving science students, researchers, scientists, investigators, technologists, and specially-gifted students." The goal of this requirement was to create an educational environment for Filipino people to thrive, to develop additional areas of expertise (especially in science and mathematics), and benefit the nation as a whole. Unfortunately, this Article has not always been recognized across the country, and services were and continue to be scarce in many areas (Republic of the Philippines, House Bill 812, 2011).

A special act entitled the Science and Technology Scholarship Act of 1994 identified the needs and desires for the country to develop more advancements in these areas. Students within the top 5% of their educational classes are provided scholarships and special programming in science and mathematics through this act, in addition to advanced teacher training and research and development funds to improve educational contexts in these areas. In 2011, a bill was proposed and passed the Fifteenth Congress that provides more financial support for Article XIV. This bill mandates that educational entities or centers:

a. Identify the gifted Filipino children and science-oriented youth at the earliest age possible;

b. Establish a Center for the identification and nurturance of Filipino gifted children and science-oriented youth;

c. Provide scholarship grants and other forms of assistance for identified Filipino gifted children and science-oriented youth;

d. Provide funds for research and development, curriculum development, training for parents, teachers and other personnel and the necessary infrastructure to carry out the objectives and programs in nurturing of the identified Filipino gifted children and science-oriented youth;

e. Provide incentives to government institutions and the private sector that will participate in the implementation of this Act; and

f. Establish and maintain linkages with national and international institutions involved in progress on giftedness. (Republic of the Philippines, House Bill 812, 2011)

**The conceptualization of giftedness in the Philippines.** As with many other ethnic groups, there has been limited research on the conceptualization of giftedness within the Filipino culture. A thesis by Baldo (1987) is the most comprehensive to date, yet should be cautiously considered because it was written decades ago. Baldo stated that the Filipino culture has strong religious components and there is a belief that the high-ability child is a gift from God. The high-ability child is often called "blessed" as well as "genius," "intelligent," and a "fast learner." In other respects, and more recently, the beliefs surrounding the causes of giftedness are similar among Filipinos and Western societies. They believe that inborn talents inherited from parents are the primary reason for giftedness (Garces-Bacsal, 2011). Additional researchers have looked at other aspects of giftedness within the Filipino culture and found that those exhibiting higher motivation are more likely to be identified as gifted (Ingham & Price, 1993). Interestingly, the Philippine Center for Gifted Education states current research projects on its website. A study on the conceptualization of giftedness within the Philippines is currently stated as "ongoing" (Philippine Center for Gifted Education, 2012).

Within Article XIV, giftedness is defined the following way. Gifted children are those who have

at least above average general intellectual ability and who have demonstrated superior achievement and/or potential abilities in any the following areas:
a. Verbal Linguistic
b. Logical Mathematic
c. Body Kinesthetic
d. Visual Spatial

    e.   Musical Rhythmic

    f.   Leadership Ability (Section 4.1).

Science-oriented youth are defined as those who have

> demonstrated at least average abilities in science and mathematics and superior ability in the following areas:
> a.   Intellectual ability and
> b.   Logical mathematical ability (Section 4.2).

**Gifted programming in the Philippines.** Although there are legal mandates regarding gifted education programming in the Philippines, I was unable to find research surrounding the educational practices currently taking place for Filipino children identified as gifted. According to Article XIV, a Center for Gifted Children and Science-Oriented Youth was established where many activities take place, such as identification of giftedness, trainings for teachers and parents, scholarships, accreditation, and research and development. However, no information about these activities could be located online or in print. In addition, no information on educational programming for high-ability children within the public school system could be found. The Philippine Center for Gifted Education lists many enrichment activities that are sponsored by the organization, including summer and weekend programs, mentoring, workshops, and counseling and assessment activities for high-ability learners and their families (Philippine Center for Gifted Education, 2012). Thus, the manner in which Article XIV is realized within the Philippines is not clearly understood.

## *The Dominican Republic*

**Legal requirements for gifted education in the Dominican Republic.** The history of education within the Dominican Republic, as with many countries, mirrors religious and political events. Catholic influences on the education system were omnipresent for many decades. Although public education has been available to children since 1844 following independence from Haiti, private schools have become more and more popular and available since this time. These private schools are often run through the Catholic Church. When possible, parents sent their children to private schools because of their distrust of the public school system. This has led to decreased attendance rates in the public schools. The Dominican Republic formally responded to this issue by creating the Plan Decenal in 1997, which included a new educational curriculum and plan for improving public education. However, after more than a decade and the improvement of some of the public school conditions, everyone who can afford it continues to go to private school (Mendoza, 2007). In 2003, the country had around 2,000 private schools (Secretaria de Estado de Educación, 2003) with 20% of children enrolled in them. However, private schools are more popular in urban areas. For example, in the city of Santo Domingo, private schools enroll more than 50% of primary education students, and 72% of all schools are private (Mendoza, 2007).

This information regarding public and private schools is reported because there are extreme differences in services and programming. Public schools in the Dominican Republic have been long ridiculed among the general population for not providing appropriate services for students and for serving those who are from lower socioeconomic classes. Thus, there are segregation and social justice issues within the country, especially within the education system. In 1997, the country combined parts of the prior (1966) education law into a new general law of education. For the first time, gifted students were noted by stating their universal right to an education that is "appropriate and free of cost, including those who are gifted, physically impaired, learning disabled and who, as such must receive special education" (General Law of Education, 1997; II.4.m). No other mention of gifted education is found within the general law of education. No other research could be located regarding the conceptualization of giftedness within the Dominican Republic.

**Gifted programming in the Dominican Republic.** Due to the discrepancies between the public and private school systems in the

Dominican Republic, programming for high-ability learners in these settings is highly variable. I was unable to find information on specific programming models within these systems, learning only that private schools typically have more opportunities for enrichment and special programming that *may* be more beneficial for high-ability learners. No information on public school gifted programming was found. In the literature, no articles exclusively about giftedness within the Dominican Republic were found, although many articles written by U.S.-based researchers included participants who are immigrants from the Dominican Republic in their samples. Thus, it is clear that more study is needed in this area.

## *El Salvador*

Minimal information about gifted education in El Salvador was located. Multiple terms for gifted and talented were searched on various Salvadorean websites and using literature searchers in both the Spanish and English languages. Special education law was found; however, it does not include gifted and talented populations (Ministerio de Educación de El Salvador, 2004). No specific information about gifted programs or services within the public school system was found. Mitchell and Williams (1987) stated that El Salvador was contacted for their study of gifted education in the world community, and that the country reported that it did not have gifted programming at that time. Although this was more than two decades ago, no more current information could be located.

## *Guatemala*

**Legal requirements for gifted education in Guatemala**. Article 74 of the Guatemalan Constitution states, "Citizens have the right and obligation to receive initial education, pre-school, primary, and basic education, within the age limits established by the law. The education is free. The State shall provide for and promote scholarships and educational credits." However, this law is not enforced. Many problems within the Guatemalan education system have been reported over the years. For example, the country has extremely low literacy rates. The overall national illiteracy rate is 52%, increasing to 85% in some rural areas (United States Department of Labor, 2012). In addition, although the law states that students have a right to receive special education services (including gifted education) if they are deemed eligible, many eligible students do not receive services. One study found that 85%–96% of students eligible for special education services in Guatemala are not receiving them (Rodriguez, Espinosa de Gaitan, & Luterbach, 2008).

The Ministry of Education (Ministerio de Educación) of Guatemala amended the special education law in 2011. Gifted education is placed under special education law in Guatemala, although it is unclear how long this has been the case. For gifted education programming, current Guatemalan law states that stand-alone Educational Centers Specialized in the Gifted Population ("Centros educativos especializados en atención de población superdotada") be formed (Minesterio de Educación, 2011b). Prior to the establishment of these centers, much of the focus of gifted education centered on the establishment of Guatemalan requirements for scholarships. For more than 50 years, Guatemalan children have been eligible to receive scholarships to attend university programs if deemed eligible. Most are for youth between the ages of 12 and 18 years (Ministerio de Educación, 2011a).

**The conceptualization of giftedness in Guatemala.** Within the special education law of Guatemala, giftedness is called superdotacion and is defined the following way:

> Aptitudes, abilities, and capacities that people with significantly superior intelligence possess over those who are considered (cognitively) normal, who are defined as talented people in one or more areas; cognitive, sports, music, emotion, spiritual, verbal, motor or math abilities, among others. (Ministerio de Educación, 2011b)

In a training document for teachers working with special education students written by the Guatemalan Ministry of Education, giftedness is also defined as "People with significantly superior intelligence that manifests as a score higher than 130 points." Although the type of score is not specifically stated, it can be inferred to be an IQ score of higher than 130 points. In addition, the guide states that children who are gifted may learn faster than other children, need an enriched curriculum, and may require more information than their classmates. Giftedness is believed to be transferred through genes, but also affected by the environment in which the child expresses his or her exceptional abilities (Ministerio de Educación, 2006).

**Gifted programming in Guatemala.** As stated earlier, gifted programming began in Guatemala in the form of scholarship programs for youth with advanced abilities. These scholarships were either for early entrance (or entrance in general) to university programs, or to attend enrichment activities typically provided at university settings. These scholarships, which began more than 50 years ago, continue to be legally and financially supported by the Ministry of Education. It is not clear when the Educational Centers Specializing in the Attention of the Gifted Population were started, although they currently are written into special education law in Guatemala. These stand-alone centers typically are not affiliated with traditional public schools. Programming within the Centers is mostly related to curriculum enrichment and the development of abilities that are specific to the needs of the individual. In addition, programs within the Centers are supposed to be based on developmental need and interest, but not necessarily on age level (Minesterio de Educación, 2011b). No information could be found on the number of Centers in Guatemala or regarding the students served in these Centers.

The Guatemalan organization Asociación Por Alumno Talentoso y Superdotado (The Association for Gifted and Talented Students), APATS, was founded in 1990 by a group of teachers, psychologists, psychiatrists, and parents. The goal of this organization is to aid in the identification of and programming for students with gifts and/or talents. The organization believes that gifted children should be provided with an individualized curriculum and services to match their needs. They also stress the importance of focusing on the social and emotional needs of this population (Aguilar & Recinos, 1996). Current information about this organization or its endeavors proved elusive.

In 1992, one of the large public universities in Guatemala, Universidad del Valle, began a program offering services to assist in identifying gifted and talented children. These services continue to this day. This university also had the first program of its kind to offer scholarships to gifted students to attend the university (Alencar & Blumen, 1993). Today, many programs for high-ability learners are run through this university, and multiple professionals (including professors) from this institution are active within the field of gifted education in Guatemala.

Lastly, it is important to mention that the Guatemalan Ministry of Education has produced recommendations for teachers regarding strategies for teaching gifted children. Some of these techniques are listed below; however, the reader is encouraged to view this resource for a more thourough understanding of recommended practices when working with gifted children in Guatemala. (Ministerio de Educación, 2006)

1. Create a dynamic intellectual environment so that students are not bored.
2. Honor flexibility in activities and schedules.
3. Make gifted children feel accepted.
4. Encourage group work with classmates.
5. Stimulate creativity within the classroom.

## *Honduras*

Minimal information about gifted education in Honduras was located. Multiple terms for gifted and talented were searched on various Honduran websites, along with Spanish and English language searches of the academic literature. Special education law was found; however, it does not mention gifted and talented or high-ability populations (Secretaria de Educacion de Honduras, 2012). In addition, no information about gifted programs within the public school system was found. An article by Mitchell and Williams (1987) stated that the country of Honduras was contacted for their study and reported that they did not have gifted programming at that time. Although this was more than two decades ago, no more recent information could be found regarding any subsequent changes.

## Diverse Cultural Perspectives on Giftedness: What Do These Mean for Educators?

Educators who are working with students from diverse cultures should understand the prior learning experiences of these learners and the educational systems in their culture of origin. This understanding will positively impact home-school collaboration, student engagement in the classroom, and matching needs to appropriate educational services. Analysis also suggests several specific implications for educators, as follows.

**Legal requirements for gifted education.** Legislated requirements vary dramatically by country, and in some countries they are legally enforced while in others they are not. A few countries do not appear to have gifted education in their educational laws at all, suggesting that conceptualizations of giftedness and programming for giftedness may be extremely limited or unknown. It also is important for teachers and schools to be aware that because the legal definitions of giftedness in other countries vary widely, a child who qualifies for services in his or her country of origin might not qualify in the U.S., and vice versa.

**Conceptualization of giftedness.** Within the countries profiled in this chapter, the conceptualization of giftedness differs from the United States federal definition. This has several implications for educators. For example, families who are aware of gifted education in their country of origin might not define giftedness the same way as educators in the United States and thus might not be speaking a common language around this topic. Other families might not appear to be advocates for their children regarding entering gifted education, when in actuality they simply might not know what to advocate for. In addition, the characteristics that are considered signs of giftedness are diverse among these profiled countries. For example, some countries cite social skills as being one of the most important aspects of giftedness. Parents in these countries might not desire pull-out or stand-alone gifted programs in which their children would be separated from typical peers. Other countries may focus on science and math or other academic achievement measures as strong signs of giftedness, which may reflect larger educational trends or political considerations, but local schools in the U.S. may emphasize different priorities for gifted or high-ability youth.

**Gifted programming.** As in the United States, the types of gifted programming that are legally mandated or mentioned in policy documents might not actually be occurring in some settings. Limited information regarding current gifted programming practices was found within many of these countries. It is clear that programming for gifted and high-ability learners varies dramatically by country, location (i.e., urban, rural), and population (i.e., socioeconomic class). The child's location in relation to these categories might be one of the most salient factors influencing access to gifted programming. It is also important to note that some countries focus on scholarships and programming geared toward older children, and thus the age at which children initially become eligible for gifted services may vary widely across countries.

Many countries do report gifted education practices that are similar to those familiar to many educators within the U.S. For example, enrichment and acceleration were cited as recommended practices within multiple countries. However, in most other countries the concept of gifted programming is a recent phenomenon, and thus the amount of training and experience that educators have with these services is likely limited. Furthermore, the parents of children within U.S. school systems might not have been exposed to these educational initiatives and gifted programs when they attended school and will likely be unfamiliar with these programs and services.

# Strategies for Improving the Educational Outcomes of Diverse High-Ability Students

In addition to understanding diverse cultural perspectives on gift-edness, there are also some promising practices within the U.S. that may promote the increased participation of culturally diverse groups in gifted education. Briggs, Reis, and Sullivan (2008) provided one of the most comprehensive reviews of these practices to date. Through their study evaluating practices and characteristics of gifted programs that increased participation of culturally, linguistically, and ethnically diverse students (CLED), these researchers found three key features that increased participation. These features include the recognition by district faculty and staff that there is an underrepresentation problem, a strong awareness of the relationship between cultural impact and academic performance, and the presence of program-level support to help educators make changes. Programs that were more successful with CLED students were those that addressed changing district demographics, made efforts to change to a strengths-based model, incorporated cultural traditions into the learning process, and worked to increase parental and community involvement in gifted education. The overarching goal among all successful programs was that they hoped to include and serve more diverse students in gifted education (Briggs et al., 2008). When districts or schools create this goal, more conversations and subsequent systematic changes will take place that will benefit all children within the district. The following sections provide educators with some additional strategies to enhance teaching supports and build relationships with culturally diverse students and their families.

## *Encourage Home–School Collaboration*

When working with diverse children and families, home-school collaboration arguably is the most important component to provid-ing an appropriate and culturally responsive educational experience. When a new family enters the school (regardless of cultural background), the school should spend time learning about the child, his or her family, and the family's educational aspirations. For culturally diverse children and their families, this is all the more important because they are likely to be less familiar with the culture of U.S. schooling than native U.S. families are. Educators should reach out to learn more about the family's culture of origin, their goals for their child's education, and their preferences regarding their involvement in the educational process. Culturally diverse children and their families should be encouraged to share past educational experiences, and educators should value and respect such shared knowledge.

Information should be disseminated regularly regarding the school's practices, including those related to the gifted education program. Sessions specifically about gifted education programming should be provided to parents, with materials translated into the native language and interpreters present. Information should also be disseminated via school newsletters, parent organizations, parent liaisons, and community groups. For more detailed information about increasing home-school collaboration, readers are encouraged to review Waterman and Harry's (2008) brief, *Building Collaboration Between Schools and Parents of English Language Learners: Transcending Barriers, Creating Opportunities,* as well as the numerous resources on the Center for Applied Linguistics website such as Short and Boyson's (2012) report, *Helping Newcomer Students Succeed in Secondary Schools and Beyond.*

## *Integrate Global Perspectives*

As demonstrated in the earlier review of various countries and their gifted education policies and practices, there is extreme diversity in how giftedness is conceptualized and promoted in public school systems in different countries. The U.S. definition of giftedness may or may not match prior experiences of the various groups educators work with. This is an exciting era, as more and more diverse learners are enrolling in U.S. public school systems. This diversity should be valued and respected. Although students will need to meet U.S. definitions of giftedness to be eligible for services, educators also need to be aware that children might exhibit different characteristics of giftedness than those traditionally valued in the U.S. Therefore, educators should learn what characteristics are promoted and valued within their students' culture(s) of origin, should value and promote those characteristics as well, and should consciously be on the lookout for culturally diverse students who demonstrate promise for exhibiting traditional gifted characteristics based on the U.S. definition.

## *Increase Professional Development*

School staff, and administrators in particular, have the opportunity to advocate for additional and more focused professional development training. Such training can occur via formal in-services, regular staff meetings, communications with staff, or support for attending external professional development opportunities (i.e., conferences, workshops). These opportunities should be woven into traditional school tasks and should not be seen as "add-ons." Topics appropriate for professional development may include creating culturally responsive classrooms, working with diverse families and communities, addressing the underrepresentation of diverse cultural groups in gifted education, and conducting self-awareness/improvement activities (Ford, Moore, & Milner, 2005).

There sometimes is a false assumption that educators who have entered the field recently will possess additional understanding and awareness regarding diversity topics. Some educators have received one or more classes related to this content, but the degree to which it has been woven into actual field experiences is likely limited. Furthermore, it is likely that educators have not taken adequate time to analyze their own personal experiences and biases when working with diverse students and families. When teachers examine cultural differences and environmental contexts, then student performance, expectations, and understanding are increased (Briggs & Reis, 2003; Frasier & Passow, 1994).

## *Practice Self-Reflection*

One of the most important tasks for educators to engage in on a regular and continual basis is self-reflection. It is not only the understanding, but also the acceptance of cultural differences that are the important aspects of self-reflection. Teachers need to come to the realization that students and families have the right to maintain their own culture and beliefs (Briggs & Reis, 2003), but this understanding cannot be externally imposed. Sometimes reaching this realization can be challenging for educators who have conflicting views, or who may not believe that a specific family's views are the most beneficial for their child's education. Educators should routinely and consistently evaluate their own beliefs by thinking critically about their own views. Self-reflection can encourage educators to recognize their own biases and to consider how these might influence teaching practices and relationships with students and their families (Ford & Trotman, 2001).

Ford and Trotman (2001) provided a list of questions to aid in self-reflection. Readers are encouraged to think about these questions on a routine basis. Having discussions with other educators about these questions is also beneficial for self-discovery.

1.  How do I feel about working with students who are different from me? What stereotypes, biases, and fears do I hold about minority students? How do they hinder teaching and learning?
2.  What aspects of my teaching and classroom practices (for example, my instructional style or reward system) hinder minority student achievement and identity?
3.  How are the expectations that I hold of minority children different from those of White children?
4.  How much time and effort (in my curriculum, instruction, and assessments) am I willing to devote to teaching about diverse groups and multicultural education?
5.  How much time and effort am I willing to commit to learning about my diverse students? (Ford & Trotman, 2001, p. 236).

## *Examine Educational Practices*

Educators' strategies when working with diverse children should differ in a variety of ways from those they usually use. One strategy involves encouraging students to utilize their own backgrounds, interests, and learning styles within assignments (Sleeter, 1990). Ford and Trotman (2001) have suggested various characteristics of a culturally responsive classroom, including a focus on equity pedagogy, a perception that knowledge is subjective, a holistic teaching philosophy, a communal "we-us-our" philosophy, a respect for the student's primary language(s), and the use of culturally congruent instructional practices. Educators should resist the temptation to focus on culture solely through holidays or celebration-of-culture weeks, which continue to be common in schools despite substantial research discrediting their effectiveness (Banks, 1993).

Ford, Moore, and Harmon (2005) have created a framework to effectively integrate multicultural content into all subject areas. Readers should consult this article to improve their own integration of multicultural practices. The authors warned that educators cannot provide an effective multicultural curriculum for culturally diverse students unless they themselves are culturally competent. Importantly, Ford and Trotman (2001) emphasized that a "culturally responsive teacher need not become an expert on every culture" (p. 239). In fact, because cultures change with time, one never can become an expert on a particular culture, but instead must continue to learn and grow. In addition, it is more important that teachers are interested in learning more about the particular individual and his or her family, rather than focusing on generalizing his or her experiences to others who share a similar cultural heritage. Being culturally responsive is about entering into individualized relationships with children and families that are built on understanding and respect.

Although it falls outside of the purview of this chapter, the reader should consider reviewing resources such as the National Center for Culturally Responsive Educational Systems' (2006) Practitioner Brief, *Becoming Culturally Responsive Educators: Rethinking Teacher*

*Education Pedagogy* for additional guidance regarding becoming a more culturally responsive teacher.

## Advocate for a Diverse Staff

The value of a diverse school staff cannot be overstated. Having diverse staff members can be valuable for *all* students, not only those who are culturally or linguistically diverse learners. For example, teachers and other education professionals who are themselves from diverse backgrounds can serve as mentors, role models, and cultural translators for students (Ford, Moore, & Milner, 2005). The under-representation of diverse staff members has been acknowledged for many years; yet, despite their value, few formal programs have been successful in remedying this issue. For more information on this topic, the reader should consider reading Achinstein, Ogawa, Sexton, and Freitas's (2010) review of 70 programs aimed at retaining teachers of color. Some practices have been shown to be effective (such as pathway programs and alternative education programs); however, many barriers continue to exist and this remains a complex issue.

## Utilize Resources

There are many existing resources that educators can use to improve their cultural responsiveness when working with diverse high-ability learners. First, it is important that educators are utilizing the resources within their district. For example, collaboration with school staff is vital yet is often overlooked as a place to begin. Educators should reach out to ESL teachers, parent liaisons, school psychologists, and other school staff members who have experiences and expertise in working with culturally diverse students. Furthermore, when educators of the gifted collaborate with others in the school or district, they become more visible and valuable to the school and community. In addition, educators should consider collaborating with community resources such as local mental health agencies, faith-based organizations, and other organizations that provide services to culturally diverse residents of the community. Of course, all educators should draw upon the expertise of parents whenever possible.

Educators should also be familiar with professional resources designed to assist teachers and schools in working with culturally diverse and high-ability learners. Many areas have a local or state gifted association, and this can be a highly valuable resource for educators and also for parents when explaining gifted services. In addition, there are multiple national and international professional organizations that educators can utilize. These include the World Council for Gifted and Talented Children, the National Association for Multicultural Education, the National Association for Gifted Children (and specifically its Special Population Network), the Council for Exceptional Children (and its Diversity Division), and state gifted associations. State gifted associations in particular may have local experts on their boards, or may bring in relevant speakers to their conferences if requested.

## *Be an Advocate*

Lastly, while being an educator can be a demanding job on its own, there is an additional role that should be promoted and valued and that is advocacy work. One straightforward way to advocate for your students is by being a part of a professional organization aimed at improving services for culturally diverse high-ability learners. In addition, teachers and parents alike may consider pursuing advocacy at the legislative level by writing letters to their elected representatives or by serving on legislative task forces. Arguably, the most important type of advocacy work that can be done is on the individual and family levels, by searching for gifts and talents within culturally diverse populations, advocating for entrance into the appropriate programming for these students, and fostering access to appropriate opportunities for talent development in the broader community. If appropriate programming does not exist in your school or district, or if there is room to improve existing services (and there always is!), educators should advocate for improvement by serving on leadership teams or other relevant committees or task forces.

# Conclusions

The demographics of the U.S. are changing rapidly and educators must be prepared for the additional challenges these changes will bring. School professionals have an obligation to learn about the prior educational experiences of the students they serve. This chapter has provided an overview of legislative support, gifted services, and attitudes about giftedness from the eight diverse countries with the largest immigrant populations in the United States. The information provided in this chapter should ultimately be used when discussing educational programming with parents, evaluating discrepancies between services in school districts and other countries, and improving transitions between programs in these countries and the United States. Educators should understand that the conceptualization of giftedness, and thus the services provided, are culturally manifested in each family's country of origin. Multiple strategies for improving the educational experiences of culturally diverse children and their families have been suggested. Although preparation is one aspect, educators must also be culturally aware, sensitive, and responsive in order to become more effective and more competent in meeting the needs of each student in our schools.

---

"If the voices of students of color, in this case gifted students, are valued, then teachers, counselors and administrators will listen to them, respect them, and address their needs." (Ford, Moore, & Harmon, 2005, p. 137)

---

To help you generalize the importance of a cross-cultural perspective on gifted education, consider asking yourself the following questions:

1. What types of cultural groups exist within your school and district? What type of data are you collecting on these groups? Are the data adequate? If not, what additional data do you need to collect?

2.  What surprised you or interested you the most when reviewing laws, conceptualizations, and programming of high-ability learners in other countries? How will you integrate this knowledge into your daily practice?
3.  Once placed in gifted programming in your school/district, are students from all cultural groups succeeding in the program? Are they succeeding in numbers proportionate to other populations within the school/district? Are these students remaining in gifted programming in numbers proportionate to other populations within the school/district? For those students who have left gifted programming, what reasons do they (and their parents) give for this decision?
4.  What strategies am I currently employing to improve my educational practices with diverse children who may be high-ability learners? What strategies from this chapter could I implement this month? This year?

# Notes

Many of the resources collected for this chapter were in Spanish. The author is fluent in English and Spanish and would like to note that that translation processes between Spanish and English were conducted by her. For all Spanish-language documents used (the author's second language), the author conducted back-translation to ensure that their intended message was conveyed in the resulting English translation.

# References

Achinstein, B., Ogawa, R., Sexton, D., & Freitas, C. (2010). Retaining teachers of color: A pressing problem and a potential strategy for "hard-to-staff" schools. *Review of Educational Research, 80*(1), 71–107.

Aguilar, G., & Recinos, L. (1996). Historia y estado actual de la psicologa en Guatemala. *Revista Latinoamericana de Psicologa, 28*(2), 197–232.

Alencar, E. M. L., & Blumen, S. (1993). Programs and practices for identifying and nurturing giftedness and talent in Central and South America. In K. A. Heller, F. J. Monks, & A. H. Passow (Eds.), *International handbook of research and development of giftedness and talent.* Oxford: Pergamon Press Ltd.

Baldo, T. (1987). *Toward a conceptualization of giftedness in the Philippine context* (Unpublished master's thesis). University of the Philippines, Diliman Quezon City, Phillipines.

Banks, J. (1993). Multicultural education: Development, dimensions, and challenges. *Phi Delta Kappan, 75*(1), 22–28.

Briggs, C. J., & Reis, S. M. (2003). An introduction to the topic of cultural diversity and giftedness. In C. A. Tomlinson, D. H. Ford, S. M. Reis, C. J. Briggs, & C. A. Strickland (Eds.), *In search of the dream: Designing schools and classrooms that work for high potential students from diverse cultural backgrounds* (pp. 5–32). Washington, DC: The National Association for Gifted Children and Storrs, CT: The National Research Center on the Gifted and Talented.

Briggs, G., Reis, S., & Sullivan, E. (2008). A national view of promising practices and programs for culturally, linguistically, and ethnically diverse gifted and talented students. *Gifted Child Quarterly, 52*(2), 131–145.

Center for Public Education (2012). *The United States of education: The changing demographics of the United States and their schools.* Retrieved from the Center for Public Education website: http://www.centerforpubliceducation.org

Donovan, M., & Cross, C. (Eds.). (2002). *Minority students in special and gifted education.* Washington, DC: National Academy Press.

Ford, D. Y., Moore III, J. L., & Harmon, D. A. (2005). Integrating multicultural education and gifted education: A curricular framework. *Theory Into Practice, 44*(2), 125–137.

Ford, D., Moore, J., & Milner, R. (2005). Beyond cultureblindness: A model of culture with implications for gifted education. *Roeper Review, 27*(2), 97–103.

Ford, D., Harris, J., Tyson, C., & Frazier, M. (2002). Beyond deficit thinking: Providing access for gifted African American students. *Roeper Review, 24*(2), 52–58.

Ford, D., & Trotman, M. (2001). Teachers of gifted students: Suggested multicultural characteristics and competencies. *Roeper Review, 23*(4), 235–239.

Frankenberg, E., & Siegel-Hawley, G. (2008). *Are teachers prepared for racially changing schools?: Teachers describe their preparation, resources, and practices for racially diverse schools.* Retrieved from http://www.civilrightsproject.ucla.edu

Frasier, M. M., & Passow, A. H. (1994). *Toward a new paradigm for identifying talent potential.* Storrs, CT: University of Connecticut, The National Research Center on the Gifted and Talented.

Frey, W. H. (2011). *A demographic tipping point among America's three-year-olds.* Retrieved from http://www.brookings.edu/research/opinions/2011/02/07-population-frey

Fry, R., & Gonzales, F. (2008, August). *One-in-five and growing fast: A profile of Hispanic public school students.* Retrieved from http://pewhispanic.org/2008/08/26/one-in-five-and-growing-fast-a-profile-of-hispanic-public-school-students

Garces-Bacsal, R. (2011): Socioaffective issues and concerns among gifted Filipino children. *Roeper Review, 33*(4), 239–251.

General Law of Education of the Dominican Republic. (1997). Ley General de Educación de Republica 66/97; 11.4 m. Retrieved from http://www.glin.gov

Government of India. (1986). *National policy on education, 1986.* Retrieved from http://education.nic.in

Harris, B., & Sanchez-Lizardi, P. (2012). Gifted law, identification, and programming in Mexico: An overview for school professionals in the United States. *Journal for the Education of the Gifted, 35*(2), 188–203. doi: 10.1177/0162353212445235

Hoefer, M., Rytina, N., & Baker, B. (2012). *Estimates of the unauthorized immigrant population residing in the United States: January 2011.* Retrieved from http://www.dhs.gov

Ingham, J., & Price, G. E. (1993). The learning styles of gifted adolescents in Philippines. In R. M. Milgram, R. Dunn, & G. E.

Price (Eds.). *Teaching and counseling gifted and talented adolescents: An international learning style perspective* (pp. 149–160). Westport, CT: Praeger.

Kea, C., Campbell-Whatley, G., & Richards, H. (2006). *Becoming culturally responsive educators: Rethinking teacher education pedagogy.* Retrieved from http://nccrest.org/Briefs/Teacher_Ed_Brief.pdf

Kindler, A. (2002). *Survey of the states' limited English proficient students and available educational programs and services.* Retrieved from http://www.ncela.gwu.edu

Marland, S. (1972). Education of the gifted and talented: Report to the congress of the United States by the U.S. commissioner of education (LC736019020). Washington DC: U.S. Government Printing Office.

Mendoza, A. (2007). Comparing school-level to private higher education: Using the Dominican Republic as a pioneer study. Retrieved from http://www.albany.edu/dept/eaps/prophe

Milner, R. (2000). Gifted education and talent development around the world: An introduction. *Roeper Review, 22*(2), 76–77.

Ministerio de Educación de Guatemala. (2006). *Manuel de atención a las necesidades educativas especiales en el aula* (Guidebook for the education of special needs children in the classroom). Retrieved from http://www.discapacidadonline.com

Ministerio de Educacion de Guatemala. (2011). *Reglamento de la ley de educación especial.* Retrieved from http://www.mineduc.gob.gt

Ministerio de Educacion de Guatemala. (2011). *Programa de Becas Solidarias.* Retrieved from http://www.mineduc.gob.gt

Ministerio de Educacion de El Salvador. (2004). *Ley General de Education 1.1* (General Education Law 1.1). Retrieved from http://www.mined.gob.sv

Mitchell, B., & Williams, W. (1987). Education of the gifted and talented in the world community. *Phi Delta Kappan, 68*(7), 531–534.

Monger, R., & Yankay, J. (2012). *U.S. legal permanent residents 2011.* Retrieved from http://www.dhs.gov

National Association for Gifted Children and the Council of State Directors of Programs for the Gifted. (2011). *2010–2011 State of the states in gifted education: National policy and practice data.* Retrieved from http://www.nagc.org/stateofthestatesreport.aspx

National Academy for Gifted and Talented Youth. (2005). *NAGTY research programme archive strand 2: summary of gifted and talented education in India.* Retrieved from http://ygt.dcsf.gov.uk

National Clearinghouse for English Language Acquisition. (2011). *The growing numbers of English learner students, 1998/99–2008/09.* Retrieved from http://www.ncela.gwu.edu/files/uploads/9/growingLEP_0809.pdf

National Commission on Excellence in Education (1983). *A nation at risk: The imperative for educational reform.* Washington, DC: U.S. Government Printing Office.

Navodaya Vidyalaya Samiti (2008). *The official website of the navodaya vidyalaya samiti.* Retrieved from http://www.navodaya.nic.in/

Pew Hispanic Center. (2009). *Hispanics of Mexican origin in the United States.* Retrieved from http://www.pewhispanic.org/files/factsheets/71.pdf

Philippine Center for Gifted Education (2012). Website for the Philippine Center for Gifted Education. Retrieved from http://pcge.ph/

Phillipson, S., Shi, J., Zhang, G., Tsai, D., Quek, C., Matsumura, N., & Cho, S. (2009). Recent developments in gifted education in East Asia. In L. Shavinina (Ed.), *International Handbook on Giftedness* (pp. 1427–1461). doi: 10.1007/978-1-4020-6162-2_75

Plucker, J., Burroughs, N., & Song, R. (2010). *Mind the (other) gap! The growing excellence gap in gifted education.* Retrieved from the Center for Evaluation and Education Policy website: http:/www.iub.edu/~ceep

Plummer, D. (1995). Serving the needs of gifted children from a multicultural perspective. In J. L. Genshaft, M. Birely, & C. L. Hollinger (Eds.), *Serving gifted and talented students: A resource for school personnel* (pp. 285–300). Austin, TX: Pro-Ed.

Raina, M. K., & Srivastava, A. K. (2000). India's search for excellence: A clash of ancient, colonial, and contemporary influences. *Roeper Review, 22*(2), 102–109.

Republic of the Philippines, House of Representatives. House Bill 812. (2011). Retrieved from the Republic of the Philippines website: http://www.congress.gov.ph

Resnick, D., & Goodman, M. (1997). *Northwest Education Research Review*. Retrieved from the Northwest Educational Laboratory website: hppt://www.nwre.org

Rodriguez, D., Espinosa de Gaitan, R., & Luterbach, K. (2008). Understanding the complexities of special needs education in Guatemala. *Journal of International Special Needs Education, 11*, 31–37.

Santibañez, L., Vernez, G., & Razquin, P. (2005). *Education in Mexico: Challenges and opportunities* [documented briefing]. Santa Monica, CA: The RAND Corporation. Available online: http://www.worldfund.org/assets/files/RAND_Education%20in%20Mexico.pdf

Secretaria de Educación de Honduras. (2012). *Website for the Secretaria de Education de Honduras*. Retrieved from the Secretaria de Education website: http://www.se.gob.hn

Secretaría de Educación Pública (2006). *Propuesta de intervención: Atención educativa a alumnos y alumnas con aptitudes sobresalientes* (Intervention Model: Educational attention for gifted students). Retrieved from The Secretaria de Educación Publica website: http://www.educacionespecial.sep.gob.mx

Secretaria de Estado de Educación (SEE). (2003). *Plan Estratégico de Desarrollo de la Educación Dominicana 2003–2012*. Santo Domingo, Dominican Republic.

Shi, J., Li, Y., & Zhang, X. (2008). Self-concept of gifted children aged 9-to 13-years-old. *The Journal for the Education of the Gifted, 31*(4), 481–499.

Short, D., & Boyson, B. (2012). *Helping newcomer students succeed in secondary schools and beyond*. Retrieved from the Center for Applied Linguistics website: http://www.cal.org

Shrestha, L., & Heisler, E. (2011). *The changing demographic profile of the United States*. Retrieved from the Congressional Research Services website: http://www.fas.org/sgp/crs/misc/RL32701.pdf

Sleeter, C. (1990). Staff development for desegregated schooling. *Phi Delta Kappan, 72*(1), 33–40.

Ting-Toomey, S. (1999). *Communicating Across Cultures*. New York, NY: The Guilford Press.

United States Department of Labor (2012). Guatemala. Retrieved from the United States Department of Education website: http://www.dol.gov

Waterman, R., & Harry, B. (2008). *Building collaboration between schools and parents of English language learners: Transcending barriers, creating opportunities*. Retrieved from the National Center for Culturally Responsive Educational Systems website: http://nccrest.org

Weinberg, M. (1997). *Asian-american education: Historical background and current realities*. Mahwah, NJ: Lawrence Erlbaum Associates.

Wright, B. (2008). *A Global conceptualization of giftedness: A comparison of US and Indian gifted education programs* (Unpublished master's thesis). Dominican University of California, San Rafael, CA.

Yasmeen, S., Raghupathi, H., Nehru, A., & Chatterjee, G. (1999). *Wasted potential of India's gifted children*. Retrieved from the Education World Online: http://educationworldonline.net

Yewchuk, C. (1992). Gifted education in China. *Roeper Review, 14*(3), 185–188.

# Chapter 4

# Latino Transnationals (Not) in Advanced Academics

## Asking Hard Questions Together

*Spencer Salas, Bernadette Musetti, & Michelle Plaisance*

In areas of the country such as metro Charlotte, NC, Latino "transnational"[1] (Suárez-Orozco & Suárez-Orozco, 2001, p. 30) schoolchildren are a small piece of a historic and ongoing demographic shift that has changed the faces of K–12 classrooms. Along the I-85 corridor between Raleigh–Durham and Atlanta, as the region's school systems struggle to meet the needs of an increasingly diverse student body, mainstream educators and the districts that employ them find themselves asked to advocate for diversity in often-unprecedented ways. Indeed, the statistically disproportionate underrepresentation of Latinos in advanced academic programming here and in other parts of the country highlights the extent to which the negotiation of diversity continues to be widely problematic (Ford, 2010; Ford, Grantham, & Whiting, 2008; Ramos, 2012; Yoon & Gentry, 2009). We begin this chapter noting the language of crisis that has colored most of the rhetoric surrounding Latinos in U.S. education—a discourse in which we too have participated in our writings about the complex issues of the achievement of children of nondominant communities (see, e.g.,

---

1 Here we employ the term "transnational" to encompass broadly the multicultural lived experiences of Latino first- and second-generation immigrants.

Musetti, Salas, & Perez, 2009a, 2009b; Portes & Salas, 2009, 2010; Salas, Portes, D'Amico, & Rios-Aguilar, 2011).

The relative dearth of focused attention on the underrepresentation of Latinos in advanced academic/gifted programming is, we suspect, not only due to the attempted legitimization of framing the education of emerging bilinguals through subtractive English Only/ First policies. Rather, somewhat limited discussions about Latino schoolchildren in advanced academic programming are perhaps due, in part, to a disciplinary resistance to labeling nondominant children as one thing or another (see, e.g., Valencia, 1997; Valencia & Suzuki, 2001; Valenzuela, 2000, 2002). Since Heath's (1983) groundbreaking ethnography of the literacy practices of North Carolina Piedmont schoolchildren, social justice oriented frameworks for language and literacy education have homed in on the asymmetry between institutionally valued communication patterns and local linguistic codes and cultural styles of thinking and doing. Activist strands of language and literacy education have since approached constructs of exceptionality—including "giftedness"—with suspicion, especially those generated by standardized measures. This is especially true for research for Latinos in education (see, e.g., Gutiérrez, Asato, Santos, & Gotanda, 2002; Gutiérrez, Baquedano-Lopez, & Alvarez, 2000; Moll & Ruiz, 2002; Valdés, 2001).

In the present collaboration, we share such hesitations and write from a place of mistrust—profoundly wary of the potential oppression that comes with the categorization of learners and their abilities, however well intentioned. As Berry (2004) cautioned, "In formal modern educational circles, the concepts of intelligence have a long-standing history, tenacious political purposes, and formidable implications for limiting democracy and social justice" (p. 237). Thus, with Valdés (2003), we argue that changing a national discourse of crisis surrounding Latinos in K–12 settings to one of achievement and potential can begin with teachers and their (re)framing of transnational Latino children's exceptionalities. We begin with a brief overview of how English First/Only thinking has created barriers for Latino transnationals' access to advanced academics. We continue with a series of reflective activities for refocusing practitioners on students' strengths rather than on their limitations, whereby more transnational children of immigration might gain greater access to advanced academics and the opportunity structures that they represent within U.S. schools.

# Beyond English Only/First

Despite an abundance of critically oriented scholarship exposing common schooling practices that have framed the success of Latino transnationals as dependent on their ability to learn English in often subtractive and reductive ways (see, e.g., Murillo, Villenas, Trinidad Galván, Sánchez Munoz, & Machado-Casas, 2010; Suárez-Orozco & Páez, 2002), there remains, nevertheless, a tremendous amount of emphasis on teaching transnational children English so they might "catch up" to their monolingual peers. In the New South, U.S. Latinos are often broadly categorized as English language learners at some moment or another in their academic careers (e.g., Portes & Salas, 2010; Salas et al., 2011). At the level of identification, state departments of education guidelines commonly require the administration of a "home language survey" upon enrollment to determine if English is a student's primary home language. Students whose native, home, or primary first language is other than, or in addition to English, are subsequently assessed for English language proficiency and then potentially labeled Limited English Proficient (LEP), even as some have suggested a more ability centered and accurate term might be "Language Enriched Person." The language assistance services that are subsequently enacted may follow a number of delivery models. However, programming for Latino bilinguals often takes an English Only/First approach with an undue amount of time spent on language instruction to the detriment of exploring talents in the academic content areas (Bohon, Macpherson, & Atiles, 2005; Portes & Salas, 2010).

At a national level, the overcharacterization of U.S. Latinos as English language learners combined with popular folklore about how languages and literacy are learned, and assimilationist rhetoric surrounding immigrants and immigration threaten a "return to the

Mexican room" in K–12 schools (Gándara & Orfield, 2010). In a survey exploring primary school teachers' conceptions of giftedness, Moon and Brighton (2008) offered participants a series of vignettes, each exhibiting characteristics of advanced academic abilities. Their composite of a young Latina illustrated a Spanish-speaking girl with intense science interest who struggled with reading. Respondents consistently and repeatedly focused on the young girl's need for ESL support and reading remediation, acknowledging her skills in science only as a means to encourage her to read more independently.

In our own lived experiences as teachers, teacher-educators, and parents, we have witnessed teachers hesitate to engage Latino transnationals who demonstrate nonnative or nonstandard features in their academic expression in higher order thinking—believing until students are able to conform to common usage, they are not capable of analysis, synthesis, or reflection in that language (see Musetti, et al., 2009a, 2009b; Musetti & Tolbert, 2010). In contrast, Valdés's (2003) landmark study of young bilingual translators highlighted the complex cognitive processes young children employ when acting as interpreters for classroom teachers, peers, and family members. Simultaneous interpretation depended, among other things, on students' well-developed working memory, selective encoding, selective combination, and selective comparison, all ongoing processes sustained over the course of the verbal exchange. One important subtheme of Valdés's work is the concept of coping when students do not possess the linguistic or experiential knowledge necessary to translate with accuracy between two languages. The cognitive process of accommodating for this lack of knowledge is, in itself, she argued, a form of giftedness, requiring that students analyze and adapt on a continuous basis.

## Examining Our Biases and Their Consequences

If students are to continue developing academically, they must engage in challenging content. A back to basics approach, therefore, not only stunts language development, but also cognitive development. Classroom teachers working in corporate climates of high-stakes testing generally focus on teaching students what they cannot do—often overlooking what they could do even better with the guided assistance of a teacher or more experienced peers in what Vygotsky (1978) called a "zone of proximal development." Although teachers express beliefs about multiple intelligences and the importance of supporting young gifted students, they may hesitate in applying these beliefs to practice or may feel constrained by broader school priorities and goals. Further, their conscious or unconscious biases and assumptions may profoundly influence teachers' agency on behalf of children of nondominant communities (Ray, 2009). There is no stronger influence on student performance than the expectations of those to whom the student looks up to for guidance—the teacher. The widely accepted concept of self-fulfilling prophecy is particularly complicated with young Latino children as they seek to redefine themselves as learners as well as individual members of school communities that are often underprepared to embrace the diversity they bring. Although entrance criteria for advanced academic programming vary from state to state, even district to district, in most cases, classroom teachers are the primary gatekeepers of these specialized programs and teachers' advocacy often supersedes standardized assessment instruments. As Moon and Brighton (2008) explained,

> In this way, whether a primary grade student receives support to develop his or her talents, and how his or her talents are developed will depend in large measure on how that student's teacher conceptualizes giftedness in young children, including those from diverse backgrounds. (p. 449)

We too argue for practitioners to begin and continue articulating and challenging their own personal subjectivities about the potential of Latino transnational children. As Ford (2010) has argued, promoting children of nondominant communities' access to advanced academics is not uniquely the job of ESL specialists or Latino activists. Rather, she explained, "It's everyone's problem . . . when underrepresentation is viewed as having personal, social, fiscal, and long-range implications, perhaps changes will be more forthcoming" (p. 31). In this final section, we offer a series of reflective exercises for engaging practitioners operating as a community of learners in the sort of introspection and courageous conversation that we believe can result in a renewal of advocacy for increased Latino access to and support within advanced academics.

## *Expectations*

It has been repeatedly demonstrated that expectations are the critically significant factor in Latino student achievement and success (Valdés, 1996, 2001; Valenzuela, 1999, 2004). In their groundbreaking work, Ruiz and Figueroa (1995) found that offering students an optimal learning environment characterized by a deep biliteracy, rich curriculum, and culturally responsive pedagogy, among other factors, allowed students who had been labeled as less academically able or in need of remediation and placed into special education to be reassessed as mainstream and able. Teachers who see their students as capable create zones of proximal development aimed at extending what their students can already do for something more.

Montalvo-Balbed (2011) documented the lives and educational trajectories of four transnational Latinas who, like herself, despite receiving messages in school such as "You're not college material!", went on to reach the highest levels in their professions as educators. We all know heartbreaking stories of low expectations like these, but with more tragic outcomes where the messages were internalized and the child's promise and potential was never developed, as with the brilliant student who invented complex machines but his giftedness was masked by his "bad" behavior and his family's working-class and immigrant status. Montalvo-Balbed's message is that we must recognize the multiple and varied types of capital that working-class transnational students bring with them, which is often harder to uncover or leverage for teachers whose conceptions of social, cultural, and intellectual capital are culturally bound within a narrow spectrum of experience and expectations.

## *Exposing Structural and Curricular Barriers to Talent Development*

Classroom teachers and administrators need to be attuned to the structural barriers that exist at schools or within districts that prevent better representation of Latino transnationals and other minorities in advanced academics. Here we would want to consider language and communication issues, school climate, and time and scheduling factors as possible barriers that prevent inclusion in high-talent programs. These are important factors to consider because we can only address them if we are aware of them. For example, how do schools accommodate students who arrive late in the year or in between identification cycles? On a day-to-day basis, when teachers offer more Latino transnationals access to sophisticated instruction and content, students often reach levels they, and we, did not know they had (Matthews & Mellom, 2012; Mayer, 2008; Shiu, Kettler, & Johnsen, 2009). A poignant example of high expectations and deeply engaging curriculum, coupled with removing structural and programmatic barriers, comes from our work with Latino English language learners in a large urban school (Musetti & Tolbert, 2010). We invited participation to any current or former ELLs from the high school who wanted to attend our summer science-based enriched program held on a college campus. No tuition, materials, transportation or food costs, or prescreening achievement (such as a particular level of English proficiency or GPA) were required. Instead, to participate students had only to attend an information session. The program goals were to promote a college-going mentality (among students who almost exclusively would be the first in their families to attend college), to promote an interest in science, and to build academic language and skills. These goals were then embedded within a rigorous thematic curriculum around water and with the program motto "Water Is Life."

The program implementers learned that at the end of the summer program these same mostly Latino students returned to their high school and started a club to teach other students the important and valuable information they had learned about academic achievement and college readiness. The students named the club FLOW, which we thought to be a continuation of the water theme that had framed the summer program. But the students explained that FLOW stood for Future Leaders of the World. The assistant principal shared that more than half of the students had contacted him to change their schedules, as they realized they were not on the college track in terms of their courses. Further, and most surprisingly, more teachers were feeling they had to "up their game" for the fall because these students now had experience in demanding courses with teachers who offered cognitively demanding lessons with high supports, both structural and emotional. Students had developed aspirations that included attending law school, becoming chemists, and joining the Atlanta ballet. Overwhelmingly, they had plans to go to college.

## *Engaging Parents*

Misperceptions about the levels and types of engagement that their families bring to instruction can negatively bias classroom teachers' interactions with children of immigration. How parents show support for education varies considerably across cultures. Within many Latino cultures, teachers are highly respected professionals deserving of parents' trust. As such, the proper role of the parent is to defer to the teacher to make sound instructional decisions and placements for students. Following the passage of the "English Only" Proposition 227 in California, when Latino parents in one elementary school were asked why they did not ask for waivers so that their children could remain in bilingual education, they responded that they trusted the teachers to do what was best for their children (Musetti, 2009). For some parents, to stop by the classroom during instructional time, to ask for updates and require accountability, and to question the education process would be seen as deprofessionalizing for the teacher and as culturally inappropriate. In the U.S., when a parent takes a hands-off stance, they are often categorized as "underinvolved."

Our own experiences as parents suggest that students' entrance into gifted programs can depend very much on their parents' (overt) involvement in their education and active lobbying for their children's gifted designation. Such involvement includes, on one end of the continuum, gathering information and being informed, to advocating, and on the other end to prepping and tutoring their child for the assessments and measures of high talent. In the U.S., "good" parents are expected to be deeply involved in such ways and their role is to advocate for their children. For newcomers to U.S. education, the very concept of gifted education might be foreign, and parents may be unaware that such programming is an option for their child. Providing communication about gifted programming to families in their primary languages is important, as is working with bilingual family liaisons to develop bilingual families' awareness of exceptionality, and how a particular school or program might be a better fit for developing their child's potential.

## Asking Hard Questions Together

We believe that promoting Latino access to advanced academic programming requires that professional educators ask hard questions together. As a starting point, we include a series of questions for reflection.

1. Recall a time when someone underestimated you or did not believe in you or your ability. Recall a time when you underestimated someone else. Tell about a time when a student surprised you. Was his or her potential masked? How? What factors prevent us from seeing or recognizing talent or giftedness among individual students and groups of students (consider issues of language, behavior, socioeconomic status, home literacy levels, ethnicity, etc.)?

2. What policy or procedural obstacles exist for English language learners and other students from culturally and linguistically diverse backgrounds? Consider issues surrounding the tools and protocols used to assess for talent and the cultural and the linguistic disadvantage those may have for some students. Consider expanding the criteria for gifted and talented at your school. For example, are there primary language and nonlinguistic assessments that can be used? Consider having

teachers in very different areas contribute to a child's "potential" portfolio by gathering evidence of a child's interests and talents across subject areas as well as across contexts, both in and out of school. What interests, expertise, types of capital, or funds of knowledge might be unrecognized or untapped?

3. Consider the extent to which all students, especially Latino bilinguals, would benefit from engaging in the deepest, richest curriculum possible, such that their interests and curiosity are heightened, thus offering more students more opportunities to succeed and to develop their gifts. Think in terms of multiple intelligences and differentiation and recognize that if students are given choices in terms of showing what they know, they are more likely to engage in academic work and further develop their talents. In what ways can the curriculum at your school be enriched for all students, but especially for Latino English language learners? How can you move from remediation to enrichment and deep engagement? How would your teaching change if you saw all students as potentially "high talent"?

4. Design an action plan for your advanced academics program with the goal of having the program reflect the school population across all categories—primary language, gender, grade levels, etc. Create a matrix showing what the gifted program would look like if this were the case and then put action steps into place to meet that goal. What would designated "Advocates for Equity in Giftedness" do at your school? Create a job description for such a position. Consider both policies and practices.

## Conclusion: Resisting the Rhetoric of Crisis

We close with a personal vignette from a colleague whose own child's native language abilities and the age at which the child began to speak English were purposely not revealed to the school district in which the child enrolled at age 6. The child's parents chose not to disclose this seemingly innocuous information because of their lived experiences in U.S. schools and their awareness of their bias toward the under-identification of giftedness among transnational children like their own. They withheld this information, but a year later their son was tested for and placed into an advanced academics program. With these parents, we suspect that this may not have been the outcome if they had informed the school that the child had only begun to learn English six months earlier. This information would likely have been used to view the child in need of remediation, rather than as bilingual and on the cusp of biliteracy (i.e., "language enriched"). Our colleague's experience is, we believe, one that challenges us all to think harder together about how we might promote greater access and equity in advanced academics by challenging a longstanding rhetoric of crisis framing Latino bilinguals first as "at risk," rather than "of great promise."

# References

Berry, K. S. (2004). Multiple intelligences are not what they seem to be. In J. L. Kincheloe (Ed.), *Multiple intelligences reconsidered* (pp. 236–250). New York, NY: Peter Lang.

Bohon, S. A., Macpherson, H., & Atiles, J. H. (2005). Educational barriers for new Latinos in Georgia. *Journal of Latinos in Education, 4*, 43–58.

Ford, D. Y. (2010). Underrepresentation of culturally different students in gifted education: Reflections about current problems and recommendations for the future. *Gifted Child Today, 33*(3), 31–35.

Ford, D. Y., Grantham, T. C., & Whiting, G. W. (2008). Culturally and linguistically diverse students in gifted education: Recruitment and retention issues. *Exceptional Children, 74*, 289–306.

Gándara, P., & Orfield, G. (2010). *A return to the "Mexican Room": The segregation of Arizona's English learner.* Retrieved from http://civilrightsproject.ucla.edu/research/k-12-education/language-minority-students/a-return-to-the-mexican-room-the-segregation-of-arizonas-english-learners-1/

Gutierrez, K. D., Asato, J., Santos, M., & Gotanda, N. (2002). Backlash pedagogy: Language and culture and the politics of reform. *Review of Education, Pedagogy, & Cultural Studies, 24,* 335–351.

Gutiérrez, K. D., Baquedano-Lopez, P., & Alvarez, H. H. (2000). The crisis in Latino education: The norming of America. In C. Tejeda, C. Martinez, & Z. Leonardo (Eds.), *Charting new terrains of Chicana(o)/Latina(o) Education* (pp. 213–232). Cresskill, NJ: Hampton Press.

Heath, S. B. (1983). *Ways with words: Language, life, and work in communities and classrooms.* New York, NY: Cambridge University Press.

Matthews, P. H., & Mellom, P. J. (2012). Shaping aspirations, awareness, academics, and action: Outcomes of summer enrichment programs for English-learning secondary students. *Journal of Advanced Academics, 23,* 105–124.

Mayer, A. P. (2008). Expanding opportunities for high academic achievement: An International Baccalaureate diploma program in an urban high school. *Journal of Advanced Academics, 19,* 202–235.

Moll, L. C., & Ruiz, R. (2002). The schooling of Latino children. In M. M. Suárez-Orozco & M. Páez (Eds.), *Latinos: Remaking America* (pp. 362–374). Berkeley: University of California.

Montalvo-Balbed, M. (Ed.). (2011). *Looking back: Tracing the trajectory of four Dominican women who learned 'to do' school.* Retrieved from http://digitalcommons.kennesaw.edu/etd/442/

Moon, T. R., & Brighton, C. M. (2008). Primary teachers' conceptions of giftedness. *Journal for the Education of the Gifted, 31,* 447–480.

Murillo Jr., E., Villenas, S. A., Trinidad Galván, R., Sánchez Munoz, J., & Machado-Casas, M. (Eds.). (2010). *Handbook of Latinos and education.* New York, NY: Routledge.

Musetti, B. (2009). *Don't question my authority: The power and pedagogy of English Only.* Saarbrucken, Germany: Lambert Academic.

Musetti, B., Salas, S., & Perez, T. (2009a). When a little knowledge is a good thing: Literacy myths and K–12 English learners. *Georgia Council of Teachers of English: Connections, 46*(1), 2–7.

Musetti, B., Salas, S., & Perez, T. (2009b). Working for and with Latino immigrant newcomers in U.S. schools. *English Journal, 99,* 95–97.

Musetti, B., & Tolbert, S. (2010). Science as springboard: Promoting achievement and aspiration among English Language Learners. In D. Sunal & C. Sunal (Eds.), *Teaching science with Hispanic ELLs in K–16 classrooms* (pp. 253–272). Charlotte, NC: IAP.

Portes, P. R., & Salas, S. (2009). Poverty and its relation to development and literacy. In L. Morrow, R. Rueda & D. Lapp (Eds.), *Handbook of research on literacy instruction: Issues of diversity, policy, and equity.* New York, NY: Guilford Press.

Portes, P. R., & Salas, S. (2010). In the shadow of Stone Mountain: Identity development, structured inequality, and the education of Spanish-speaking children. *Bilingual Research Journal, 33,* 241–248.

Ramos, E. (2012). Let us in: Latino underrpresentation in gifted and talented programs. *Journal of Cultural Diversity, 17,* 151–153.

Ray, J. M. (2009). A template analysis of teacher agency at an academically successful dual language school. *Journal of Advanced Academics, 21,* 110–141.

Ruiz, N., & Figueroa, R. (1995). Learning-handicapped classrooms with Latino students: The Optimal Learning Environment (OLE) project. *Education and Urban Society, 27,* 463–483.

Salas, S., Portes, P. R., D'Amico, M., & Rios-Aguilar, C. (2011). Generación 1.5: A cultural historical agenda for research at the 2-year college. *Community College Review, 39,* 121–135.

Shiu, A., Kettler, T., & Johnsen, S. K. (2009). Social effects of Hispanic students enrolled in an AP class in middle school. *Journal of Advanced Academics, 21,* 58–82.

Suárez-Orozco, C., & Suárez-Orozco, M. M. (2001). *Children of immigration.* Cambridge, MA: Harvard University Press.

Suárez-Orozco, M. M., & Páez, M. (2002). *Latinos: Remaking America.* Berkeley: University of California Press.

Valdés, G. (1996). *Con respeto: Bridging the distances between culturally diverse families and schools: An ethnographic portrait.* New York, NY: Teachers College Press.

Valdés, G. (2001). *Learning and not learning English: Latino students in American schools*. New York, NY: Teachers College Press.

Valdés, G. (2003). *Expanding definitions of giftedness: The case of young interpreters from immigrant communities*. Mahwah, NJ: Lawrence Erlbaum.

Valencia, R. R. (1997). *The evolution of deficit thinking: Educational thought and practice*. London, England: Falmer Press.

Valencia, R. R., & Suzuki, L. A. (2001). *Intelligence testing and minority students: Foundations, performance factors, and assessment issues*. Thousand Oaks, CA: Sage Publications.

Valenzuela, A. (1999). *Subtractive schooling: U.S.-Mexican youth and the politics of caring*. Albany: State University of New York Press.

Valenzuela, A. (2000). The significance of the TAAS test for Mexican immigrant and Mexican American adolescents: A case study. *Hispanic Journal of Behavioral Sciences, 22*, 524–539.

Valenzuela, A. (2002). Reflections on the subtractive underpinnings of education research and policy. *Journal of Teacher Education, 53*, 235–241.

Valenzuela, A. (2004). *Leaving children behind: Why Texas-style accountability fails Latino youth*. Albany: State University of New York Press.

Vygotsky, L. S. (1978). *Mind in society: The development of higher psychological processes* (M. Cole, V. John-Steiner, S. Scribner, & E. Souberman, Trans.). Cambridge, MA: Harvard University Press.

Yoon, S. Y., & Gentry, M. (2009). Racial and ethnic respresentations in gifted programs. *Gifted Child Quarterly, 53*, 121–136. doi:10.1177/0016986208330564

# Chapter 5

# Motivation and the Academically Able English Learner

*Michael S. Matthews*

## Introduction

Motivation can present one of the most problematic issues for teachers of students with gifts and talents. What can the teacher do with a student who obviously has a high aptitude for the course content, but does not want to complete homework or other assigned class tasks? There also is a related issue, relevant specifically for students who are ELLs, in that some teachers may perceive that these students are not going to achieve academically regardless of any additional help the teacher may offer. One may hear statements such as "These students are just going to drop out when they get to high school, so why should we make any extra efforts to help them achieve," or "Their families are going to move away as soon as the peach crop is harvested," or "Those parents just don't value the education we are offering their children." Although there is perhaps a kernel of truth to these views—Latino students, the largest ELL group in the U.S., in general do have far higher high school dropout rates and lower college attendance rates than many other groups (Aud, Fox, & KewalRamani, 2010)—there also are compelling examples of individuals having the same general background and life experiences who have become academic success stories, completed graduate degrees, and become eminent educators, professionals, scholars, and leaders in their adult lives. Indeed, retrospective studies suggest that the influence of a single committed teacher or family member, or a mentor or older successful sibling, often is what made the difference between achievement and lack of achievement for learners at risk of poor educational outcomes who have gone on to achieve success as adults. Every student deserves to have the opportunity to feel supported in his or her learning!

## Perspectives on Achievement and Motivation

There are multiple theoretical perspectives on motivation (e.g., Ryan & Deci, 2000), and each perspective uses similar but not identical terms to describe its own proprietary ideas. Some findings appear to hold true across theories; for example, we know that in general, high-ability learners report higher levels of motivation than average-ability learners do (Garn, Matthews, & Jolly, 2010, 2012), although clearly there also are substantial within-group differences in motivation that may be larger than the differences between these groups. We know, despite a paucity of research on parenting and gifted learners (Jolly & Matthews, 2012), that parents and families exert a strong influence on the academic motivation and other attitudes their children develop toward teachers and schools (Campbell & Verna, 2007; Garn et al., 2010). We know that this familial influence also holds true for Latino students (Valenzuela, 1999), as well as for students of many other cultural and linguistic backgrounds (Campbell & Verna, 2007). Taken together, these diverse perspectives can yield a multifaceted understanding of motivation and its relationships with achievement that the reflective teacher can apply in her or his practice in order to improve educational outcomes for all learners. Selected perspectives are described in the sections that follow; I encourage the reader to follow up by referring to the primary sources for more information on any perspective that may be of interest.

## *Intrinsic and Extrinsic Motivation*

Theorists long have recognized a distinction between two broad types of motivation, internal (intrinsic) and external (extrinsic). In essence, intrinsic motivation is when one does something for the enjoyment of it, while extrinsic motivation is when an external factor (such as a reward or threat of punishment) causes one to do something; it is the difference between "I want to learn about dinosaurs because I think they are cool" and "I have to learn about dinosaurs because there will be a test on them tomorrow." Intrinsic motivation is considered the healthiest form and is associated with a variety of positive long-term academic and mental health outcomes.

## *Anthropological Perspective on Motivation*

Anthropology considers the broader cultural positions within which motivation may be studied. Such consideration is particularly important when we consider how to deal with motivation in culturally pluralistic settings, as with the education of students who are linguistically and culturally diverse (whose teachers, in the U.S., come largely from culturally and economically mainstream backgrounds). Zusho and Clayton (2011) described three epistemological stances or positions drawn from anthropological theory—absolutist, universalist, and relativist—from within which motivation may be viewed. Stated briefly, the absolutist position assumes that motivation is the same across cultures and that it arises from individual factors rather than from cultural influences. The relativist position, in contrast, assumes that motivational processes are highly dependent on the social and cultural context surrounding the individual and that motivation may vary widely across cultures rather than being a trait residing within the individual. The universalist position lies between these two extremes; it assumes that the processes underlying motivation are universal, but that they may be expressed differently in different cultural settings, and that both the individual and his or her cultural context are important in studying motivation. Of these three positions, Zusho and Clayton suggested that the universalist position is most useful in developing theories of motivation, and this likely also is the most helpful perspective for teachers who seek to understand the motivations of the linguistically, culturally, and economically diverse students in their classrooms and schools.

## *Resiliency Theory*

Resiliency refers to a trait of those individuals who demonstrate high achievement or who otherwise thrive despite encountering obstacles, adversities, and challenges that would harm or severely hamper the average person's ability to succeed in life. For students who are ELLs, challenges may take the form of traumatic memories of the immigration process, economic hardships in the family due to relocation, or stresses related to the immigration status of themselves or other family members, in addition to many other stressors shared in common with non-ELL children. There is some evidence that good cognitive functioning—including a high IQ—may increase the likelihood of a child developing resiliency, although other authors (López & Sotillo, 2009) have not found support for this idea.

Regardless of whether high ability helps or makes no difference in the process, the existence of positive relationships with other individuals in the child's life is the key factor in developing resiliency, and it is here that the caring teacher can make a tremendous difference (Kitano & Lewis, 2005). Specific strategies can include connecting students with appropriate mentors, supporting learners' friendships with high-achieving peers, encouraging students' engagement with family and community members, and providing instruction in specific skills to foster effective teamwork, positive coping strategies, and mutual respect among students. Teachers also should look to the research literature to identify culturally specific strategies that may be effective with the unique mix of cultural backgrounds represented in their classroom or school.

High motivation may be related to resiliency, although indirectly. Learning environments that provide high expectations for student achievement (from the teacher as well as from peers) and student choice in learning goals are associated with resiliency and also with increased motivation. Lastly, supporting students' pride in their heritage (including their use of the home language) and validating students' experiences with social injustices and bias (for example, by discussing specific incidents and modeling appropriate coping strategies) can also help increase students' resilience in the face of adversity.

### *Achievement Goal Theory*

Achievement goal theory considers motivation and achievement from the point of view of students' purposes or reasons for completing academic tasks. As with the intrinsic/extrinsic distinction, two types of achievement goals initially were suggested: mastery goals and performance goals. A learner who has mastery goals focuses on his or her learning for its own sake, while learners who have performance goals focus on demonstrating their learning to those around them. More recently, these two goals each have been subdivided into approach and avoidance goals. Approach goals focus on achieving mastery or performance objectives, while avoidance goals in both areas focus on not losing ground in these areas.

Mastery-approach goals are considered the healthiest, as these are associated with positive behavioral and learning outcomes. Research suggests that performance-approach orientations may sometimes lead to higher academic achievement, while performance-avoidance goals have uniformly negative effects; mastery-avoidance goal orientations can lead to both positive and negative achievement outcomes (Zusho & Clayton, 2011).

### *Mindset*

Mindset is the term used by psychologist Carol Dweck (2006) to describe how individuals view their own intelligence and other abilities. One's mindset may exist as one of two general approaches, known as fixed or as incremental. Individuals who hold a fixed view of intelligence believe that it is something one is born with, and that it cannot be changed. Individuals who hold an incremental (or growth) view believe that intelligence and other abilities can be developed through study and other efforts to practice, and that working hard to improve one's intelligence is more important than how much innate ability a person may have.

Mindset is important for educators to understand because it influences how people react to failure, and also because it is malleable and therefore can be influenced through the use of appropriate teaching strategies. People who hold a fixed view of intelligence believe failures reflect on their shortcomings as a person, and hence they strive to avoid them. But for those who hold an incremental view, failure implies a need to try harder to achieve mastery. The mindset theory implies that teachers should emphasize the importance of hard work. For example, rather than telling a student that he did a good job because he is smart, the teacher should say that he did a good job because he worked hard. This will encourage the student to adopt an incremental perspective on his learning, rather than a fixed one, and this perspective in turn will help motivate the student to work harder in future situations that may involve failure in their early stages.

## *Grit*

Psychologist Angela Duckworth has identified persistence or stamina, in the form of long-term motivation and perseverance to achieve goals, as an essential feature of successful individuals that she has labeled *grit* (Duckworth, Peterson, Matthews, & Kelly, 2007). In Duckworth's view, grit is what makes the difference between successful individuals and those who are of equal intelligence but are less successful. Interestingly, her research finds grit is associated with the personality trait of conscientiousness, but is not significantly correlated with IQ scores. The construct of grit explains about one twentieth of the variation in individuals' success rates across a variety of different outcomes.

## *Self-Determination Theory*

Self-determination theory (SDT; Ryan & Deci, 2000, 2002) builds on the broad distinction between intrinsic and extrinsic motivation by further dividing extrinsic motivation into four subtypes based on the amount of control (or internalization) the individual feels. Specifically, SDT postulates two self-determined forms of extrinsic motivation, known as integration and identification, and two non-self-determined forms of extrinsic motivation labeled introjection and external. In the two self-determined forms, the behavior is consistent with the student's internal values or personal commitment, while in the two non-self-determined forms, the behavior is imposed by others' values (i.e., parental or peer pressure), or is completed solely for a reward or avoidance of punishment. For the reader interested in learning more, Garn et al. (2012) provided examples of what each of these forms of motivation might look like in the classroom setting, and they also summarized some other competing theories of motivation.

The basis for all motivational states, according to SDT, lies within three basic human needs: the desire to choose one's behavior, the wish to interact effectively with the environment, and the need to feel a shared connection to others. When these needs are not satisfied, SDT also recognizes an additional class that it labels amotivation; this state is characterized by a lack of intent, leading to the failure to complete a task or to passive (as opposed to active or engaged) behaviors.

## Issues Related to Motivation

Motivation can predict academic achievement beyond the contribution of IQ alone (Duckworth et al., 2007; Gottfried & Gottfried, 2004), so clearly a high IQ alone is not sufficient to explain high achievement. Of course, motivation does not exist in a vacuum; many other related factors also influence achievement. Research suggests that student perceptions of their own academic competence, their perceptions of educational opportunities in their surroundings, and (specifically for ELLs and other cultural minority students) the level of stress they feel with regard to acculturation pressures (Lopez, 2010) also may influence their academic performance. As the selected practices listed in Table 5.1 should suggest, the variety of perspectives on motivation imply numerous and varied suggestions for what teachers

## Table 5.1

### Classroom Practices Supported by Varied Models of Academic Motivation and Achievement

| Model | Sources for Further Study | Supported Practices |
|---|---|---|
| Self-Determination Theory | Garn et al., 2011; Reeve, 2002; Ryan & Deci, 2000, 2002 | Provide choices<br>Encourage students to solve their own problems, but provide assistance (scaffolding) as needed<br>Reduce control and pressures<br>Take the student's perspective |
| Co-regulation of Emergent Identity | McCaslin, 2008, 2009 | Provide social and cultural environments that validate students' actions<br>Offer opportunities that are challenging and that support risk-taking and the development of self-confidence<br>Foster the development of supportive relationships with teachers |
| Gifted Education Differentiation | Widely known; e.g., Stepanek, 1999 | Differentiate content<br>Differentiate student products<br>Differentiate the learning process<br>Differentiate the learning environment |
| Mindset | Dweck, 2006 | Provide constructive feedback that helps solve the problem, rather than labeling the student as insufficient<br>Foster students' love for challenge<br>Teach that intelligence grows (like a muscle) with use<br>Focus feedback on the process of learning, not the products<br>Convey expanding one's skills as a goal, not praising one's innate talent |

and schools can do to support academic achievement by the students in their care. It should be evident that there is substantial overlap between the practices and approaches suggested, regardless of whether they are intended for learners of high ability or of average ability, or intended for English learners or for native speakers of the language. Importantly, motivation should be viewed as a state of mind, rather than as a consistent trait that individuals possess to varying degrees

(Dai, Moon, & Feldhusen, 1998). Motivation depends heavily on the specific situation, and it also is subject to change; teachers and other caring adults can foster the development of motivation among learners who are not exhibiting it in their current setting.

# Three Instructional Approaches That Foster Intrinsic Motivation

Self-determination theory and most other theories of motivation concur that educators should strive to foster intrinsic forms of motivation among their students. Specific instructional approaches can be used to meet this goal. For example, the underlying desire to choose one's own behavior supports the gifted education practice of allowing students to choose their assignment from among a variety of options, and thoughtful instructional design by the teacher will ensure that any option a student selects will allow him or her to meet the specific curricular objectives for that lesson or unit. Through this approach, the learner has the opportunity to pursue his or her intrinsic interests to a far greater extent than when only one undifferentiated assignment option is offered.

**Differentiation.** In gifted education practice, differentiation may occur in the areas of content, process, product, and learning environment; it is focused on student strengths, rather than on remediation of areas of weakness. Importantly, this is a very different conceptualization of what differentiation is, in comparison to the way it usually is framed (i.e., as a form of remediation) in general and special education practice. Although a thorough treatment of differentiation in the gifted education context is beyond the scope of this chapter, there are many resources available in print and online that can be consulted for further information on this topic (e.g., Rebora, 2008). Sidebar 5.1 offers one example of what differentiation might look like in practice.

---

## Sidebar 5.1: First-Grade Differentiation Example: Herminda

Herminda's teacher, Ms. Anthem, has noticed how much Herminda likes to read and write about animals. Because Herminda has already worked ahead and completed next week's story about horses, an animal she is particularly fond of, Ms. Anthem decides to differentiate the content and product of next weeks' unit for Herminda so that she remains interested in her school work.

Their state has adopted the Common Core Standards, so Ms. Anthem decides that the first grade standard "Range of Reading and Level of Text Complexity" (see http://www.core-standards.org/the-standards/english-language-arts-standards/reading-literature/grade-1/) offers an appropriate focus for differentiation. Specifically, she decides to focus on the descriptor, "RL.1.10. With prompting and support, read prose and poetry of appropriate complexity for grade 1" (National Governors Association Center for Best Practices & Council of Chief State School Officers, 2010, para. 5). Searching online for a few minutes, Ms. Anthem locates a selection of poems about horses that are appropriate, and she makes a list of the vocabulary in the poems that she thinks may be terms new to Herminda's experience and beyond the vocabulary in the horse reading that she completed earlier. In class, while other students read the horse story, Herminda reads the selected poems and looks up definitions for the new vocabulary words. Then, while her classmates are copying a letter to the author of the horse story, Herminda works on composing a poem of her own that uses the new vocabulary she has learned.

---

**Joint productive activity.** Joint productive activity (JPA) is an instructional strategy that has been suggested as being particularly useful for students who are ELLs. In this approach to group work, students work collaboratively with one another in pairs or small groups to complete instructional activities. The "joint" part of the name comes from the fact that the activities students are offered require collaboration with one another and with the teacher (or another content expert) to complete. The rationale for JPA is that it provides a "context that allows students to develop common systems of understanding with the teacher and with one another" (Center for Research on Education, Diversity & Excellence, 2002, p. 1). The authors note that JPA is especially important when teachers and students come from different backgrounds, which often is the case for ELLs and their teachers. JPA allows students to develop their communication skills in English, and in the process to connect what they are learning in school to everyday and real-world problems and issues (McIntyre, Kyle, Chen, Kraemer, & Parr, 2009). This latter feature is shared with other pedagogical approaches, such as problem-based learning and creative problem solving, which have long been promoted in gifted education practice. This means that JPA clearly is appropriate for high-ability learners. The elements of student choice, real-world problems, and reliance on collaborative communication all foster students' development of intrinsic motivation to learn.

**Academic acceleration.** Acceleration, particularly when used in concert with ability grouping (see below), offers a very effective set of approaches for increasing students' learning. Academic acceleration also is a low-cost approach that can be implemented relatively easily within the existing school structure.

In its most widely known form, grade skipping, acceleration allows students (those who are both academically and socially ready) to move up into the next higher grade level, where they receive the same instruction that already is being offered to students in that grade. Although full-grade acceleration (or grade skipping) is widely known, there are a number of other approaches to acceleration that also have been shown to be effective (Colangelo, Assouline, & Gross, 2004). These approaches include early entrance to kindergarten or first grade, acceleration in a single subject area, online or correspondence course-work, and, at the high school level, Advanced Placement courses and concurrent or dual enrollment in both high school and college coursework. Each of these approaches helps students to achieve the background knowledge and prerequisite credits that will free up their learning time to pursue in greater depth those areas of study that they find most interesting, and to pursue these interests at an appropriate (faster) pace that itself will reduce boredom and increase the motivation to learn.

# Grouping Practices and Motivation

The origins of the practice of grouping students together for shared instruction are shrouded in time. The underlying premise of grouping is that placing students of similar ability levels together will reduce the range of ability in the group, and that this reduction in range will make the teacher more effective in providing instruction at the appropriate level. This is because each learner in a similar-ability group receives correspondingly more of the teacher's instructional attention than he or she would in a group comprised of a broader range of ability levels. Thus, learning occurs more rapidly in ability-grouped settings.

Research in gifted education strongly supports the effectiveness of flexible grouping by ability level (Kulik & Kulik, 1992; Lee, Olszewski-Kubilius, & Peternel, 2010). For academically gifted students, the benefit of spending one year in an ability-grouped classroom may be as little as one month (i.e., a gain of 1/9 year on standardized test scores) when ability grouping alone is used, without additional curricular differentiation. But, when used in conjunction with other instructional modifications such as content acceleration, ability grouping can produce gains in academic growth averaging approximately half a year. This suggests that students could potentially complete 3 years' content in a 2-year span of time. Research on accelerated instruction within the talent search setting (Matthews, 2007) also lends support for this finding.

## *How Ability Grouping Fosters Motivation*

The appropriate level of instruction for a given learner falls within the theoretical "Zone of Proximal Development" or ZPD (Vygotsky, 1978). The ZPD describes the range between the highest level of pace and complexity of tasks a child can complete independently, and the level at which he or she can master the material with assistance from a teacher, adult, or other more experienced learner. This range moves over time, as learners master more complex material and their learning grows; grouping learners allows a greater proportion of the instruction provided by the teacher to fall within the ZPD of each group member.

Grouping's connection to motivation lies not only in increasing the amount of appropriately leveled instructional attention students receive from the teacher, but also in reducing students' boredom in the classroom. Boredom is a powerful demotivator, and especially for high-ability learners, having to sit through multiple repetitions of material they already have mastered while waiting for other learners to catch up proves very frustrating. In the ability grouped setting, group members all are closer to the same level, and the teacher is able to speed up the pace accordingly.

As is alluded to in Chapter 4, some parents and teachers view the very idea of gifted education with suspicion, and this is particularly the case with the practice of ability grouping. Despite strong research evidence documenting positive student outcomes from ability grouping (see Colangelo et al., 2004), the practice has been subject to vehement opposition from some quarters. Some parents believe their child must be gifted, and for these parents it doesn't matter if there is no evidence that their child is above average in either academic ability or performance. At the opposite extreme, other parents and even some teachers resist the idea that anyone can be above average, or that a child may need advanced academic opportunities beyond those offered to the average learner. This may be in part due to cultural values, such as the egalitarian impulse in U.S. culture that values equity over the pursuit of excellence. Despite these beliefs, no one wants to be operated on by the doctor who graduated last in his or her medical school class! U.S. culture values high achievement in some arenas, but generally opposes it in the context of public education. Other cultures may hold beliefs such that anything that sets one person over another is a form of showing off and therefore in poor taste, or that hard work is more important than ability; these perspectives and others all can influence beliefs about ability grouping, but they do not change the underlying research findings that support it.

## Grouping and Academically Advanced ELL Students in Inclusive Settings

For students who are ELLs, schools should take particular care to ensure that flexible grouping, rather than tracking, is being practiced. There are, of course, some shared instructional needs that can be met most efficiently by placing ELLs together for a portion of the day (the reader may refer to Chapters 2 and 7 for some of these needs); but we also know that English language development is fostered most effectively through regular interaction with native-English-speaking peers. Thus, school schedules should be designed to provide opportunities for ELL students to engage with like-ability peers who are native English speakers within content-area instructional settings. Because academically advanced learners characteristically tend to have developed a more advanced vocabulary than their age peers of average ability, high-ability learners who are also ELLs may find interactions with these learners to be especially helpful in advancing their own English language proficiencies. For the learner who already is intrinsically motivated, access to advanced learning opportunities will enable rapid progress in acquiring English language skills and their associated content knowledge. For the high-ability learner who is not intrinsically motivated at the moment, the teacher may find it helpful to emphasize the importance of seizing opportunities when they present themselves.

---

## Sidebar 5.2: Single Subject Acceleration Example: Joaquin

Joaquin appears to be doing fine so far in his on-grade-level placement in seventh grade, and his skills in using English for both social and academic purposes are advancing rapidly.

Although his grades are in the low A range in math, his ESOL teacher, Ms. Arrieta, is beginning to think that the regular seventh-grade math curriculum may not be posing much of a challenge for him. Joaquin has been sharing with her the complex and whimsical drawings he likes to make, and when prompted, he tells her that he draws them in math class "while the teacher goes over the same problem again and again for the kids who don't understand." Ms. Arrieta knows that Joaquin still occasionally stumbles over unfamiliar terms (confusing the homophones "chord" and "cord," for example), but realizes that he has few if any difficulties with computation once he has learned the associated vocabulary. She talks over with him the idea of moving to a more challenging placement for math, but Joaquin is hesitant to leave his two bilingual friends who are in the general education math class with him.

Ms. Arrieta talks with the teacher who teaches the school's two sections of seventh-grade pre-Algebra, and finds that one section is offered during the same period and just down the hall from his current class. She also learns that a friend of Joaquin's—who he knows through the cross country track team—is in this section, and she guesses that Joaquin probably will be willing to change sections once he learns that he already knows someone in this new placement. She convenes a meeting with the assistant principal, both math teachers, and Joaquin and his mother to discuss the idea, and within the next month everyone agrees to try moving him to the higher level math class for the next grading period. Over the upcoming winter break, his friend from the cross country team agrees to review with him the topics they have covered in class that fall that were not covered in Joaquin's general math course. Once the new placement begins in January, Ms. Arrieta will continue to work closely with Joaquin and his new math teacher to anticipate the new and advanced vocabulary used in the class, so that she and Joaquin can work together to learn these new terms before he encounters them in class.

**Assessment and ability grouping.** Ability grouping may be implemented within the classroom, across all classrooms at a given grade level (i.e., using Total School Cluster Grouping; Gentry & Mann, 2009), or at both of these levels simultaneously. A key feature of effective ability grouping is regularly scheduled, ongoing reassessment of student placement. Such assessment should happen at least annually at the school level, and it may happen as often as every few days or weeks for instructional groupings within the classroom.

Importantly, assessment within the classroom should not require additional work for the teacher, although it may require a subtle change in mindset or modifications to some specific evaluation practices. For example, the teacher may offer students the opportunity to choose alternative assignments (such as continuing their independent work on a long-term project like a science or math fair display) if they can demonstrate mastery on a pretest of unit skills. The teacher should not have to develop a whole new set of tests for this purpose; the pretest can be the same as the unit posttest, allowing advanced learners to make themselves familiar with the material ahead of time if they wish to test out of a given unit to devote their time to other work. All students should be given the pretest at the beginning of each instructional unit; even if no one places out of the unit, the pretest will provide the teacher with an ability profile of the entire class. This profile then can be used to design instructional groups for that unit and to address specific subareas within the topic that may need additional instruction, while minimizing the amount of time devoted to learning objectives that most students already have mastered. In addition to pretests, existing student products may also serve as assessments of students' readiness to be grouped at a particular level for subsequent assignments. Again, by providing students the opportunity to learn something new each day, ability grouping increases motivation by decreasing the student boredom caused by repetition of material they already have mastered.

# Sidebar 5.3: High School Differentiation Example: Minh

Minh has been placed in the ninth-grade World History class even though he has excelled in history classes in his native language before moving with his parents to the U.S. He reads copiously, and has finished reading the history textbook by the end of the third week of school. Even now, halfway through the school year, he tends to keep quiet in class unless his teacher, Coach T., directly asks him a question. When he is asked, Minh usually can offer a complete and correct response if given a few moments to formulate his thoughts. Minh's written homework always demonstrates a strong factual knowledge of the subject and keen insight because of the time and effort he puts into completing it, although often it requires multiple corrections for English grammar and style.

Coach T. realizes that Minh probably already knows more about world history than any of his classmates, because of the strong educational background he brings from his home country. He decides that Minh probably would get more out of his education if he were able to learn more about U.S. history in particular. He arranges with Mr. Bosquet, who teaches AP U.S. History across the hall, for Minh to sit in on the AP lectures but to continue completing the World History homework and tests. By remaining enrolled in World History until he can take AP U.S. History the following year, Coach T. can continue to foster Minh's English writing and speaking skills so that he will be prepared to be successful on the exams in AP U.S. History the following year.

# Role of the Teacher in Fostering Motivation

## *Teacher Self-Reflection*

There are several reflective questions that teachers can pose for themselves to informally evaluate their own progress toward greater fostering of motivation among their students. These questions might include, for example: Do I consistently organize the content so that it is personally meaningful and relevant to my students? Do I consistently develop learning experiences in which inquiry, curiosity, and exploration are valued? Do I regularly reinforce and reward effort, rather than only completion or obtaining the "right" answer? Why do I think it is important to provide the opportunity for students to develop and pursue their own questions within the curriculum? In addition to reflecting on these questions directly, thinking about the types of evidence that would answer these questions also can lead toward changes that improve instructional practice. For example, consider: What does it look like when the teacher rewards effort rather than simply completion? Making specific changes to the language within a grading rubric might be one answer. Sharing famous quotations (such as the widely known statement by Einstein about genius being 1% inspiration and 99% perspiration) might offer a second way for a teacher to convey the value of effort to her or his students. This sort of reflective instructional planning can be especially valuable if teachers are able to sit down together to consider these questions and issues in a shared planning session. Teachers also should query their own mindsets and beliefs regarding motivation, effort, and ability in order to understand any unconscious or overt biases they may hold regarding these areas.

## *Classroom Expectations and ELLs*

For advanced learners who also are learning English, the teacher needs to be aware of (and consciously reject) the premise that strong English writing skills are a necessary prerequisite for content-area expertise. After all, around the world there are content experts in nearly every discipline who don't know any English at all. Students who are ELLs will require targeted feedback about specific writing issues, and these issues may depend in part on the structures they have acquired in their native language (as the reader may recall, there is further discussion of this issue in Chapter 2). Students learning English also may be hesitant to speak up in class, especially early on in the language acquisition process when much of their attention is being devoted to receptive rather than expressive aspects of English.

Assignment rubrics are another area that the responsive teacher may need to tweak, as specific adjustments may be needed both for advanced learners and for students learning English. Many times the rubrics found in textbooks or online sources emphasize completion of a task or product, no matter how shoddy the work may be, rather than evaluating the quality of the student's contribution. In my experience, the best procedure for evaluating a rubric can happen only after it has been used. Start by finding two student products whose quality you believe is not the same, but that received similar grades on the rubric. Then, think about what was different that was not reflected on the rubric. Perhaps one of the projects was the student's own idea, while the other was a "canned" project that you've seen many times before. In this case, you would add categories and descriptors for different levels of originality, perhaps, or for the student's contributions to the development of the project idea.

Although these points may seem to have strayed from the central theme of this chapter, they actually are closely related to motivation. Most people only rarely put forth their best effort (perfectionists excepted); students in general will seek to learn what will be "good enough" in a given assignment or for a given teacher, and that is the level of work they will produce. When a grade or other feedback does not recognize the amount of effort we have put into something, it becomes demotivating. In self-determination theory terms, by removing the learner's internal commitment to his or her work it shifts the motivation from being either intrinsic or extrinsic but self-determined, to being extrinsic and non-self-determined (i.e., imposed by other's values). For the effective teacher, the goals should be two-fold: to recognize exemplary work in the first place, and to foster the motivational attitudes that lead students to continue producing it in the future.

## Chapter Summary

This chapter began by examining what motivation is and suggested some strategies for encouraging the development of intrinsic motivation among students of high ability. The self-determination theory of motivation provides a useful perspective through which to differentiate the various aspects of motivation and to consider instructional approaches designed to produce intrinsic motivation. Other relevant perspectives include resiliency theory, achievement motivation theory, anthropological theory, and mindset.

In general, all students (but especially those of high academic ability) will respond to being offered guided choices within specific content objectives, and to appropriate grouping practices and instructional placements designed to reduce boredom arising from time wasted on unnecessary repetition. The chapter concludes with some suggestions for how teachers should modify their instructional practices and their own perceptions in order to more closely meet the needs of their students who are ELLs of high academic potential.

## References

Aud, S., Fox, M. A., & KewalRamani, A. (2010). *Status and Trends in the education of racial and ethnic groups* (NCES 2010-015). U.S. Department of Education, National Center for Education Statistics. Washington, DC: U.S. Government Printing Office. Retrieved from http://nces.ed.gov/pubs2010/2010015.pdf

Campbell, J. R., & Verna, M. A. (2007). Effective parental influence: Academic home climate linked to children's achievement. *Educational Research and Evaluation, 13,* 501–519.

Center for Research on Education, Diversity & Excellence (2002). *Joint Productive Activity: Teacher and students producing together.* Berkeley, CA: Author. Retrieved from http://gse.berkeley.edu/research/credearchive/standards/1jpa.shtml

Colangelo, N., Assouline, S. G., & Gross, M. U. M. (2004). *A nation deceived: How schools hold back America's brightest students.* Iowa City: University of Iowa, The Connie Belin and Jacqueline N. Blank International Center for Gifted Education and Talent Development. Retrieved from http://www.accelerationinstitute.org/nation_deceived/

Dai, D. Y., Moon, S. M., & Feldhusen, J. F. (1998). Achievement motivation and gifted students: A social cognitive perspective. *Educational Psychologist, 33*(2–3), 45–63. doi:10.1207/s15326985ep3302&3_1

Duckworth, A. L., Peterson, C., Matthews, M. D., & Kelly, D. R. (2007). Grit: Perseverance and passion for long-term goals. *Journal of Personality and Social Psychology, 92,* 1087–1101. doi:10.1037/0022-3514.92.6.1087

Dweck, C. S. (2006). *Mindset: The new psychology of success.* New York, NY: Random House.

Garn, A. C., Matthews, M. S., & Jolly, J. (2010). Parental influences on the academic motivation of gifted students: A self-determination theory perspective. *Gifted Child Quarterly, 54,* 263–272. doi:10.1177/0016986210377657

Garn, A. C., Matthews, M. S., & Jolly, J. L. (2012). Parents' role in the academic motivation of students with gifts and talents. *Psychology in the Schools, 49,* 656–667. doi:10.1002/pits.21626

Gentry, M., & Mann, R. L. (2009). *Total School Cluster Grouping and differentiation: A comprehensive, research-based plan for raising student achievement & improving teacher practices.* Waco, TX: Prufrock Press.

Gottfried, A. E., & Gottfried, A. W. (2004). Toward the development of a conceptualization of gifted motivation. *Gifted Child Quarterly, 48,* 121–132. doi:10.1177/001698620404800205

Jolly, J., & Matthews, M. S. (2012). A critique of the literature on parenting gifted learners. *Journal for the Education of the Gifted, 35,* 259–290. doi:10.1177/0162353212451703

Kitano, M. K., & Lewis, R. B. (2005). Resilience and coping: Implications for gifted children and youth at risk. *Roeper Review, 27,* 200–205.

Kulik, J. A., & Kulik, C.-L. C. (1992). Meta-analytic findings on grouping programs. *Gifted Child Quarterly, 36*(2), 73–77. doi: 10.1177/001698629203600204

Lee, S. Y., Olszewski-Kubilius, P., & Peternel, G. (2010). The efficacy of academic acceleration for gifted minority students. *Gifted Child Quarterly, 54,* 189–208. doi:10.1177/0016986210369256

López, F. (2010). Identity and motivation among Hispanic English language learners in disparate educational contexts. *Education Policy Analysis Archives, 18*(16). Retrieved from http://epaa.asu.edu/ojs/article/view/717

López, V., & Sotillo, M. (2009). Giftedness and social adjustment: Evidence supporting the resilience approach in Spanish-speaking children and adolescents. *High Ability Studies, 20*(1), 39–53.

Matthews, M. S. (2007). Talent search programs. In C. M. Callahan & J. A. Plucker (Eds.), *Critical issues and practices in gifted education* (pp. 641–653). Waco, TX: Prufrock Press.

McCaslin, M. (2008). Learning motivation: The role of opportunity. *Teachers College Record, 110,* 2408–2422.

McCaslin, M. (2009). Co-regulation of student motivation and emergent identity. *Educational Psychologist, 44,* 137–146.

McIntyre, E., Kyle, D. W., Chen, C-T., Kraemer, J., & Parr, J. (2009). *6 principles for teaching English language learners in all classrooms.* Thousand Oaks, CA: Corwin Press.

Musetti, B., & Tolbert, S. (2010). Science as springboard: Promoting science achievement and aspiration among Latino English language learners in the secondary school. In D. W. Sunal, C. Sunal, E. L. Wright (Eds.), *Teaching science with Hispanic ELLs in K–16 classrooms* (pp. 253–272). Charlotte, NC: Information Age.

Rebora, A. (2008, September). Making a difference. *Education Week, 2*(1). Retrieved from http://www.edweek.org/tsb/articles/2008/09/10/01tomlinson.h02.html

Reeve, J. (2002). Self-determination theory applied to educational settings. In E. L. Deci & R. M. Ryan (Eds.), *Handbook of self-determination research: Theoretical and applied* (pp. 183–203). Rochester, NY: Rochester Press.

Ryan, R. M., & Deci, E. L. (2000). Intrinsic and extrinsic motivations: Classic definitions and new directions. *Contemporary Educational Psychology, 25*, 54–67.

Ryan, R. M., & Deci, E. L. (2002). An overview of self-determination theory. In E. L. Deci & R. M. Ryan (Eds.), *Handbook of self-determination research: Theoretical and applied* (pp. 3–36). Rochester, NY: Rochester Press.

Stepanek, J. (1999). *Meeting the needs of gifted students: Differentiating mathematics and science instruction.* Portland, OR: Northwest Regional Educational Laboratory. Retrieved from http://educationnorthwest.org/webfm_send/755

Vygotsky, L. S. (1978). *Mind in society: The development of higher psychological processes* (M. Cole, V. John-Steiner, S. Scribner, & E. Souberman, Trans.). Cambridge, MA: Harvard University Press.

Zusho, A., & Clayton, K. (2011). Culturalizing achievement goal theory and research. *Educational Psychologist, 46*, 239–260. doi:10.1080/00461520.2011.614526

# Building Collaborative Partnerships in Schools and Communities

*Vicki K. Krugman & Linda Iza*

Collaboration and collaborative partnerships that support an inclusive classroom hold tremendous potential in addressing the needs of highly able diverse student populations, in particular ELLs. In this chapter, we will focus on collaboration and collaborative partnerships a classroom teacher and school can develop to engage highly able students, specifically building the potential of ELLs. We will discuss comprehensive integrated services, instructional relationships, organizing for a collaborative classroom, and student-centered instruction. Practical solutions that impact classroom instructional environments for ESL and gifted program services will be described throughout the chapter. Special education will also be discussed in a limited degree to describe the nature of a comprehensive approach.

## Definition of Collaboration

Collaboration and collaborative partnerships have been defined in the resource areas of gifted education, ESL, special education, and other educational arenas using a variety of terminology and practices within their program domains. The characteristics of successful collaboration may differ slightly, but encompass trust, communication, accountability, planning, responsibility, and common goals. Interpreting collaboration in a broad manner is important to understanding the variety of relationships that develop in an educational setting. However, the description of collaboration by Hughes and Murawski (2001, p. 196) better defines and guides who, what, and how collaboration works when providing support services for students:

> Collaboration is a style for interaction that includes dialogue, planning, shared and creative decision making, and follow-up between at least two coequal professionals with diverse expertise, in which the goal of the interaction is to provide appropriate services for students, including high-achieving and gifted students.

The above description helps educators better understand collaboration and to begin to develop a shared language to facilitate communication and practices when working in an inclusive classroom. Teachers often say successful school and classroom collaboration initiatives hinge on positive collaborative relationships.

## Need for Comprehensive Collaboration Services

It is essential to consider the design and implementation of collaborative relationships in the educational setting in a comprehensive manner across schools, programs, and classrooms to efficiently meet the needs of students and families. Reflecting on the interaction of the relationships relative to the common goal of student achievement is imperative to working more efficiently in schools. Looking at the different support groups and personnel that collaborate with classroom teachers, it is imperative their terminology, practices, and relationships to establish a common foundation and guide for improving student achievement serve as an important starting point. Many instructional decisions are made individually in the design of a program of services for gifted, ESL, special education, and other students. Each group has standards, terminology, and practices that are at times very confusing to a classroom teacher who has students receiving a variety of services. Ideally, inclusion and other classroom support services will be on a continuum with seamless options that address ascending levels of challenge in similar ways with the same goals. Figure 6.1 shows the inclusive classroom in the center of a number of support services that are working together to flow into classroom instruction. Understanding each program and how they can integrate is an important aspect of seamless services.

Gifted program services focus on challenging able learners, ESL program services focus on teaching language and culture, and special education program services focus on overcoming barriers to learning. All of the program services have the common goal of successful academic achievement for students. The programs have much in common in their approach, delivery, and mission to create a relevant and motivating educational environment. Additionally, other school personnel such as media specialists, lead teachers, coaches, and specialists collaborate with classroom teachers to support students. Collaboration with the classroom teacher is foundational to their work of serving students directly and indirectly.

Classroom instruction must support multiple needs of students with a variety of services, while a positive instructional climate is instrumental in promoting their academic growth. Gifted programs and all resource service programs need to develop positive working relationships that complement their work with and in classrooms. Gifted programs working collaboratively with ESL and special education programs need to build stronger instructional relationships and processes for addressing the language and cultural issues of the highly able ELLs and the barriers highly able students in special education may encounter in classrooms. It is important to build systems for recognizing and meeting a spectrum of needs that have not traditionally been served in gifted programs. The systems would be similar to a special education team planning an Individualized Education Program (IEP), but blend services for efficiency and effectiveness in the inclu-

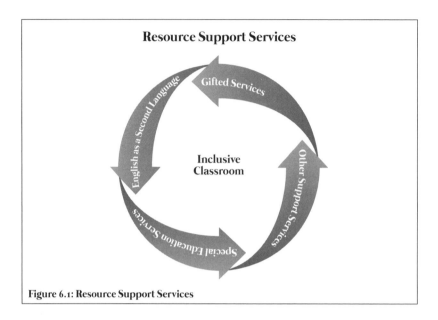

**Figure 6.1: Resource Support Services**

sive classroom. Gifted, ESL specialists, and classroom teachers would follow a team approach, blending supports for highly able ELLs. For example, highly able ELLs need differentiation for language that facilitates access to rigorous content and addresses the cultural differences of their prior school experiences. In the situation in Sidebar 6.1 there was a system for the team to collaborate and blend support services through common curriculum and standards to effectively meet the needs of the student. The planning responsibilities were shared and the combined expertise provided engaging and comprehensible curriculum and instruction for the student.

## Sidebar 6.1: Juan and Mathematics Learning

Juan arrived from Colombia a few weeks ago. Upon administering the language proficiency test, his ESL teacher, Mrs. Scott, determines that Juan is at the very beginning levels of English language development. Juan is entering fifth grade this school year in the United States. Juan's previous grades are excellent and his teachers' comments praise Juan's progress and capacity to grasp difficult concepts in math and other content areas.

Mrs. Scott and the collaborating team met with Juan's parents to discuss his educational background. Juan made excellent progress in school and scored at the top of his class in his native country. Juan's parents were especially proud of the fact that Juan excelled in math and expressed concern that he would not be challenged in his fifth-grade classroom because they have viewed the fifth-grade curriculum on the district's website. They want their son to have a successful experience in school and continue to make progress.

Mrs. Scott and Mrs. Phillips, the gifted specialist, collaborate with Juan's homeroom teacher, Mr. Hammond, once a week to plan for upcoming lessons. In a recent meeting, Mr. Hammond expresses concern for Juan's math after viewing the results of a preassessment to determine the students who need more advanced instruction. Mr. Hammond came to the conclusion that Juan does not understand division, commas, or decimals. Furthermore, he believes that Juan does not seem to know how to copy numbers correctly and confuses his 7's and 1's. He gave the following example problem: $3{,}786.15 \div 13 = \underline{\hspace{2cm}}$

Juan's answer:

$$
\begin{array}{r}
3786{,}15\overline{)13} \\
118 \qquad \overline{291{,}24} \\
016 \\
31 \\
055 \\
03
\end{array}
$$

Mrs. Scott explains, "ELLs with prior school experiences in their countries of origin may find that familiar symbols, expressions, and methods differ from those they encounter in U.S. classrooms" (Egbert & Ernst-Slavit, 2010, p. 124). She knows that it is important for Juan's teachers to understand that "Mathematics is performed differently around the world (such as in the case of long division)" (Gottlieb, 2012, p. 66). She begins to explain some differences in representations and computing methods in math that are evident in Juan's method of solving long division problems. As they analyze Juan's work, Mrs. Scott creates a chart noting the differences in operational methods used by Juan and those used in Mr. Hammond's and other classrooms.

| Mismatch of Languages | In other countries | In the U.S.A. |
|---|---|---|
| Numbers written differently | $7 \quad 1$ | $7 \quad 1$ |
| Multiples of thousands are separated by different symbols | Commas are used to separate tenths, hundredths, etc.<br><br>291,24 | Decimals are used to separate tenths, hundredths, etc.<br><br>291.24 |
| Division problems are solved using different methods and representation of problems | $321(6$ | $6\overline{)321}$ |
| Ways of "showing work" vary | Mental math is used in the multiplication and subtraction portions of long division<br><br>$\begin{array}{l} 321,0)6 \\ \phantom{3}21 \quad \overline{53,5} \\ \phantom{32}30 \\ \phantom{320}0 \end{array}$ | All work is shown. Both multiplication and subtraction portions are recorded<br><br>$\begin{array}{r} 53.5 \\ 6\overline{)321.0} \\ \underline{30} \\ 21 \\ \underline{18} \\ 30 \end{array}$ |

Adapted from Egbert and Ernst-Slavit (2010, p. 125)

Mr. Hammond and the other members of the collaborative group recognize that it is important to build on Juan's prior knowledge and understanding of math to instruct and challenge him. As they begin to brainstorm strategies, Mr. Hammond suggests using the think-aloud strategy he has seen Mrs. Scott model during their collaborative/coteaching time in social studies. The team agrees that he could model his thinking to demonstrate how he solves long division problems, emphasizing the set-up of the problem and showing his problem-solving method step by step. They decide to develop a graphic organizer that compares Juan's current symbols, expressions, and methods that differ from those he will encounter in his current classroom. Initially, Mr. Hammond will fill in the organizer and

Juan can add drawings or symbols that will help him remember the differences.

Furthermore, the gifted specialist, Mrs. Phillips, knows that Mr. Hammond uses cooperative groups and she thinks giving Juan the opportunity to work with a partner in think-pair-share activities and other cooperative problem-solving activities will assist him in discussing his thinking and processing on the advanced problems. Additionally, the group work will help Juan develop his academic language proficiency in the area of math as well as assist him in understanding the operational methods used in his class. Mr. Hammond confirms that he has noticed progress in Juan's comprehension and use of academic language and content knowledge during and after working in small groups and with a partner. The team determines that this will also assist Juan once he is presented with advanced word problems that will be challenging.

One team member suggests the use of a visual content word wall for math similar to the one the class has been creating for science. They begin to work with Mr. Hammond to create the visual/content wall with the language and symbols of math operations such as add, plus, altogether, in all, total. Mrs. Scott believes the students should play an active role in this process in their cooperative groups and the collaborating team plans to include this activity in the lessons. Mrs. Scott emphasizes that the visual/content wall will assist Juan when reading, writing, speaking, and listening during math class. The collaborating team ends the meeting feeling confident they have a better understanding of the language of math and how to plan for highly able ELLs such as Juan.

---

School programs should collaborate together to meet these needs by expanding each special area with a collective focus on integrated services that promote better parent awareness, a proficiency view of what students can do that builds on strengths to reach academic goals, and a relevant curriculum that infuses multicultural and global understandings with sensitivity to language proficiency. Schools and/or teachers can immediately impact the inclusive classroom's collaboration across resource groups and personnel by organizing how the groups interact and work together.

# Better Parent Awareness

Better parent awareness is gained when collaborating support personnel understand all of the services a child is receiving at school. Gifted, ESL, and other areas can share data and other information on students in the classroom and meet with the classroom teacher together when planning or discussing students and/or instruction. Just meeting together is a good starting point; however, discussing student needs and curriculum planning will help all school personnel understand the huge tasks a classroom teacher encounters in a culturally diverse classroom. Sharing data information and meeting together will help gifted, ESL, and other areas communicate an understanding of the specific terminology of special services among themselves and ultimately with parents. Support for parents of highly able ELLs is as important as it is for the students. Collaboration is an excellent benefit to parent awareness because gifted, ESL, and other areas know the combined services a student is receiving, rather than just their own. Parents receive one collective message rather than multiple and possibly conflicting messages. This may be helpful for parents new to the U.S. school system.

Meetings with parents should include representatives from gifted, ESL, and other service areas that impact a child's instructional day. Parent awareness can best be achieved when communicating in the parents' heritage language. It is important to have a fully bilingual interpreter. This can be a school employee, family member, community member, or parent liaison. Care should be given to ensure that the interpreter understands the educational jargon used and is able to interpret in a comprehensible fashion. When sending written communication, do not rely on software; make sure a competent translator prepares all information sent from the school.

Parents will immediately see the broad support a school provides and the school personnel will better articulate the full picture of services a student receives in one day and across time during the school year. Parents will be able to see the connections of services with an opportunity to ask questions or get information during one visit to the school. Often, parents meet to learn about one service area (gifted, ESL, special education) and what the provider does for the child. If the child receives multiple services, it can be a challenge for parents to sort out the support the child is receiving during school. The parents can get more complete information when the gifted, ESL, and classroom teacher work collaboratively and each person can discuss the shared services and needs of the child.

## Proficiency View of Students

Integrated collaboration services function effectively for highly able ELLs when all teachers focus on the proficiencies of students. Gifted programs are based on the premise that services are built on strengths and interests. Gifted services meet student needs through differentiation of instruction with advanced, supplemental, or extensions of the regular curriculum. Gifted programs see what the students can do in the identification process and build on the information.

ESL programs are focused on developing a second language for students to be successful in U.S. schools. Students are expected to learn social language for interpersonal exchanges and academic language to specifically understand the content of the multiple disciplines of science, math, social studies, and English, among others. ELLs arrive at schools with varying backgrounds in education and language abilities. Some enter school with extremely high academic ability and/or potential and rich school backgrounds, while others have limited formal schooling. The ESL identification system (i.e., English language proficiency assessments) targets language proficiency and not general academic ability as is done in gifted and special education programs. However, ESL programs do gather information on the background of ELLs and realize it is critical to understanding their classroom needs. The process for collecting information is informal and has a number of barriers (Waterman & Harry, 2008) that impede a thoughtful perspective of what ELLs can do in their native language. Teachers often have difficulty getting records from schools in other countries, the records may come in a foreign language, and courses may also have different names and content than U.S. schools. The differences in schooling can impact the grade level and/or academic credit received in the U.S. Additionally, parents may be new to the country, not speak English, and not understand how schools work. Arranging for interpreters, explaining resource programs, and discussing needs can be challenging for parents and schools. It is important to note that ESL data collection does not address cultural strengths, motivation, or creative abilities that could provide insight into engaging highly able ELLs.

The integrated collaboration approach will require teachers to deepen their understanding of ELLs to effectively capitalize on the strengths they bring to school. Information on ELLs needs to be expanded to include their interests and general academic ability. Teachers can gain information through authentic learning activities and products incorporating alternative ways for ELLs to express their understanding. This collection of information will take time and can be part of a student's initial month of learning activities. As a quicker way to get information, some schools use the Renzulli Learning System (Renzulli, 2012). The online program surveys students on a broad array of information and provides a learning profile that includes their top three interest areas, learning styles, and product styles, with many targeted activities that the students may be interested in completing. Capturing such information will enable teachers to engage highly able ELLs and all students in what they like and ultimately make positive school connections with learning. Once abilities, interest, and learning styles are thoroughly understood, more targeted instructional approaches and curriculum differentiation can create an environment for highly able ELLs to express their academic talents. Hence, their proficiencies are evidenced and integrated in daily instructional practices.

The proficiency view becomes more complicated in special education. Gifted students who also qualify for special education are known as "twice exceptional." This situation can be perplexing to a teacher.

Special education identification uses the term *disability*, which can be misconstrued into a deficiency view of the academic abilities of students. However, special education gathers good information about the student during the identification process, including general academic ability. Gifted and highly able special education students have data that show their proficiencies, strengths, and most often, their interests. Teachers will need to focus on these strengths to differentiate instruction while using coping skills to impact the disability. In some cases, the most successful highly able special education students come from programs that recognize their disabilities but focus on their strengths to build coping skills and ways to compensate. Students often select to move toward their area of strength and will ultimately do well if they use their strengths to accommodate their disabilities (Foley Nicpon, Allmon, Sieck, & Stinson, 2011).

## Infuse Multicultural and Global Understandings with Sensitivity to Language Learning

When considering student strengths, collaborators will want to understand how to capitalize on cultural backgrounds and language development for highly able ELLs. Although schools may have a dominant culture, classroom demographics are changing and offer an opportunity for teachers to build a bigger picture with multicultural and global understanding for all students. The school's dominant culture is only one of countless cultures across the U.S. and the world (Noel, 2005). Collaborating teachers will want to become familiar with the cultural background of their students to best understand how to create an instructional environment that will engage them in learning. Infusing meaningful experiences can be as easy as having students and families different from the dominant culture share their customs and traditions (Moll, Amanti, Neff, & Gonzalez, 2005). However, deeper understandings are necessary to expand classroom experiences with a global perspective. The Asia Society and the

Council of Chief State School Officers (2011) have developed Global Competence Matrices containing four areas for teachers to frame a global classroom. One matrix articulates lessons with big ideas in the content areas and another can frame global competency in any discipline. Students become engaged through areas that investigate the world, recognize perspectives, communicate ideas, and identify actions designed to impact issues. Collaborators will find that highly able ELLs will more readily connect to curriculum that compares the dominant culture to their own and others. The connection can also impact children's individual identities in reference to the world around them and their heritage. A global classroom environment encourages critical thinking for all students and motivates highly able ELLs to participate because it connects them to familiar experiences.

Inclusive classrooms are heterogeneous and have a range of language abilities and strengths. Within a single class, ELLs may have varying second language skills. Because of this varying ability, all students need differentiation to meet their language needs and to effectively access or extend the curriculum. Teachers need to be sensitive to the specific instructional needs of ELLs by understanding their language proficiency levels and by being able to challenge them with complex thinking skills and advanced content. Collaboration can help a classroom teacher embed a full range of language experiences and services by combining the expertise of ESL, gifted, and other support personnel throughout the instructional day.

## *Comprehensive Resource Collaboration Team*

Reorganizing and rethinking services in an inclusive classroom with a Comprehensive Resource Collaboration Team (CRCT) approach for all resource support areas (expanding on the special education child study team) will maximize human resources and provide a common foundational approach for each student's learning needs. This approach will defragment instruction and content for students and build an instructional plan that is highly focused on students' overall needs. The collective effort of resource service areas such as gifted, ESL, and special education, for example, allow for school personnel to work closely together with classroom teachers to develop shared instructional objectives and goals. We recommend schools design a CRCT group to work jointly with classroom teachers in a well-coordinated support system for students. The group will bring a laser focus to the needs of students through a bevy of direct academic and other related services.

## *Building a Comprehensive Resource Collaboration Team*

To build a strong CRCT, it is essential that resource teachers have an understanding of all available school services. In most cases, gifted, ESL, and special education teachers are focused on their own area of expertise in both training and professional learning. However, when working with comprehensive services for highly able ELLs, it is important to note that "Language forms the heart of instruction; thus all teachers are language teachers" (Gottlieb, 2012, p. 5).

Read the description of Marion Elementary in Sidebar 6.2. Then, consider how this hypothetical school might meet the needs of its fourth graders this year. What would a CRCT look like in this setting?

---

## Sidebar 6.2: Marion Elementary

Marion Elementary fourth-grade teachers are reviewing the students in their classrooms for the coming year. They will have a significant group of ELLs, highly able students, and some special education students that have varying needs for differentiation. In previous years, it has been difficult to arrange for services and provide the support to effectively meet their needs.

The teachers have been contacted by the special education, gifted, and ESL teachers individually for a meeting to discuss the specific needs of their students and how to best support their academic success this year. The fourth-grade teachers recall the problems of working with so many different people and how they were never sure what their students were doing with the specialist when leaving the classroom. Most of the teachers only had their students in class for a few hours of the day and many missed math, social studies, or science periods. This year, the teachers are discussing keeping their students in class and working collaboratively with at least some of the specialists in their classrooms. The fourth-grade teachers want to have a meeting with all of the support personnel to discuss a more effective way to meet the needs of their students.

The fourth-grade teachers see the value of having additional support in the classroom during team-teaching so students will be more closely connected with the curriculum and benefit from differentiated instruction as a community of learners. The teachers want the support specialists to blend services so students' multiple needs will be met and opportunities for differentiation can be developed through classroom units. Some of their ELLs need language support and challenging instruction and curriculum. Several of the teachers collaborated with the ESL teacher last year and recognized how enriching the experience was for the entire class. The units engaged students with different perspectives and provided a base for understanding a variety of languages. Teachers shared responsibilities for developing and delivering lessons, enabling them to do more motivating activities without additional work. This year they would like to add more collaboration and learn how to be more efficient working with multiple specialists to blend support for students.

---

First and foremost, to build a CRCT, the school's resource teachers will want to work together to gain knowledge of the basic foundations of identification, characteristics, eligibility, and instructional perspectives of each area. Engaging in professional learning is the initial step to building a CRCT. "Action research" is a very effective professional learning approach when teachers are designing a systemic process, because the team will be reflecting on current practices while problem solving how each person's activities can become part of a complement of services. Teachers seek a common foundation while working together. Utilizing action research will build the teacher relationships necessary for the CRCT to function once the foundation is in place. Classroom teachers are critical to the success of a CRCT and should also be a part of its professional learning process. Teachers can initiate and sustain action research in a number of ways that best fit the people working together. Professional learning communities, program retreats, and/or quarterly sessions centered on each program are all possible starting points for collaborative learning. Common readings and follow-up discussions can help teachers become knowledgeable in multiple areas. One salient piece of this work is that all resource services are built around the same general curriculum standards. Resource services in an inclusive environment are built on the curriculum of the classroom (i.e., district). Whatever professional learning approach selected by the team, the focus is on finding commonality in services, reducing redundancy, and developing a collective perspective on the approach to best serve students.

Building a CRCT takes time and commitment to common goals and understanding how to integrate the instruction into a school day, week, and year. The team can be comprised of resource program teachers (as described previously), lead teachers, coaches, media specialists, or any support personnel in a school. Administrators and teachers will want to work together to develop formal systems that integrate collaboration into the school instructional environment. Honigsfeld and Dove (2010) discussed a number of formal instructional and noninstructional practices and systems that will need to be in place for successful integrated collaboration. Joint planning centered on discussing student information, developing curriculum and instructional materials, and determining the best instructional model is a key element to successful collaboration. The CRCT can be built in phases to ensure a strong base for growing and sustaining an effective collaboration system. In some situations it may be best to start small, collaborating with two resource programs or even one person to develop the underpinnings of coordinating a collaborative classroom environment. As stated earlier, whether a school or group of teachers decides to build a CRCT with two, three, or more programs or support personnel, the collaboration process requires formal systems.

Gifted and ESL programs are a good place to begin building effective collaborative systems to meet the needs of highly able ELLs. The best gifted and ESL programs look at students' proficiencies and build on their strengths. Teachers in these programs know that ELLs' native language proficiency can facilitate the development of a second language and academic success in the process. ELLs have the unique opportunity to develop complex thinking when adding a second language. The cognitive process of switching from one language to another has been shown to promote a high level of thinking and academic success in school (Reyes & Crawford, 2012). It is important to note that gifted ELLs' and highly able (potentially gifted) ELLs' needs are met differently than typical English speaking students' needs are. Gifted programs can learn from ESL programs about the best approach to instruction and blend the programs with challenging and motivating curriculum.

We noted earlier that CRCT building starts with a shared understanding of each resource program. During the initial professional learning time, it is important to concurrently develop instructional relationships, organization systems, and student-centered classrooms. The three distinct areas are closely intertwined in a CRCT and can capitalize on existing school structures. Relationships are what make collaboration work. Schools can have the best organization for learning with excellent curriculum, but the success of student learning rests on the people delivering the services.

## *Teacher Relationships*

In today's schools, the roles of ESL and gifted resource teachers are constantly changing to meet the demands for increasing student achievement. Gifted and ESL teachers are connecting more closely to classroom teachers and curriculum as schools focus on mastery of standards based on broad ideas in curriculum. Schools are recognizing that services for highly able students are necessary to meet their needs regardless of if they are labeled gifted or ELL or if evidence shows they have advanced abilities. Teachers view their pedagogy through the eyes of students and student learning. The central question is,

"Who are my students and how well are they achieving?" The role of today's teacher is to facilitate differentiated experiences by creating an environment that is open-ended, relevant, challenging in a risk-taking safe environment, and enables students to actively engage in learning. Highly able ELLs have unique needs that can be addressed by combining gifted and ESL services in a collaborative relationship with a classroom teacher.

The collaboration of gifted, ESL, and homeroom teachers builds the capacity of classrooms for more effective teaching, assessment, and evaluation of highly able ELLs. These teacher-to-teacher relationships need to be built and maintained as they grow and mature. Formal structures for gifted, ESL, and classroom teachers to discuss beliefs, styles, and philosophies need to be in place before, during, and after collaboration is implemented. Inclusive classrooms require close teacher relationships that evolve and grow as they focus on the enhancement of student learning. Gifted, ESL, and classroom teachers have strengths to contribute to the shared goals for supporting highly able ELLs in the collaborative relationship. Although the teachers will have many informal instructional conversations, more formal structures with facilitation guides help move the collaboration discussion to a professional level focused on student learning. We recommend the following three guides to help build a professional teaching relationship between gifted, ESL, and classroom teachers.

Guide 6.1 is Teacher-Held Beliefs. This is a simple scale for gifted, ESL, and classroom teachers to independently mark a point that best represents their beliefs on some broad practices. The scale facilitates a discussion that helps professional educators share personal beliefs with one another. The purpose of the scale is to begin communicating some basic tenets that will impact the instructional culture in a classroom.

# Guide 6.1: Teacher-Held Beliefs

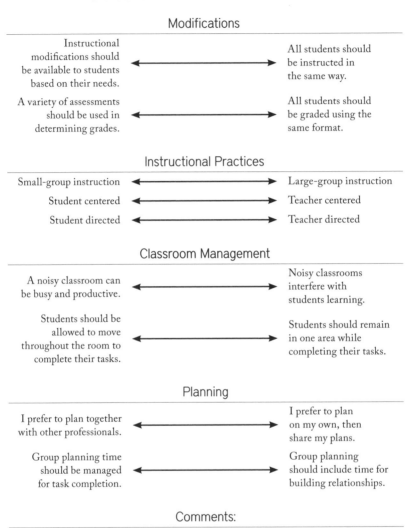

## Modifications

| | |
|---|---|
| Instructional modifications should be available to students based on their needs. | All students should be instructed in the same way. |
| A variety of assessments should be used in determining grades. | All students should be graded using the same format. |

## Instructional Practices

| | |
|---|---|
| Small-group instruction | Large-group instruction |
| Student centered | Teacher centered |
| Student directed | Teacher directed |

## Classroom Management

| | |
|---|---|
| A noisy classroom can be busy and productive. | Noisy classrooms interfere with students learning. |
| Students should be allowed to move throughout the room to complete their tasks. | Students should remain in one area while completing their tasks. |

## Planning

| | |
|---|---|
| I prefer to plan together with other professionals. | I prefer to plan on my own, then share my plans. |
| Group planning time should be managed for task completion. | Group planning should include time for building relationships. |

## Comments:

*Note.* Developed based on *The Power of 2: Making a Difference Through Co-Teaching, Facilitator's Guide* (Friend, 2005).

Guide 6.2, Classroom Practices Inventory, enables gifted, ESL, and classroom teachers to discuss their beliefs and current practices with regard to incorporating differentiation into instruction. Differentiation of curriculum and instruction is required to effectively meet the needs of highly able ELLs. Gifted, ESL, and classroom teachers will bring a different perspective and have varying experiences and understandings of differentiation. Initially, teachers will mark the place on the continuum representing their current practices to gain an understanding of each person's experiences and discuss target areas for developing differentiation practices. Teachers will want to maximize differentiation practices for highly able ELLs. This guide, therefore, can set a baseline by identifying the selection of areas that can be implemented immediately, and teachers can also note areas to learn more for implementation in later units. Differentiation is a key skill for all the collaborating teachers to master in student-centered classrooms in order to respond effectively to varying learning needs.

Guide 6.3, Collaboration "Must-Have" Conversations, is for gifted, ESL, and classroom teachers to express more specific information about everyday instructional decisions necessary for effective collaboration. Teachers discuss the questions to enable a detailed conversation on their roles in the classroom in reference to what each person would be doing and how the classroom would function. This is a time to recognize that ESL, gifted, and classroom teacher information are equally important to the relationship and individual strengths can complement one another. A basic tenet of collaboration is that the instructional decisions should result in a plan so that each teacher has a purpose and an active role in teaching students at all times. The professional conversation proactively develops a shared vision for the collaborative relationship in a classroom. The decisions made at this time will influence the culture of the classroom and its instructional environment.

# Guide 6.2: Classroom Practices Inventory

Use this inventory to look at what you are already doing in your classroom to differentiate instruction. Mark an "X" on each line to show where your current teaching practices lie on the continuum.

| Traditional Classroom | | Differentiated Classroom |
|---|---|---|
| Covering the curriculum is my first learning priority and directs my teaching. | ←——————→ | I base my teaching on students' needs as well as on the curriculum. |
| Learning goals remain the same for all students. | ←——————→ | Learning goals are adjusted for students based on their needs. |
| I emphasize mastery of content and skills. | ←——————→ | I emphasize critical and creative thinking and the application of learning. |
| Students use the same informational resources (books, articles, Web sites). | ←——————→ | I match students to specific informational resources based on their learning needs and abilities. |
| I primarily use whole-class instruction. | ←——————→ | I use several instructional formats (for example, whole class, small groups, partners, individuals). |
| I tend to group students heterogeneously. | ←——————→ | As appropriate, I group students for instruction based on their learning needs. |
| All students move through the curriculum together and at the same pace. | ←——————→ | The pace of instruction may vary, based on students' learning needs. |
| All students complete the same activities. | ←——————→ | As appropriate, I give students opportunities to choose activities based on their interests. |
| I tend to use similar instructional strategies day to day. | ←——————→ | I use a variety of instructional strategies (for example, lectures, manipulatives, role plays, simulations, readings). |

| Traditional Classroom | Differentiated Classroom |
|---|---|
| All students complete all activities. | Students complete different activities based on their needs or learning preferences. |
| All students are involved in all instructional activities. | I use methods for testing out of work and for compacting (speeding up, eliminating, replacing) work, as appropriate. |
| My enrichment work provides more content or more application of skills. | My enrichment work demands critical and/ or creative thinking and the production of new ideas , thoughts, and perspectives. |
| In re-teaching, I provide more practice using a similar instructional method. | In re-teaching, I use a different instructional method from the one I used to teach the material the first time. |
| My re-teaching activities typically involve lower-level thinking– knowledge and comprehension– to reinforce basic skills and content. | My re-teaching activities demand higher-level thinking while reinforcing basic skills and content. |
| I assume that students have limited knowledge of curriculum content. | Before beginning a units, I use pre-assessment strategies to determine what students already know. |
| I usually assess students' learning at the end of an instructional sequence. | I use ongoing assessment to check students' learning throughout an instructional sequence. |
| I typically use the same assessment tool, product, or project for all students. | I allow for learner differences by providing a variety of ways to show learning. |

# Guide 6.3: Collaboration
# "Must-Have" Conversations

All teachers respond to the questions individually and then have a conversation before, during, and after collaboration lessons.

## Conversations Before Collaborating

- How do you envision your role in the classroom?
- How do you envision my role in the classroom?
- What positive and negative collaborative teaching experiences or perceptions do you have?
- How can we present constructive criticism to each other?
- What is appropriate teacher interaction in the classroom?
- To what depth do you plan your lessons?
- What is your teaching philosophy?
- What is your teaching style?
- What instructional strategies will we use?
- Who is responsible for conferencing with parents?
- What behavior plan will be in place?

## Conversations During Collaboration

- Are the instructional strategies being used effective?
- Are all student needs being met?
- How do you think the pace of the instruction is going?
- Are classroom norms/rules being utilized?
- How will we respond to one another's directions, lessons, insights within the classroom?
- Be aware of the involvement of your collaborative teacher. Is he or she standing in the back twiddling his or her thumbs?
- Are the assignments addressing the proficiency levels of the students?

## Conversations After Collaboration

- How are the students progressing?
- Are there any special needs to address? If so, how will **we** address them?
- Was the lesson effective? Did the students understand the content? What is our evidence?
- Are there any changes that **we** need to make to the lessons/units? How should **we** change this lesson to make it more effective next time it is implemented?
- What is the next step to take for the lesson?
- Are there any behavior issues that need addressing? If so, how will **we** address them?
- Were the assessments: appropriate, differentiated, comprehensive, etc. . . . ?
- What are the next assessments we will give to the students? When?
- Do we need to make any adjustments regarding differentiation, remediation, extension, etc. . . . ?

- Did the students accomplish the learning goals and meet/exceed standards?
- Do we need any additional resources or collaboration with other teachers/staff regarding our upcoming lessons?
- How could **we** have collaborated more effectively?

*Note.* Adapted from "Conversations we must have: General education and ESOL teachers," 2009, by B. Braude and G. Johnson. Presentation at the 8th Annual ESOL Conference, Kennesaw, GA.

## *Organizing for Collaboration*

Formal organizational structures are necessary to effectively coordinate collaboration in the inclusive classroom. The structures define and outline a framework of how people work together and the roles and responsibilities of each person. Collaboration is heavily dependent on professional teacher relationships and needs clarity of purpose as well as clear understandings of what will be done and how the plans will be implemented. To be successful collaborators, teachers will need to be flexible within the formal structures that guide the process. Schools and classrooms by nature are dynamic because they are responding to the needs of students and the school community. Additionally, a collaboration system requires that the support of administrators be outlined, discussed, and shared across the school. Gifted, ESL, and classroom teachers will want to understand what expectations will be in place and how they will interact in the collaborative process with co-teachers, students, and parents. Working with administrators to formally clarify the organization of collaboration is essential. In our experiences teachers and staff have important questions that address organizing issues. Below we list some of the concerns that teachers have expressed when embarking on collaboration.

- Will the entire school be organizing for collaboration, one or more grade levels, or individual classes?
- How will professional learning be organized?
- How will collaboration information be communicated between collaborators and across the school?
- How much time will be allocated for preparation and how will it be organized?

- How will instructional time be organized?
- Will there be guides to organize how planning and other meetings will be conducted?

Administrators will want to work closely with the gifted, ESL, and classroom teachers on the initial decisions. Collaboration practices will evolve during the first year and adjustments are generally necessary to respond to the specific needs of the students and school situations.

A comprehensive collaboration model's goal is to blend existing school structures and/or systems into a more efficient system that better meets the needs of highly able ELLs. The structures promote shared teacher responsibilities for planning and implementing curriculum and instruction. Here are some criteria to consider that we recommend from our experiences and that others have found essential when organizing for collaboration (Honigsfeld & Dove, 2010; Landrum, 2002; Risko & Bromley, 2001):

- open and transparent communication systems;
- clear roles, responsibilities, and goals;
- organization and clarification of teacher planning;
- seamless implementation of services;
- shared responsibilities;
- models for instruction; and
- differentiated curriculum that infuses culture, global insight, and language proficiencies into complex challenging tasks.

The Inclusive Collaboration Model (Figure 6.2) is one way to organize how gifted, ESL, and classroom teachers can collaborate with each other. Each frame outlines how collaborators will work individually and together with a balanced plan for delivery of services to students. The model is designed so schools can use it for various resource services that come together in the inclusive classroom.

The organization of how gifted, ESL, and classroom teachers will interact for the purpose of integrating services for highly able ELLs begins with individual preparation that leads to group/shared preparation, provides for communication, and outlines a balanced plan for

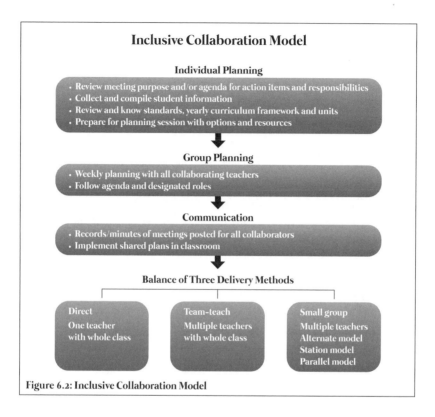

**Inclusive Collaboration Model**

**Individual Planning**
- Review meeting purpose and/or agenda for action items and responsibilities
- Collect and compile student information
- Review and know standards, yearly curriculum framework and units
- Prepare for planning session with options and resources

**Group Planning**
- Weekly planning with all collaborating teachers
- Follow agenda and designated roles

**Communication**
- Records/minutes of meetings posted for all collaborators
- Implement shared plans in classroom

**Balance of Three Delivery Methods**

Direct
One teacher
with whole class

Team-teach
Multiple teachers
with whole class

Small group
Multiple teachers
Alternate model
Station model
Parallel model

Figure 6.2: Inclusive Collaboration Model

the implementation of comprehensive collaboration services. When addressing highly able ELLs, team members will specifically want to blend gifted and ELL services so they share common goals. Group preparation occurs when the gifted, ESL, and collaborating teachers devise a plan for organizing initial and ongoing student information. However, gathering and compiling the information into portfolios or folders (paper or electronic) is completed individually and discussed during group preparation. This information should let teachers know the strengths, interests, learning styles, and specific instructional needs of their students. Ongoing assessments, project work, and other information will be continually added to inform decisions for instruction. Individual preparation is also recommended so that each teacher can review and understand the content standards, the approved curriculum framework, and instructional units for a class/grade. Teachers will want to plan at least 2–3 weeks prior to starting a collaborative unit of study to have enough preparation time to organize and gather resources. The gifted and ESL teachers will want to specifically prepare differentiation options to blend and/or develop complementary services. The individual preparation will result in more productive group meetings.

## *Planning for Instruction*

The efficient use of time should drive the organization of integrated collaboration services planning for highly able ELLs. In the model, individual planning provides time to prepare student information, review standards and curriculum, and develop options and resources to share during group planning. Gifted, ESL, and classroom teachers will want to have a structured meeting with defined roles, a shared agenda, and clear goals. The collaborating team will need to determine the role each person will have in the meeting.

A common planning template completed during the meeting is a good practice for follow-up communication and efficiency, as is access to the curriculum framework, standards, and multiple resources that expedites session planning. Minutes, records, and documents created should all be available to the collaborating team in an accessible location at all times. The best option is to keep everything electronic and stored for easy referencing in any central location. Keeping the meeting professional is imperative to saving time and staying focused on the goals, and a positive spirit among collaborators will create a climate conducive to producing materials and plans all collaborators will want to implement. Agendas should be developed at the end of each planning session for the next meeting and should include what was discussed, any actions that need to be completed with a deadline, and who is responsible for the action. All completed work should be cited on the agenda for future records and referenced to all collaboration team members when moving forward with units and lessons.

Lastly, the collaboration model outlines the implementation of the planning through a balance of three delivery models. The Inclusive Collaboration Model emphasizes the importance of balancing this time with direct whole-group instruction, team-teaching, and small-group instruction in an effort to create opportunities for classrooms to meet a variety of interests, learning styles, and teaching strategies. Murawski's (2009) coteaching models support inclusion services and assist in organizing structures that will ultimately incorporate differentiated strategies and curriculum content to best meet the needs of students.

## *Delivery Model Descriptions*

Direct instruction occurs when the regular classroom teacher delivers differentiated instruction without assistance from colleagues, team-teaching is when collaborating teachers are in the room together, and small-group work can occur in the classroom or outside the classroom. All of the instructional models provide different environments as a first step for differentiating learning experiences for highly able ELLs. They also offer a multitude of options for learning and can be adapted by teachers for effective collaboration.

The whole class model is when one teacher leads a lesson using targeted differentiated strategies that blend into the instruction to address the needs of highly able ELLs in a specific content area. Strategies include the use of visuals, repetition, graphic organizers, manipulatives, and gestures to emphasize vocabulary and concepts that facilitate understanding of content. Differentiation is organized to challenge highly able ELLs at their language proficiency level and bridge what they know to the next level. Complex concepts will need to be comprehensible so students can be challenged with both language and content. The one-teacher delivery model can be a combination of whole-group instruction with time for individual practice and/or station activities. Even though only one teacher is in the classroom, the entire team works together in planning the supports necessary to meet the needs of highly able ELLs. Generally, at least one designated instructional period during the day for specific differentiation targeting highly able ELLs is organized by the collaboration team. However, classroom teachers often incorporate support strategies throughout the school day after they master the differentiation process through collaboration with the ESL and gifted specialist. The classroom teacher's expertise in differentiation for highly able ELLs is enhanced during planning sessions and implementation of coteaching and small-group teaching.

Team-teaching occurs when both teachers are working side by side to teach the whole group in the classroom. Lessons are delivered simultaneously, alternating the lead and utilizing the content and instructional strengths of the teachers. Two or more teachers model working together using high-level questioning, thinking aloud, and playing devil's advocate while incorporating differentiation strategies. The teaching process is a lead, question, listen, and respond strategy that supports making content comprehensible for highly able ELLs.

Collaborating teachers can also organize into several different small-group configurations. *Parallel teaching* is when students are divided into two groups and are taught the same material by each teacher. Differentiation of the process and content is used to learn the same concepts. *Station teaching* is when the instructional content is divided into two or more groups for differentiation; each teacher takes responsibility for a learning station while one is specifically designed as an independent learning station. The last small-group delivery model, *alternative teaching*, is used when one teacher works with a group of students who have specific needs for differentiation, while the other teacher works with the large group (Friend, 2005). The power of small groups is that student needs can be more specifically differentiated, allowing for more participation, specific checking for understanding, and targeting of feedback to improve comprehensibility of content.

The most significant part of the model for teachers to integrate is the idea of balance and meeting student needs. The different delivery models for instruction create a variety of environments for learning that respond to specific needs of students while keeping a close connection to the classroom curriculum. Alternating the delivery models creates a more engaging differentiated environment for students.

Collaborating teachers will need to identify the models they will use to deliver services. When this is done, they can move ahead with developing the supporting formal structures for working together before, during, and after teaching. Teachers will want to decide which of the models will best support the instructional plan for meeting the needs of students and consider their own strengths within the model. One important note is that teachers will save time by efficiently sharing the responsibilities for planning, teaching, and assessing. Dividing the responsibilities among the collaborating team is critical to the success of collaboration.

---

## Sidebar 6.3: What Does the CRCT Look Like in Practice?

Excited about her new role as member of the CRCT fourth-grade team, Mrs. Alistair, the ESL teacher, prepares for a meeting to discuss the upcoming unit in social studies and English language arts. Mrs. Alistair gathers up the student profiles she has written based on students' language proficiency scores, and information gathered from interviews with students and parents concerning former education, interests, etc. She has included copies of descriptors stating what her students can do at their given proficiency level through the domains of listening, speaking, reading, and writing, and a list of strategies and scaffolds that teachers can use during instruction and assessment.

Previously, the team has discussed the idea of scaffolding in great depth and everyone agreed that, with scaffolding, the students, even those at the pre-emergent and emergent stage, will be able to comprehend and demonstrate higher order thinking skills even at low proficiency levels. Ms. Alistair will demonstrate this even further as she works with the activities and assessments planned for this unit:

- *Essential Question:* How can literature show us the world through the eyes of others?
- *Task:* Establishing elements of myths and traditional literature from different cultures.

Focusing on the essential question the team has identified for the unit, "How can literature show us the world through the eyes of others?", Mrs. Alistair sees a great opportunity to incorporate literature from cultures represented in the classrooms, school, and beyond. The team has selected literature from the example unit on the state website which focuses mostly on legends of the Native American culture. Although Mrs. Alistair sees this as an opportunity for her English learners to explore literature based on the culture of Native Americans, she will recommend that the teachers expand the unit to include other cultures as well. Mrs. Alistair gathers several books from her personal and school library to take to the team meeting. In previous meetings, the idea of literature being both a mirror and a window to learning has been expanded to include text from all content areas.

Mrs. Alistair has provided the teachers with specific information on the strengths and needs of each student's language proficiency level from both summative and formative assessments and background knowledge of prior education and interests. The students are at the beginning levels of language acquisition with scores ranging from levels 2 to 3 in the four domains of listening, speaking, reading, and writing, with writing being the lowest score for most of her students.

Mrs. Alistair recognizes that she can build on her students' higher scores and abilities in the domain of speaking to increase their writing scores. She will recommend a plan for discussion groups prior to reading using anticipation guides and other strategies. Additionally, Mrs. Alistair will recommend to follow-up the reading with discussion groups that allow her students to practice their language skills, consolidate their knowledge, and build on their understanding based on their discussions with others in the group. She will discuss ways students can demonstrate their comprehension. For example, one of her students, Samuel, is able to communicate his understanding and thinking through elaborate drawings. Mrs. Alistair has met with Samuel's mother several times and knows that his mother is a talented botanical artist. Samuel has shown a great interest in plants as well. He has also expressed concern about the town's recent drought and its effect on the plants in the area. Samuel has noticed that many of the plants on the school grounds are dying due to the drought. Following his example, several of the students have been using their recess time to water and care for some of the plants.

Mrs. Alistair will suggest the unit include opportunities for the students to build on their interest in school plants and the current drought. Some project ideas she will share include organizing a proposal to install rain barrels and/or investigating the current plants and landscaping plans at the school to develop a play, song, or naturalist's journal incorporating legends of plants or wildflowers.

The next steps include determining when, where, and how collaborating teachers will plan, teach, assess, and reflect on instruction and curriculum units. Scheduling time for each of these components is imperative for the success of collaborative instruction. When implementing collaboration, good planning makes for good instruction in classrooms. All teachers need to know what is being taught and how it will be taught with a clear understanding of the goals and objectives for every unit/lesson. Each collaborating teacher will need to know his or her role and responsibility for the learning plan and be reliable in completing his or her part. Teachers will also need a schedule with collaborating times and locations. Fortunately, collaboration can be a timesaver for teachers because the responsibilities for instruction are shared and when working together they can utilize each other's expertise to develop effective instructional ideas. ESL and gifted teachers collaborating with the classroom teacher can utilize their special area knowledge to create meaningful units and lessons. However, this will only happen if teachers carefully prepare for and focus their time in the meetings, keep good records of each meeting, and recognize that each person must accept and take responsibility for working together.

## *Student-Centered Classrooms and the Mirror/Window Analogy*

Student-centered classrooms for highly able ELLs can best be described and understood through the following analogy of a mirror and window:

> Literature can act as both mirror and window for its readers . . . Although it is true that literature allows readers to envision themselves and those different from themselves, perhaps the best books offer an experience that is more like looking through a window as the light slowly fades. At first, one sees clearly through the window into another's world—but gradually, as the light dims, one's own image becomes reflected as well. (Galda, Liang, Sipe, & Cullinan, 2013, pp. 47–48).

As educators, we believe that it is imperative that we include text and experiences that are both a mirror and a window, but most importantly that our curriculum is based on that same premise. Our curriculum needs to be an inclusive one in which students can "see" others but also "see" themselves. As a mirror, students focus on themselves, their own cultural group and experiences, and their language. As a window, the students focus on other cultural groups, new experiences, and new languages. Furthermore, we need to know our students can make connections that support a relevant learning environment that expands thinking. " . . . We must build the habit of always looking through a 'sociocultural lens' to get to know our students" (Zwiers, 2008, p. 16). Purcell-Gates (1995, p. 6) stated,

> How can we understand why so many children do not learn what the mainstream schools think they are teaching unless we can get "inside" the learners and see the world through their eyes? If we do not try to do this, if we continue to use the mainstream experience of reality as the perspective, we fool ourselves into believing that we are looking through a window when instead we are looking into a mirror.

Using the mirror/window analogy, we come to understand that a student-centered classroom needs to focus on big ideas in which all perspectives are included and that learning about others also helps us learn about ourselves—our strengths, interests, and challenges. In this classroom, highly able ELLs learn through relevant, motivating, and empowering experiences; "when our children feel empowered to learn, they take control of and responsibility for their own education" (Schmidt & Lazar, 2011, p. 23).

In order to build a student-centered classroom that provides highly able ELLs with different ways of demonstrating their talents, we need to examine what we teach and how we teach. What is the best way to teach gifted and talented ELLs? Consistent with constructivist thinking, and based on our research and experiences, we believe that students learn best by constructing their own knowledge rather than having someone else construct it for them.

Students build new knowledge upon previous knowledge. In the constructivist approach, educators understand that students approach learning with prior knowledge. They are not a *tabula rasa*, or blank slate, upon which new information is engraved. ELLs enter a new situation with knowledge learned from previous experiences. This previous knowledge influences how they approach new information or knowledge. If new learning is inconsistent with prior knowledge, the ELL has to note these inconsistencies and either modify or construct new knowledge based on these new experiences. For highly able ELLs, prior knowledge can come from a variety of sources, such as content, language, culture, and so on. Oftentimes, classroom teachers assume that highly able ELLs are aware of these building blocks; however, it has been our experience that, sometimes, we need to point out to students that they already know how to conduct an experiment or use cognates to understand vocabulary in English.

In a student-centered classroom, educators and learners recognize that learning is an active process rather than a passive one. Learners are actively engaged in the process of constructing new knowledge based on prior experiences. Highly able ELLs learn best by trying to make sense of information with the teacher and peers as guides to help them along the way. In this active process, highly able ELLs become aware of the elements from their prior experiences that can be applied in new situations. For example, in the content area of math, they come to understand that even though the procedures used in the new learning environment may appear to be different, the solution remains the same. In the language arts classroom, highly able ELLs can infer and come to conclusions from text in any language. As educators in a student-centered classroom, we need to be cognizant of our role. We are not transmitters of knowledge, but rather, providers of opportunities in which students are allowed to construct understandings and knowledge through a differentiated environment.

In order to build on students' prior knowledge, it is imperative that we know as much about the students' prior knowledge as possible. We need to build on what Gonzalez, Greenberg, and Velez (2012), following the findings of Luis C. Moll, referred to as "funds of knowledge." These researchers, quoting Moll, agreed that "existing classroom practices underestimate and constrain what Latino and other children are able to display intellectually" (Gonzalez et al., 2012, p. 1). Moll believed the secret to "instruction is for schools to investigate and tap into the 'hidden' home and community resources of their students" (Gonzalez et al., 2012, p. 1). Teachers gather data about the knowledge and skills in the community and homes of their students through conversations with "family members in order to learn about the personal and labor history of the family" (Gonzalez et al., 2012, p. 2). Using this information, in Moll's lab/study group, "teachers began to treat the students as 'active' learners using and applying literacy as a tool for communication and for thinking" (Gonzalez et al., 2012, p. 3). Teachers also involved parents and other members of the community to share their knowledge by "teaching through the community" (Gonzalez et al., 2012, p. 4). Parents and community members became what Moll called "a cognitive resource for the class" (Gonzalez et al., p. 5). Furthermore, students became researchers within the classroom to study topics of interest to them related to curriculum goals. These connections with community partners are a resource that students can use to further their interests, strengths, and areas of giftedness. As Roby, Rivera, and Lewis (2012) suggested, students can pursue their area of giftedness by connecting with community partnerships in which students can engage in activities and resources offered by members of the community to develop professional mentorships or other real-world opportunities to explore their interests, strengths, and areas of giftedness.

Another source of information on students' prior knowledge comes from assessments. It is important to know the proficiency levels of our students in the domains of listening, speaking, reading, and writing, as well as content knowledge and understanding, in order to scaffold what they know and are able to do. Recognizing the knowledge that highly able ELLs possess is a key factor in identifying them as gifted. However, understanding their language proficiency is only one aspect of understanding how to motivate and create relevant learning experiences for them. A student-centered classroom builds a learning environment that incorporates the interest, learning styles, and strengths of its students.

Vygotsky's (1978) theory of learning is one of the foundations for constructivism that expands the student-centered classroom through social interactions and learning. He proposed that students acquire language and content knowledge through actions and shared social interaction with a more knowledgeable peer or teacher. Students are capable of moving from their actual level of development to what Vygotsky referred to as the zone of proximal development. The zone of proximal development has been defined as "the distance between the actual developmental level as determined by independent problem solving and the level of potential development as determined through problem solving under adult guidance, or in collaboration with more capable peers" (Vygotsky, 1978, p. 86). The more knowledgeable peer or teacher provides the scaffold for students to learn beyond their actual level. The students continue to think about their learning through metacognition and are then able to perform tasks independently.

Scaffolding is a key element in the zone of proximal development theory. By providing highly able ELLs with the necessary scaffolds, students are able to achieve deeper understanding of language and content. Although these scaffolds are usually thought of for ELLs, we posit that the scaffolds of learning also provide a window and mirror into different ways of understanding for native speakers of English as well. While working with peers and in cooperative groups, all students construct knowledge from interactions with others. They are able to consolidate their understanding by reflecting on the information presented by others and their own understanding or knowledge. When highly able ELLs are comparing perspectives gained from working with students who come from different backgrounds, they learn how to frame their own learning. For example, they adjust their misconceptions and perspectives of content knowledge and build linguistic understanding of how language is used and expressed in different situations and for different purposes.

Cooperative learning is a commonly used strategy for scaffolding. It also builds on some cultural aspects of learning. In cultures in which group memberships are important, students tend to learn better and work harder in order to reach group goals. Examples of collaborative learning techniques are reciprocal teaching, think-pair-share, jigsaw, and sequence chains. When using visual scaffolds in cooperative groups, highly able ELLs can demonstrate their knowledge (talents) in the same way that the scaffold provided the student with comprehensible input or understanding. For example, when he or she is given visuals to understand complicated texts or tasks in a cooperative group, the student can demonstrate his or her comprehension and critical analysis by illustrating his or her thinking.

In a student-centered classroom, teachers need to provide students with a curriculum based on students' interest. When teachers offer students opportunities to interact with their peers, students can consolidate their learning based on these interactions. By comparing their understanding with that of their peers, students are able to become viewers, as we discussed earlier.

We believe the student-centered classroom encompasses the elements of constructivism and differentiation found in ESL, gifted, and special education. Constructivism is a way of learning. Reyes and Crawford (2012) described constructivists as educators who "conceive learning as a process of reconciling prior knowledge and understandings of the world with new experiences and social interactions, resulting in new knowledge and new understandings" (p. 335). They realized that students come to school with a vast amount of knowledge about their own language, culture, and ways of knowing and learning. Highly able ELLs at the very beginning levels of English language acquisition possess knowledge that needs to be assessed in order to further learning and promote talent development. When a teacher utilizes a student's own culture and funds of knowledge in the classroom, students gain knowledge of other cultures and are exposed to multiple ways of thinking that expand the learner's vision. That vision then becomes an important foundation for learning and critical thinking. In a student-centered classroom setting, information is not presented to the student in facts to be memorized but rather through avenues to discovery and exploration. Knowledge, meaning, and understanding of the world can be addressed in the classroom from both the point of view of the individual learner and the collective view of the entire class (Cobb, 1995; Gredler, 1997; Kim, 2001).

In closing, we propose the student-centered inclusive classroom for highly able ELLs should build on students' strengths as language learners and potential as gifted students, blending both resource areas in the following ways:

- connects to real-world problems with global perspectives;
- seeks multiple solutions with no single answer to any given question;
- allows for student decision making;
- leads to understanding rather than memorization;
- promotes risk-taking in a safe environment where mistakes are valued in language and content learning as a way to build knowledge;
- highly values social and cooperative group learning;
- builds on student's prior knowledge, interests, and culture; and
- requires collaboration among students, teacher, and possibly community members.

Collaborating teams of ESL specialists, gifted specialists, and classroom teachers can make content more comprehensible for highly able ELLs in a student-centered classroom. Connecting prior experiences to curriculum, creating cooperative and collaborative learning experiences, and focusing on problem solving serve as meaningful ways to build talent.

# Summary

Building collaboration and collaborative partnerships is a challenging and rewarding way to meet the needs of highly able ELLs. The potential for providing multiple support services in an inclusive classroom is endless. Inclusive classroom instruction demands professional collaborative relationships focused on the multiple needs of students with differentiated services.

A Comprehensive Resource Collaboration Team works in concert to build targeted support that promotes better parent awareness and a proficiency approach to instruction and that infuses multicultural and global understandings with sensitivity to language learning. Teachers complement their strengths in a coteaching environment, bringing efficiency and more effective differentiation with expertise from multiple specialists and the classroom teacher. The relationships of ESL, gifted, and classroom teachers create an opportunity for highly able ELLs to receive targeted support and challenging curriculum at all language proficiency levels.

Organization of collaboration in an inclusive classroom brings clarity of purpose to teachers, students, and parents. Using the classroom as a center that resource services wrap around throughout an instructional day builds the capacity of the teachers and the school to best meet the needs of highly able ELLs.

Student-centered classrooms open the door for highly able ELLs to immediately access curriculum and engage in classroom instruction. Students see relevancy and are highly motivated by connections made to their interests and strengths. The classroom is an inviting place to expand on current knowledge and investigate new ideas in a different language and culture. As in the analogy of the window and the mirror, collaboration in an inclusive classroom opens the potential for excellence to teachers, parents, and most importantly, students.

In a final note, it is important to recognize that collaboration requires many curriculum decisions to bring a collaborating team together with common goals for student learning. We believe that beliefs, philosophies, organization, relationships, and practices are some of the underpinning constructs of effective collaboration. However, it is the people and their work that impact the effectiveness of collaboration. Most importantly, "collaboration can only be as good as the questions teachers ask each other—and themselves—about the quality of their work and the curriculum basis for their collaboration" (Risko & Bromley, 2001, p. 85).

# References

Asia Society, & Council of Chief State School Officers. *Global competencies.* Retrieved from http://www.edsteps.org/ccsso/ManageContent.aspx?system_name=I5nka44NofDD3IY38QBonx%20Crwfdw%20uF&AspxAutoDetectCookieSupport=1

Braude, B., & Johnson, G. (2009). *Conversations we must have: General education and ESOL teachers.* Paper presented at the meeting of the 8th Annual ESOL Conference, Kennesaw State University, Kennesaw, GA.

Cobb, P. (1995). Continuing the conversation: A response to Smith. *Educational Researcher, 24*(6), 25–27.

Egbert, J., & Ermst-Slavit, G. (2010). *Access to academics planning for instruction for K-12 classrooms with ELLs.* Boston, MA: Pearson Education/Allyn & Bacon.

Foley Nicpon, M., Allmon, A., Sieck, B., & Stinson, R. (2011). Empirical investigation of twice-exceptionality: Where have we been and where are we going? *Gifted Child Quarterly, 55,* 3–17. doi:10.1177/0016986210382575

Friend, M. (2005). *The power of 2: Making a difference through co-teaching* (Facilitator's manual, 2nd ed.). Bloomington, IN: The Forum on Education Publication & Elephant Rock Productions.

Galda, L., Liang, L., Sipe, L., & Cullinan, B. (2013). *Literature and the child.* (8th ed.) Belmont, CA: Wadsworth/Cengage.

Gonzalez, N., Greenberg, J., & Velez, C. (2012). Funds of Knowledge: A look at Luis Moll's research into hidden family resources. Retrieved from http://www.usc.edu/dept/education/CMMR/FullText/Luis_Moll_Hidden_Family_Resources.pdf

Gottlieb, M. (2012). *Common language assessment for English learners.* Bloomington, IN: Solution Tree.

Gredler, M. E. (1997). *Learning and instruction: Theory into practice* (3rd ed). Upper Saddle River, NJ: Prentice-Hall.

Heacox, D. (2002). *Differentiating instruction in the regular classroom: How to reach and teach all learners, grades 3-12.* Minneapolis, MN: Free Spirit.

Honigsfeld, A., & Dove, M. (2010). *Collaboration and co-teaching: Strategies for English learners.* Thousand Oaks, CA: Corwin Press.

Hughes, C., & Murawski, A. (2001). Lessons from another field: Applying co-teaching strategies to gifted education. *Gifted Child Quarterly, 45,* 195–204. doi:10.1177/001698620104500304

Kim, B. (2001). Social constructivism. In M. Orey (Ed.), *Emerging perspectives on learning, teaching, and technology.* Retrieved from http://projects.coe.uga.edu/epltt/index.php?title=Social_Constructivism

Landrum, M. (2002). *Consultation in gifted education: Teachers working together to serve students.* Mansfield, CT: Creative Learning Press.

Roby, D., Lewis, L., & Rivera, A. (2012). *Identifying & serving culturally and linguistically diverse gifted students.* Waco, TX: Prufrock Press.

Moll, L. C., Amanti, C., Neff, D., & Gonzalez, N. (2005). *Funds of knowledge for teaching: Theorizing practices in households, communities, and classrooms.* Mahwah, NJ: Lawrence Erlbaum.

Murawski, W. (2009). *Collaborative teaching in secondary schools: Making the co-teaching marriage work!* Thousand Oaks, CA: Corwin Press.

Noel, J. (2005). *Developing multicultural educators.* Long Grove, IL: Waveland Press.

Purcell-Gates, V. (1995). *Others people's words: The cycle of low literacy.* Cambridge, MA: Harvard University Press.

Renzulli, J. (2012). *Renzulli Learning System* [Computer software]. Retrieved from http://www.compasslearning.com/renzulli

Reyes, S., & Crawford, J. (2012). *Diary of a bilingual school: how a constructivist curriculum, a multicultural perspective, and a commitment to dual immersion education combined to foster fluent bilingualism* [Kindle Edition]. Retrieved from http://www.amazon.com/dp/B006T3LLZK/ref=rdr_kindle_ext_tmb

Risko, V., & Bromley, K. (2001). *Collaboration for diverse learners: View points and practices.* Newark, DE: International Reading Association.

Schmidt, P. R., & Lazar, A. M. (Eds.). (2011). *Practicing what we teach: How culturally responsive literacy classrooms make a difference.* New York, NY: Teachers College Press.

Vygotsky, L. S. (1978). *Mind in society: The development of higher psychological processes* (M. Cole, V. John-Steiner, S. Scribner, & E. Souberman, Trans.). Cambridge, MA: Harvard University Press.

Waterman, R., & Harry, B. (2008). *Building collaboration between schools and parents of English learners: Transcending barriers, creating opportunities.* Retrieved from http://nccrest.org/Briefs/PractitionerBrief_BuildingCollaboration.pdf

Zwiers, J. (2008). *Building academic language: Essential practices for content classrooms.* San Francisco, CA: Jossey-Bass.

# Chapter 7

# Using Service Learning to Support High-Ability English Language Learners

*Paul H. Matthews*

## Introduction

ELLs in U.S. classrooms are already a very heterogeneous group, representing many possible dimensions, including home language background, educational history, time in the U.S., social and academic English proficiency, and academic ability. As this volume's anecdotes of Herminda, Joaquin, and Minh suggest, ELLs are in need of high-quality content-area and English language instruction, already a challenging scenario for many schools and classroom teachers. When such students are academically talented, with potential for significant academic gains and advanced achievement beyond their peers, we are faced with an additional question: What kinds of pedagogical activities can support the talent development of high-ability ELLs, especially in settings where no sheltered content, gifted, pull-out English, or other special "program" tailored to the needs of such students exists? In this chapter, I suggest that the incorporation of academic service learning into their education holds significant promise for fostering the unique constellation of linguistic and academic talents and challenges for such students, whether in specialized or inclusive class settings.

---

## Sidebar 7.1: Service Learning: Herminda

After hearing how it might benefit all of her students, including Herminda, Ms. Anthem decided to incorporate service learning into her first-grade class throughout the year. She identified the local "no-kill" animal shelter as a willing, nearby community partner and worked with her students to investigate its services and needs through a field trip and follow-up research. The students then collaborated in small heterogeneous groups to identify a particular concern that they felt passionate about, and wanted to address through a service activity.

For instance, Herminda's group learned that the shelter needed more families to adopt or temporarily foster pets. When Herminda asked, she found out that almost no one from the local Latino community ever came to the shelter for this purpose. She led her group to write, illustrate, and distribute bilingual posters and flyers throughout her neighborhood and to the shelter, showing how many pets were awaiting a home and why and how families could get involved. The shelter was pleased with the results and displayed the students' posters.

Ms. Anthem noticed this helped her students meet a number of first-grade performance standards, including those in mathematics (measurements, estimations, graphs/charts), science (characteristics of living things, basic needs of living things), and English/language arts (persuasive, informative, and narrative writing). She integrated other activities with the shelter, reflecting on the experience as an ongoing interdisciplinary theme throughout the year. Herminda continued to develop advanced cognitive and language skills, taking on additional projects such as helping draft bilingual descriptions for the local newspaper accompanying photos of pets available for adoption.

---

# What Is Service Learning?

*Academic service learning* entails applying academic skills and knowledge to address a community need, providing benefit to the community while at the same time enhancing student learning. Service learning is often defined as a course-based educational experience in which students participate in an organized service activity meeting identified community needs, and reflect on the activity to deepen their understanding of the academic links and to enhance their sense of personal values and civic responsibility (Bringle & Hatcher, 2005). Identified as a high-impact practice (Kuh, 2008), service learning shows positive outcomes across a range of variables, from personal and social development to civic responsibility, academic learning, and school climate (Billig, 2000; Eyler & Giles, 1999; Warren, 2012). In her handbook for K–12 teachers, Kaye (2010) presented examples, best practices, and advantages of service-learning pedagogy. She noted that students participating in service learning can:

- apply academic, social, and personal skills to improve the community;
- make decisions that have real, not hypothetical, results;
- grow as individuals, gain respect for peers, and increase civic participation;
- experience success no matter what their ability level;
- gain a deeper understanding of themselves, their community, and society; and
- develop as leaders who take initiative, solve problems, work as a team, and demonstrate their abilities while and through helping others. (p. 9)

Because service learning can manifest in many different ways (e.g., direct vs. indirect service; through individual, small-group, or whole-class activities; during regular class time or outside of normal school hours; as a one-time project or an ongoing service activity), it is highly flexible and therefore somewhat challenging to characterize definitively. Billig, Root, and Jesse (2005) have identified 11 "essential elements" for service learning best practices (see Table 7.1); in their research, they found the greatest correlations between measures of positive student outcomes and "student engagement in challenging tasks; activities that meet genuine needs of the community; valuing diversity; direct contact with the community; and student preparation" (p. 40).

Service experiences "can range from performing direct, simple services to advocating for social change" (Lewis, 1996, p. 73). It is important to emphasize, however, that academic service learning intends to move well beyond volunteer work or charitable community service, in that the service activities should be meaningfully selected and intentionally linked to student learning outcomes. Indeed, in their large-scale quantitative study, Vogelgesang and Astin (2000) found that while both service learning and community service had positive effects on all of the affective, leadership, and academic student outcomes they investigated for university students, "for all academic outcomes as well as for some affective ones, participating in service as part of a course ha[d] a positive effect over and above the effect of generic community service" (p. 29). Thus, to fully deliver on its potential, service learning should be carefully integrated into academic coursework (Eyler & Giles, 1999). Kaye (2010) provided one common model showing five stages of developing and carrying out service learning in classroom contexts (Table 7.2).

## *Who Takes Part in Service Learning?*

As a pedagogy, service learning has become relatively frequent in classrooms across the country; more than a quarter of U.S. schools report using academic service learning, especially in middle and high schools, and two thirds of schools involve students in some aspect of community service (Scales & Roehlkepartain, 2004). In the schools offering academic service learning, principals estimated that some 35% of students, and 30% of teachers, are involved in this work (Scales & Roehlkepartain, 2004). Proponents of service learning suggest that the pedagogy is for everyone: it "works with kindergartners and college students as well as every grade in between. Students of all ages

# Table 7.1.

## *Essential Elements for Service Learning*

| Essential Elements |
|---|
| 1. Clear educational goals that require the application of concepts, content, and skills from the academic disciplines and involve students in the construction of their own knowledge. |
| 2. Student engagement in tasks that challenge and stretch them cognitively and developmentally. |
| 3. Assessment used as a way to enhance student learning as well as to document and evaluate how well students have met content and skill standards. |
| 4. Student participation in service tasks that have clear goals, meet genuine needs in the school or community and have significant consequences for themselves and others. |
| 5. Formative and summative evaluations employed in a systematic evaluation of the service effort and its outcome. |
| 6. Student voice in selecting, designing, implementing and evaluating the service project. |
| 7. Value of diversity as demonstrated by its participants, its practice and its outcomes. |
| 8. Direct communication and interaction with the community. |
| 9. Students prepared for all aspects of their service work including a clear understanding of task and role, the skills and information required by the task, awareness of safety precautions, and knowledge about and sensitivity to the people with whom they will work. |
| 10. Student reflection before, during, and after service, using multiple methods that encourage critical thinking, and serving as a central force in the design and fulfillment of curricular objectives. |
| 11. Multiple methods designed to acknowledge, celebrate, and validate students' service work. |

*Note.* Adapted from *The impact of participation in service-learning on high school students' civic engagement* by S. Billig, S. Root, and D. Jesse, 2005, Denver, CO: The Center for Information & Research on Civic Learning & Engagement, p. 2. Copyright 2005 by the Center for Information & Research on Civic Learning & Engagement.

and most ability levels can participate successfully, and almost every subject or skill can be enhanced through the practice" (Kaye, 2010, p. 9).

## Table 7.2.

### Five Stages of Service Learning

| Stage | Description |
| --- | --- |
| 1. Investigation | Learn about student resources, community need, and related details |
| 2. Preparation and Planning | Build background knowledge, make connections to the curriculum, and detail project steps |
| 3. Action | Carry out the community service activity |
| 4. Reflection | Make ongoing connections between the experience, students' own lives, and the classroom |
| 5. Demonstration | Hold a public celebration or presentation of the activities and resulting learning |

*Note.* Adapted from *The complete guide to service learning: Proven, practical ways to engage students in civic responsibility, academic curriculum, & social action* (2nd ed.), by C. B. Kaye, 2010, Minneapolis, MN: Free Spirit Publishing. Copyright 2010 by Free Spirit Publishing.

However, opportunities for service learning are not uniformly available, and indeed, without additional intentional effort on behalf of schools and teachers serving high-ability ELLs, such students may not yet be engaged with this pedagogy. For instance, "low-income students tend to have fewer service opportunities in schools . . . [and] schools serving mostly low-income students tend to engage fewer of their students in service learning than schools that serve fewer low-income students" (Scales & Roehlkepartain, 2004, p. 36). Given that ELLs as a group tend to be low income and to attend segregated high-poverty schools (Arias, 2007; Orfield & Lee, 2006), many such students may well have less access to service learning and its benefits. There are also disparities based on ethnicity. In their review of literature on participation in community service, Webster and Worrell (2008) noted, "although the number of minorities who participate in service activities is growing, these numbers are still small in comparison to Whites" (p. 173). This also mirrors longstanding challenges for high-ability ELL and minority student participation in traditional gifted and talented programs (Lockwood, 1998), as well as Advanced Placement (AP) and International Baccalaureate (IB) programs (Kyburg, Hertberg-Davis, & Callahan, 2007). Disparate participation in service learning does not seem to reflect a lack of interest among underrepresented students, but rather, a lack of opportunity:

> [G]lobal attitudes toward service were not related to ethnicity, grade level, or SES, suggesting that attitudes toward service are positive and generally equal across these demographic groups. Thus, differences in participation in service activities may be related to the ease of opportunity to participate rather than to attitudes toward these activities. (Webster & Worrell, 2008, p. 178)

---

## Sidebar 7.2: Service Learning: Joaquin

In Joaquin's seventh-grade math class, his teacher decided to incorporate service-learning options into the required standards for developing statistical understandings of data, as well as enhancing student geometry and algebra skills. After pre-teaching key vocabulary and concepts, the teacher challenged students individually or in small groups to take on a series of preselected but real issues around the school that would allow for developing and demonstrating their competencies.

Joaquin decided to address his town's recent drought, and analyzed rainfall and reservoir levels monthly for the past several years to show their relationship and trend. He created a poster representing the data in different ways, applying not only the statistical concepts and tools his teacher had focused on but additional ones he learned about on his own. Next, after analyzing his school's roof and gutter system, Joaquin estimated the quantity of water that could likely be harvested from the roof runoff each month and calculated the cost to the school for purchasing this quantity of water for irrigation through the local water authority. Finally, he diagrammed the proposed sizes, dimensions and locations for cisterns and rain barrels to capture roof runoff, and investigated the costs of purchasing them on the Internet. With feedback from his teacher, Joaquin presented his project to the PTA, and later to the school board, encouraging them to act on his proposal to save costs and help conserve water.

---

Fostering more use of service-learning pedagogy with academically advanced ELLs might, then, help counteract some of the lack of resources and attention otherwise directed toward this group, while simultaneously being fully appropriate for other students as well. In addition to its well-documented overall student learning outcomes (e.g., Eyler & Giles, 1999; Warren, 2012), in what ways does academic service learning hold promise for specifically meeting student needs from both the perspectives of gifted education and English to speakers of other languages (ESOL)?

# Review of Literature

## *Service Learning and Advanced Academics*

Many authors have proposed and documented potential benefits of service learning for meeting needs of high-ability students. For instance, Bernal (2003) advocated for a focus on developing the talents and abilities of students in real-world settings, in order that program "alumni were not just smart, but were also getting things done" (p. 185), with service learning as one promising program element to accomplish this.

Service learning has been promoted as exemplifying a differentiated curriculum for academically talented students, serving as "an experience that interests and challenges them, encourages critical thinking, and stimulates them to contribute in areas of passionate interest to them" (Lewis, 1996, p. 71). Service-learning projects are touted as allowing for true differentiation, with various roles and activities connected to the experience, and not solely for academically advanced students; "service provides opportunities for other students in a classroom to join in at different levels of ability and interest" (Lewis, 1996, p. 74). Likewise, Reis and Renzulli (2004) noted that "numerous strategies can be used to make the classroom environment more challenging and developmentally appropriate for gifted students while simultaneously improving education for *all* children" (p. 121, emphasis in original), including "using high-interest content and hands-on activities to create high engagement and creativity" (p. 121)—certainly a possibility with academic service-learning activities. Although not all service-learning projects allow for individualized selection of the community service component, several authors (e.g., Bruce-Davis & Chancey, 2012; Terry, 2003) suggest that student-selected service-learning projects in particular can exemplify "Type III" enrichment in Renzulli's Enrichment Triad ("providing opportunities for applying interests, knowledge, creative ideas and task commitment to a self-selected problem or area of study"; Reis & Renzulli, 2004, p. 125).

Additionally, service learning has been proposed to counter academically able students' potential underachievement, through maintaining and developing student interest in the educational process (Bruce-Davis & Chancey, 2012). "Because service-learning projects involve substantial aspects of student choice and interest, they may be particularly effective in reversing underachievement and thereby motivating students to develop positive skills, such as task commitment" (Bruce-Davis & Chancey, 2012, p. 719). Involvement with engaged and caring adults and peers in joint productive activity—already a tenet of research-based effective education (e.g., Dalton, 2008)—may also help service learning counteract academic underachievement. For instance, Terry (2003) suggested that creative-problem-solving-focused service learning "enhanced attitudes, student development, and commitment" among high-ability middle school students taking part in her program (p. 301).

Given the opportunities for various roles in contextualized group and community engagement, leadership skills of academically talented students might also be developed by these community service activities (e.g., Terry, 2000; Wade & Putnam, 1995; Zinskie, 2003, cited in Matthews, 2004). However, the studies of Lee, Olszewski-Kubilius, Donahue, and Weimholt (2007, 2008) of short-term summer programs for high-ability students did not find consistent evidence for differences in leadership development between participants engaged in service learning and other classes. These findings may suggest a need to include a focused leadership development component within service-learning programs in order to produce measurable changes in leadership skills.

As moral concerns are suggested to be especially salient for highly academically able students (Terry, 2008, p. 46), some research has focused on the role of service learning in helping high-ability students develop and display qualities of caring and moral development (Terry & Bohnenberger, 2003) as well as an orientation toward civic responsibility (Lee et al., 2007, 2008). Stewart and Bai (2010) found higher gains in self-efficacy for service among adolescents taking part in service learning than for those in other classes in the same summer residential program for academically talented youth. Similarly, Lee et al. (2007) found that high-ability students who participated in a summer service-learning program demonstrated enhanced civic responsibility, awareness of issues, and connection to the community, compared with similar students participating in a non-service-learning academic program.

## *Service Learning and Language Acquisition*

Service learning is also an advantageous pedagogy for language-learning students. For instance, it carries many of the same academic benefits for ELLs as those found in more general studies (e.g., development of critical thinking; Martin, 2011), enhanced motivation, and higher order thinking skills through the reflection accompanying the service-learning experience (Russell, 2007). Briggs, Reis, and Sullivan (2008) investigated programs across the country successfully serving high-ability, linguistically and ethnically diverse students; among their findings of factors that contributed to successful identification and participation of these students was the use of curriculum and instructional designs that enabled student success, including service learning (p. 139). Although not focused on language learning, another large-scale national study of (mostly Latino) high school students (Billig et al., 2005) found a range of impacts from service learning on students' civic knowledge, skills, and dispositions when compared with similar students who did not take part in service learning.

Service learning's "use in English language learning contexts appears relatively unexplored . . . [yet] can be a powerful combination, yielding significant benefits for students" (Minor, 2002, p. 10). Both in the realm of ESOL (Hamstra, 2010; Minor, 2002; Russell, 2007) and foreign language (Kaplan & Pérez Gamboa, 2004; Lizardi-Rivera, 2005; Tacelosky, 2008), practitioners have described their efforts to incorporate service learning and the benefits they see for language learners. For instance, Minor (2002) described how his university's intensive English programs incorporated service-learning activities for international students, including work in a soup kitchen, visiting and sharing cultural information with local elementary schools, tutoring, and work with Habitat for Humanity. Ellwell and Bean (2001) incorporated service learning benefiting migrant field workers into a community college, immigrant ESL course focused on reading the novel *Of Mice and Men*. Russell (2007) described service-learning projects her ELL students took part in, including creating community-specific bilingual phrasebooks, implementing reading programs with younger children, and teaching computer skills to older adults.

Service learning also provides a natural context for *authentic language experiences* with community members and peers, beneficial for effective second language acquisition (Russell, 2007; Tacelosky, 2008). "When service learning and the associated reflection activities are done well, opportunities for authentic dialogue are created" (Tacelosky, 2008, p. 878) that can help drive language development. Hamstra (2010) found significant improvement in ELL students' writing skills in English from service-learning participation, hypothesized to come from increased background knowledge through participation in service-learning projects, as well as through students' enhanced sociolinguistic competence developed through their "authentic language experiences in authentic contexts" (p. 80). Service-learning activities might also help "international students adjust to the American culture" (Hamstra, 2010, p. 64; see also Ellwell & Bean, 2001). Kaplan and Pérez Gamboa (2004) likewise cited the community knowledge and linguistic confidence gained by students in their undergraduate Spanish service-learning courses to practice that language in real-world settings.

Although more research studies empirically testing service learning's impact on language learning are needed, this pedagogy's best practices relate well to those for developing second-language competence. Second language acquisition is a complex and long-term process; however, certain elements of practice seem to have a particularly strong impact in driving its development. Access to authentic and understandable language "input," contextualized support for language use, opportunities for negotiation of meaning and obtaining feedback, and the development of academic as well as social language (e.g., Echevarria & Graves, 2007; Levine & McCloskey, 2009; Mullaney, 2005) are necessary for successful mastery of a new language (see Table 7.3 for one set of principles recommended for supporting second language acquisition); each of these aspects of language acquisition is at least as salient in service-learning contexts as in the traditional classroom.

The Sheltered Instruction Observation Protocol (SIOP) model, perhaps the best known and most elaborated model for developing and implementing appropriate content-area instruction for ELLs (Echevarria, Vogt, & Short, 2000), includes some 30 features organized around eight components, intended to develop both academic English proficiency and subject-matter expertise. Service learning dovetails well with SIOP recommendations, including meaningful activities that integrate lesson concepts with language practice: "Because sheltered instruction is student centered, students are assigned real-life activities . . . with lots of opportunities for listening, speaking, reading, and writing" (Echevarria & Graves, 2007, p. 62). Likewise, service learning seems a good fit for accomplishing other key parts of sheltered instruction, such as building students' background knowledge and related vocabulary; incorporating a variety of hands-on techniques to ensure that language is made comprehensible; building higher-order thinking skills into activities; providing opportunities for interaction and discussion with teacher, peers, and others; maintaining student engagement with the lesson; and incorporating practice/application opportunities for using new content knowledge and language (Echevarria et al., 2000).

# Table 7.3.

## Principles of Integrated Language Teaching and Learning

| Principle | Representative Description |
|---|---|
| 1. Active Engagement | "Language is learned while doing something with it, not just learning it" (p. 27). |
| 2. Cultural Relevance | "Respect and incorporate the cultures of learners in the classroom while helping them to understand the new culture of the community, the school, and the classroom" (p. 28). |
| 3. Collaboration | "Two-way experiences through which learners solve problems, negotiate meaning, and demonstrate what they have learned" (p. 29). |
| 4. Learning Strategies | "Allow learners to control and direct their own learning ... They are generally oriented toward solving problems and can involve many aspects of language to be learned beyond the cognitive" (p. 30). |
| 5. Comprehensible Input With Scaffolding | "Provide rich input with appropriate context and support, to make that input comprehensible to learners, and appropriately and increasingly more challenging" (p. 30). |
| 6. Prior Knowledge | "Help learners use their prior knowledge of language, content, and the world to develop new language and increase learning" (p. 32). |
| 7. Content Integration | "Language learning is integrated with meaningful, relevant, and useful content" (p. 34). |
| 8. Differentiation | "Accommodate different language, literacy, and cognitive levels and incorporate many dimensions of learning" (p. 36). |
| 9. Clear, Appropriate Goals and Feedback | "Set and communicate attainable goals for learners and provide students with appropriate and consistent feedback on their progress in attaining these goals" (p. 37). |

From Levine, L. N., & McCloskey, M. L. (2009). *Teaching learners of English in mainstream classrooms (K–8): One class, many paths.* Boston, MA: Pearson.

# Connecting Service Learning to Supports for High-Ability ELLs

Thus, prior research supports the value of academic service-learning experiences for improving personal, civic, and academic outcomes for high-ability students (as well as others), and as an appropriate strategy for supporting ELLs. Weaving together these two strands of support, I next offer considerations for implementation of service learning with high-ability ELLs.

## *Program Settings for Service Learning*

Ideally, service learning should not be viewed as an add-on to work that teachers and students are already doing, but rather, it should be integrated into the curriculum and school day as a methodology for carrying out desired teaching and learning goals regardless of program context. Bernal (2003) has advocated for improving talent development instruction in ways that do not open programs to charges of elitism, noting that "gifted children are rarely served in inclusive settings because teachers make no or few modifications of instruction to assist them and almost never incorporate differentiated or individualized instruction" (p. 184). Readily incorporated into mainstream classroom instruction, service learning thus has potential for significantly enhancing the experiences and talent of English learners in entirely inclusive settings.

Additionally, this pedagogy could support ELL students who are placed in gifted programs with English-only peers—a challenging situation both for teachers and for students (Castellano, 2002). Service learning can provide high-ability minority students in AP and IB courses with the requisite contextualized and high-interest "scaffolding to support and challenge" them while also allowing them to build their background knowledge, as research recommends (Kyburg et al., 2007, p. 204). Indeed, the International Baccalaureate model seems a particularly promising venue for service learning. For instance, its Middle Years program explicitly incorporates both a focus on "community and service" as well as completion of an individualized "personal project," with curriculum promoting intercultural awareness, communication, and holistic learning (International Baccalaureate Program Organization, 2013).

The English language development needs of ELLs of all ability levels are nominally addressed through a wide range of programs—pullout ESOL classes, newcomer programs, cotaught immersion settings, bilingual or dual-language programs, sheltered content instruction, etc. (e.g., Rennie, 1993)—intending to promote language development and, ideally, allow students to also access appropriate content knowledge. However, the diversity of ELL student backgrounds in a given school (Echevarria & Graves, 2007) may mean that students are placed into support programs based more on their grade level or for scheduling convenience than on comparable language proficiency or academic ability. Fortunately, many features of effective practice for ELLs (Edvantia, 2009; Levine & McCloskey, 2009; Rennie, 1993) and students with high academic potential—both at the classroom level (e.g., high expectations for all students, academically rigorous learning environments, thematic organization of content, prioritizing interaction and communication, focusing on language development) and school or district level (professional development for all teachers, supportive school leadership)—also mesh with service learning.

## *Possible Service-Learning Activities to Foster Advanced Academics for ELLs*

What kinds of service activities merit particular consideration for high-ability ELLs? Although the range of possible project areas is vast (Kaye, 2010, proposed more than a dozen themes and related resource materials for grades K–12, ranging from AIDS education to animal protection, immigration, literacy, and emergency readiness), direct service with communities of interest may appeal in particular to high-ability students due to their potential for consideration and application of moral, ethical, and civic issues (Fishman & Swanson, 2011; Terry & Bohnenberger, 2003). These areas may also resonate strongly with Latino ELLs, given the importance of care/caring in the education of such students (Valenzuela, 1999). "Interest-based service-learning projects have the potential to address factors leading to underachievement and set the stage for gifted behaviors" (Bruce-Davis & Chancey, 2012, p. 716); topics such as immigration and immigrant rights, which may have a personal connection for many ELLs, can stimulate this interest, while also fulfilling best practices for English language development such as cultural relevance and prior knowledge (Levine & McCloskey, 2009). Such interest-based topics also meet overall service-learning goals of diversity, impact, and meaningful service (Kaye, 2010).

One potentially high-impact focus of service learning for high-ability ELLs entails using and developing students' dual-language skills to help the community. Matthews and Matthews (2004) have argued that, because developing bilingual competence holds academic benefits, programs (such as "heritage language" courses) that foster students' proficiency in both home and school languages can help enhance or develop high ability, serve as an appropriate venue for easier identification of high ability, and support and develop student motivation for academic success. Although the extent to which being bilingual results in linguistic and cognitive advantages that carry over beyond specific tasks (Bialystok, 2009) is still under active investigation by researchers, the benefits of strong first-language and literacy development in assisting English language progress are well documented (e.g., Cummins, 1991; Thomas & Collier, 2002). Indeed, Valdés (2003) has proposed that bilingual children who successfully serve as interpreters between their family and community are demonstrating gifted behaviors compared to their peers. She encourages schools to consider ways to identify, foster, and celebrate such students' accomplishments.

Service-learning opportunities that draw upon and develop the specialized language abilities of bilingual ELLs (e.g., providing interpretation between local agencies and their clients, translating materials for school use [Lizardi-Rivera, 2005], or fostering dual-language literacy development of younger students) are thus well worth considering. As the earlier review of research suggests, the element of student choice vis-à-vis the service activity is likely vital for stimulating student interest and motivation, and is a best practice for service learning; "service-learning programs and projects that affect factors such as curricular relevance, social connections, attitudes toward school, and academic goals may help students develop and display gifted behaviors and/or reverse patterns of underachievement" (Bruce-Davis & Chancey, 2012, p. 718). Although the particular grade level, content area, resources available, and desired learning outcomes from the teacher's perspective will necessarily constrain the range of choices available to students, incorporation of bilingual language use seems possible across the majority of themes proposed by Kaye (2010) and others.

Finally, service learning's emphasis on critical reflection (Eyler & Giles, 1999; Fishman & Swanson, 2011), and on sharing lessons learned through the process in the "celebration/demonstration" stage (Kaye, 2010), benefits both language and talent development. Reflection, whether through journaling, discussions, visual products, theater, or other methods (Eyler, Giles, & Schmiede, 1996), can provide a driver for fostering higher order thinking skills, ethical and civic development, and creative problem solving that incorporates classroom and community resources. Reflection strategies and reporting on service activities and outcomes can likewise support the breadth of language domains (i.e., listening, reading, writing, and speaking) for ELLs, as well as maximize exposure to and practice with general and content-specific academic and social language with authentic audiences.

## Sidebar 7.3: Service Learning: Minh

Minh's ESOL teacher, Mr. Berm, decided to build on Minh's interests and advanced knowledge of social studies to help him further develop his social and academic English skills through service learning. Every Thursday, Minh and other students from his class walked across the street to the middle school to tutor sixth-grade ELLs during their study skills time. Minh helped two sixth-graders with their social studies readings and homework, which focused primarily on European and Asian history and geography.

Using a copy of the middle school students' textbook, on Monday through Wednesday Minh applied the skills, strategies, and topics Mr. Berm was teaching Minh's class. These included identifying key vocabulary, language structures, patterns, and concepts, and creating graphic organizers such as timelines, illustrations, and personal dictionaries. Minh was able to share these with the sixth graders, as well as additional insights about the material outside of the textbook from his own prior knowledge and readings. With one student who was originally from Haiti, Minh also drew upon his French knowledge to make connections and help clarify the content.

On Fridays, Mr. Berm incorporated art- and language-based reflective activities with his students to allow them to debrief and share their experiences, successes, and challenges as tutors. They also focused on English language structure and function in support of their work and readings, and demonstrated their own growing language proficiency. After several weeks, Minh's world history teacher also confirmed to Mr. Berm that Minh's content vocabulary and his language skills were improving steadily as well.

---

# Summary

Extensive research supports academic service learning's overall benefits. Service learning is also highly flexible; it can be implemented across a host of school-based programs and settings, in regular, "inclusive" mixed-ability classes, as well as within specialized programs (e.g., ESOL, sheltered instruction, IB, AP, gifted and talented, etc.). As a pedagogy that develops academic, personal, and civic learning outcomes through service in response to community needs, it promotes and provides effective differentiation for language and academic development.

From the perspective of supporting second language acquisition, service learning offers a valuable setting for contextualized and meaningful language input and interaction, in both home and school languages. The planning, action, reflection, and demonstration aspects of the activity provide an authentic context and audience for language use, production, and products. Service learning also supports advanced academics, motivation, and achievement by allowing students to select service activities connected with deep individual interest; to work with peers, teachers, and community members on collaborative problem-solving activities; and to connect learning with moral, ethical, civic, and academic issues. Thus, engaging students with the community through academic service learning is a high-impact practice that holds considerable potential for enhancing the education, language acquisition, and talent development of high-ability ELLs at all levels of schooling.

# References

Arias, B. (2007). School desegregation, linguistic segregation and access to English for Latino students. *Journal of Educational Controversy, 2*(1). Retrieved from http://www.wce.wwu.edu/Resources/CEP/eJournal/v002n001/a008.shtml

Bernal, E. M. (2003). To no longer educate the gifted: Programming for gifted students beyond the era of inclusionism. *Gifted Child Quarterly, 47,* 183–191.

Bialystok, E. (2009). Bilingualism: The good, the bad, and the indifferent. *Bilingualism: Language and Cognition, 12*(1), 3–11.

Billig, S. (2000). Research on K–12 school-based service-learning: The evidence builds. *Phi Delta Kappan, 81,* 658–664.

Billig, S., Root, S., & Jesse, D. (2005). *The impact of participation in service-learning on high school students' civic engagement.* CIRCLE Working Paper 33. Denver, CO: The Center for Information & Research on Civic Learning & Engagement. Retrieved from http://eric.ed.gov/PDFS/ED495215.pdf

Briggs, C. J., Reis, S. M., & Sullivan, E. E. (2008). A national view of promising programs and practices for culturally, linguistically, and ethnically diverse gifted and talented students. *Gifted Child Quarterly, 52,* 131–145.

Bringle, R., & Hatcher, J. (1995). A service-learning curriculum for faculty. *Michigan Journal of Community Service Learning, 2,* 112–122.

Bruce-Davis, M. N., & Chancey, J. M. (2012). Connecting students to the real world: Developing gifted behaviors through service learning. *Psychology in the Schools, 49,* 716–723.

Castellano, J. A. (2002). Gifted education program options: Connections to English-language learners. In J. A. Castellano & E. I. Díaz (Eds.), *Reaching new horizons: Gifted and talented education for culturally and linguistically diverse students* (pp. 117–132). Boston, MA: Allyn & Bacon.

Cummins, J. (1991). Interdependence of first- and second-language proficiency in bilingual children. In E. Bialystok (Ed.), *Language processing in bilingual children* (pp. 70–89). New York, NY: Cambridge University Press.

Dalton, S. S. (2008). *Five standards for effective teaching: How to succeed with all learners, grades K–8.* San Francisco, CA: Jossey-Bass.

Echevarria, J., & Graves, A. (2007). *Sheltered content instruction: Teaching English language learners with diverse abilities* (3rd ed.). Boston, MA: Allyn & Bacon.

Echevarria, J., Vogt, M., & Short, D. (2000). *Making content comprehensible for English language learners: The SIOP model.* Boston, MA: Allyn & Bacon.

Edvantia. (2009). *Effective practices for teaching English language learners: A resource document for North Carolina's ELL work group.* Charleston, WV: Appalachia Regional Comprehensive Center at Edvantia. Retrieved from http://www.edvantia.org/publications/arcc/EffectiveELLPractices031109.pdf

Ellwell, M. D., & Bean, M. S. (2001). Editors' choice: The efficacy of service-learning for community college ESL students. *Community College Review, 28*(4), 47–61.

Eyler, J., & Giles, D. E., Jr. (1999). *Where's the learning in service-learning?* San Francisco, CA: Jossey-Bass.

Eyler, J., Giles, D. E., Jr., & Schmiede, A. (1996). *A practitioner's guide to reflection in service-learning: Student voices & reflections.* Nashville, TN: Vanderbilt University.

Fishman, T., & Swanson, L. (2011). *Teachable moments: Ethics and reflection in service-learning.* Clemson, SC: National Dropout Prevention Center/Network.

Hamstra, M. D. P. (2010). *The impact of service-learning on second language writing skills.* (Doctoral dissertation). Retrieved from http://hdl.handle.net/1805/2496

International Baccalaureate Program Organization. (2013). *Middle years program curriculum framework.* Retrieved from http://www.ibo.org/myp/curriculum/index.cfm

Kaplan, B., & Pérez Gamboa, T. (2004). Más allá del salón de clase: Una experiencia de integración de aprendizaje de español y servicio comunitario en UGA. *Hispania, 87*(1), 137–138.

Kaye, C. B. (2010). *The complete guide to service learning: Proven, practical ways to engage students in civic responsibility, academic curriculum, & social action* (2nd ed.). Minneapolis, MN: Free Spirit.

Kuh, G. D. (2008). *High-impact educational practices: What they are, who has access to them, and why they matter.* Washington, DC: Association of American Colleges and Universities.

Kyburg, R. M., Hertberg-Davis, H., & Callahan, C. M. (2007). Advanced Placement and International Baccalaureate programs: Optimal learning environments for talented minorities? *Journal of Advanced Academics, 18,* 172–215.

Lee, S.-Y., Olszewski-Kubilius, P., Donahue, R., & Weimholt, K. (2007). The effects of a service-learning program on the development of civic attitudes and behaviors among academically talented adolescents. *Journal for the Education of the Gifted, 31,* 165–197.

Lee, S.-Y., Olszewski-Kubilius, P., Donahue, R., & Weimholt, K. (2008). The Civic Leadership Institute: A service-learning program for academically gifted youth. *Journal of Advanced Academics, 19,* 272–308.

Levine, L. N., & McCloskey, M. L. (2009). *Teaching learners of English in mainstream classrooms (K–8): One class, many paths.* Boston, MA: Pearson.

Lewis, B. A. (1996). Serving others hooks gifted students on learning. *Educational Leadership, 53*, 70–74.

Lizardi-Rivera, C. (2005). Learning the basics of Spanish translation: Articulating a balance between theory and practice through community service. In J. Hellebrandt & L. T. Varona (Eds.), *Construyendo puentes (building bridges): Concepts and models for service-learning in Spanish* (pp. 107-121). Sterling, VA: Stylus.

Lockwood, A. T. (1998). *Talent and diversity: The emerging world of Limited English Proficient students in gifted education.* Washington, DC: U.S. Department of Education.

Martin, C. (2011). *Service-learning pedagogy as an instructional tool for Latino student education.* (Master's thesis). Retrieved from https://etda.libraries.psu.edu/paper/11877/7143

Matthews, M. S. (2004). Leadership education for gifted and talented youth: A review of the literature. *Journal for the Education of the Gifted, 28*, 77–113.

Matthews, P. H., & Matthews, M. S. (2004). Heritage language instruction and giftedness in language minority students: Pathways towards success. *Journal of Secondary Gifted Education, 15*, 50–55.

Minor, J. (2002). Incorporating service learning into ESOL programs. *TESOL Journal, 11*(4), 10–14.

Mullaney, J. (2005). Service-learning and language-acquisition theory and practice. In J. Hellebrandt & L. T. Varona (Eds.), *Construyendo puentes (building bridges): Concepts and models for service-learning in Spanish* (pp. 49–60). Sterling, VA: Stylus.

Orfield, G., & Lee, C. (2006). *Racial transformation and the changing nature of segregation.* Cambridge, MA: The Civil Rights Project at Harvard University. Retrieved from http://www.swannfellowship.org/research/files07/racialtransformation.pdf

Reis, S. M., & Renzulli, J. S. (2004). Current research on the social and emotional development of gifted and talented students: Good news and future possibilities. *Psychology in the Schools, 41*(1), 119–130.

Rennie, J. (1993). *ESL and bilingual program models.* Washington, DC: Center for Applied Linguistics. Retrieved from http://www.cal.org/resources/digest/rennie01.html

Russell, N. M. (2007). Teaching more than English: Connecting ESL students to their community through service learning. *Phi Delta Kappan, 88,* 770–771.

Scales, P., & Roehlkepartain, C. (2004). *Community service and service learning in U.S. public schools, 2004: Findings from a national survey.* Retrieved from http://www.peecworks.org/PEEC/PEEC_Research/S0179AAA9-0179AAB7

Stewart, T., & Bai, H. (2010). Community service self-efficacy and summer service-learning: Comparative analyses among academically talented youth. *Gifted Education International, 27,* 149–160.

Tacelosky, K. (2008). Service-learning as a way to authentic dialogue. *Hispania, 91,* 877–886.

Terry, A. W. (2000). An early glimpse: Service learning from an adolescent perspective. *The Journal of Secondary Gifted Education, 11,* 115–134.

Terry, A. W. (2003). Effects of service learning on young, gifted adolescents and their community. *Gifted Child Quarterly, 47,* 295–308.

Terry, A. W. (2008). Student voices, global echoes: Service-learning and the gifted. *Roeper Review, 30,* 45–51.

Terry, A. W., & Bohnenberger, J. A. (2003). Service learning: Fostering a cycle of caring in our gifted youth. *Journal of Secondary Gifted Education, 15,* 23–32.

Thomas, W. P., & Collier, V. (2002). *A national study of school effectiveness for language minority students' long-term academic achievement final report: Project 1.1.* Retrieved from http://crede.berkeley.edu/research/crede/research/llaa/1.1_final.html

Valdés, G. (Ed.). (2003). *Expanding definitions of giftedness: The case of young interpreters of immigrant communities.* Mahwah, NJ: Erlbaum.

Valenzuela, A. (1999). *Subtractive schooling: U.S.-Mexican youth and the politics of caring.* Albany: State University of New York Press.

Vogelgesang, L. J., & Astin, A. W. (2000). Comparing the effects of community service and service-learning. *Michigan Journal of Community Service Learning, 7*(1), 25–34.

Wade, R. C., & Putnam, K. (1995). Tomorrow's leaders? Gifted students' opinions of leadership and service activities. *Roeper Review, 18,* 150–151.

Warren, J. L. (2012). Does service-learning increase student learning? A meta-analysis. *Michigan Journal of Community Service Learning, 18*(2), 56–61.

Webster, N. S., & Worrell, F. C. (2008). Academically talented students' attitudes towards service in the community. *Gifted Child Quarterly, 52,* 170–179.

Zinskie, C. D. (2003, April). *Evaluating the impact of service-learning on the leadership ability of gifted middle school students.* Paper presented at the annual meeting of the American Educational Research Association, Chicago.

# Chapter 8

# Working Within the System to Build Effective Policies and Procedures

*Jaime A. Castellano & Erik M. Francis*

When primary stakeholders communicate and collaborate as a matter of routine, the school's ability to develop talent and potential increases exponentially. Within such a framework, everyone is a partner, trusting and respecting one another. Educational and instructional leaders know that what matter most in the development of student skill and talent are solid teachers trained in effective strategies that promote success. Ultimately, in a school context, it is the quality of teaching in each classroom that determines whether the diverse range of student talent is brought to the forefront. Even in isolation, the efforts of effective teachers are relevant and meaningful, and students benefit from the structured opportunities these teachers provide. However, when the teacher is part of a larger, comprehensive programmatic infrastructure with multiple levels of support, the opportunities to develop and maximize talent and potential are limitless. This is especially important for special populations of gifted and talented students, including (among others) economically, culturally, and linguistically diverse students.

In this chapter, we present a framework (see Figure 8.1) that develops student talent and potential by systematically promoting a

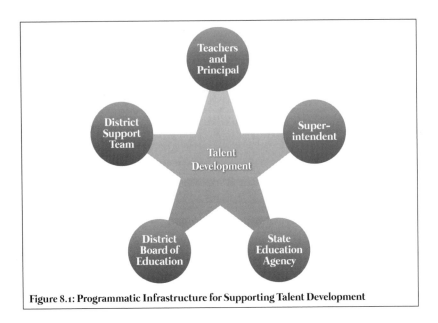

**Figure 8.1: Programmatic Infrastructure for Supporting Talent Development**

programmatic infrastructure designed to strengthen programming, operationalize identification procedures, and advocate for all students. We offer recommendations for each key player and we clarify their implications for accountability, practice, and assistance.

# Supporting Talent Development: The Role of the State Education Agency (SEA)

Although the primary role of state educational agencies (SEAs) has been to act as an intermediary between state government and local school districts in establishing and managing a statewide education system, the focus of the SEA also changes based upon the shifting demands of social and political climate, culture, and traditions within its individual state context (Institute for Educational Leadership, 2011; Seashore-Louis, Leithwood, Wahlstrom, & Anderson, 2010).

## Challenges at the State Level

**Focus.** In the last 10 years, SEAs have evolved into increasingly bureaucratic organizations that are characterized as understaffed, underfunded, and overly focused with monitoring compliance rather than providing assistance and guidance (Brown, Hess, Lautzenheiser, & Owen, 2011). The SEAs have focused their efforts on monitoring the progress and services provided to low-achieving students or at-risk subgroups such as Title I, special education, and ELLs, groups that are counted as part of efforts to evaluate the constituent local education agencies' (LEAs) performance. Little to no attention is devoted to the progress of, or services for, high-ability or high-potential students.

**Lack of monitoring capacity.** According to the National Association for Gifted Children (NAGC) and Council of State Programs for the Gifted (CSDPG, 2011), the lack of accountability the federal government requires of the states has resulted in many states not only failing to collect and report data on how high-performing learners are faring in school, but failing even to be aware of the programs and services its schools offer to meet these learners' needs. Twenty states reported to the NAGC and CSDPG as of 2011 that they do not monitor district gifted and talented education programs, and 14 reported they do not collect information on students identified as gifted and talented. This inevitably has caused the needs of high-ability and high-potential students to be limited, overlooked, or even completely neglected in many states.

**Inconsistency.** Gifted and talented education is plagued by inconsistency, both nationwide and within the individual states. As with many policies, procedures, and practices in education, the definition and governance of gifted and talented education (sometimes abbreviated G.A.T.E.) have been delegated to the states individually, which has caused disparity in both clarity and oversight. In 22 states, gifted education has been included under the designation of "exceptional students" (NAGC & CSDPG, 2011). Although inclusion under this category has allowed gifted education to reap some benefits from the large funding sources supporting this category, the states' major focus is placed on monitoring services for students with disabilities rather than on gifted and talented students (Gallagher, 2002). Only 26 states mandate service for G.A.T.E. (NAGC & CSDPG, 2011), and many of these mandates are unfunded.

State policies regarding teacher certification are also diverse and disjointed; 24 states do not require gifted and talented credentials for professionals teaching in specialized gifted and talented programs (NAGC & CSDPG, 2011). Within the states, even those having mandates, decision making for gifted education has been delegated mostly to the local level. This has caused further inconsistency in the areas of accountability, identification, and progress monitoring.

**Inadequate or eliminated funding.** Drastic cuts in federal and state funding to support gifted education have also affected the SEA's role in gifted education. The elimination in 2008 of federal funding allocated to the states under the provisions of Title V of the Elementary and Secondary Education Act of 1965 (ESEA) further shifted the focus of SEAs away from working with LEAs to develop, implement, and fund innovative programs that increase student achievement, teacher effectiveness, and overall school performance. Around the same time, elimination of funding for the Jacob K. Javits Gifted and Talented Students Education Act, which was the only federal grant program dedicated to addressing the needs of gifted and talented education, seriously depleted the SEA's ability to maintain even limited accountability and monitoring, as well as affecting directly the services provided to high-ability learners. At the state level, many SEAs also have had their state funding supporting gifted education reduced or even eliminated: 14 states have had their funding drastically reduced, while 10 states reported they no longer receive state funding for gifted education (NAGC & CSDPG, 2011).

**Limited political support and staffing.** Lack of political and accompanying fiscal support has also reduced the SEA's capacity to monitor and support gifted and talented education programs. Of the 45 states that responded to the NAGC and CSDPG (2011), only 17 states reported having one or more full-time staff members whose sole responsibility is the oversight of gifted education within the SEA. The majority of staff members working in gifted education at the state level maintain either part-time or shared responsibility for other programs not associated with gifted education. The SEA's lack of support and capacity has reduced its ability to monitor for progress and compliance, limited its service to an advocacy or advisement capacity, and relegated the SEA's role to merely a source of information and referral service to institutions and organizations that can provide further guidance and assistance.

## *Overcoming Challenges at the State Level*

**Add accountability for advanced learners.** To increase the state's ability to provide oversight in gifted and talented education, there must be a more comprehensive, systematic approach that not only clarifies what gifted and talented truly means in legislative terms, but that also establishes criteria for accountability, for practice, and for service delivery. The SEA and LEA must work together in establishing a system that ensures not only the existence of criteria for identification, accountability, and monitoring for compliance, but also diligence and service in their application. As with other programs servicing special populations, such as Title I, Title III (ELLs), Title VII (Native Americans), and special education, the SEA should require LEAs to develop action steps that detail how the needs of high-ability and high-potential students will be addressed and to implement strategies by which the LEA can support these students in meeting and exceeding state academic standards.

Equitability of services and support is a key goal of federal and state policies governing education. The SEA must extend its focus to monitoring and compliance of programs and services provided to high-ability and high-potential students with the same diligence the agency extends to programs supporting students and populations identified as academically at-risk. State accountability systems should be modified to include the progress of top-performing students in measures of student achievement, teacher effectiveness, and overall school performance. Some states already are making progress in this direction; for example, the North Carolina Department of Public Instruction began including students identified as gifted in its progress monitoring efforts for the first time beginning in 2012–2013. The

SEA must further ensure high-ability and high-performing students who are minorities or in low socioeconomic neighborhoods are appropriately identified, serviced, and supported (Miller, 2004; Slocumb & Payne, 2000).

**Restructure for collaboration and expertise.** The SEA itself must also undergo organizational restructuring to become a more proactive, transparent, and collaborative organization. It must become a source of information where stakeholders can obtain guidance, support, and training on how to improve overall school performance and meet the needs of all students, particularly those identified with having advanced aptitude, ability, and/or potential. The agency must actively recruit individuals who possess the expertise to guide and assist LEAs in implementing comprehensive school reform that identifies, services, and supports high-ability and high-potential students.

Unfortunately, SEAs are often hindered from hiring these highly qualified individuals due to bureaucratic and economic barriers and obstacles (Seashore-Louis et al., 2010). State superintendents are restricted by "state hiring rules, salary scales and caps, and civil service guidelines, and are responsible to multiple parties such as the governor and state legislators, making it difficult to attract and recruit talented people to their agencies" (Brown et al., 2011, p. 4). These factors prevent SEAs from recruiting and retaining highly qualified men and women with the expertise to provide the guidance and assistance their constituent LEAs need. SEA employees should be leaders in their field of study with expertise in serving certain populations and addressing specific needs, and they should be skilled not only in best practices and instructional strategies but also in training adult learners on how to implement such practices and strategies.

The same principles that apply to developing student talent also apply here: identifying "talented" individuals/experts within the agency and giving them opportunities to develop their talent. If the SEA is held accountable to the same requirements as LEAs to recruit and retain highly qualified professionals, this not only will strengthen the SEA's ability to provide technical assistance effectively, but also will increase its constituents' confidence in the agency's value as a service provider.

**Maintain flexibility of funding.** Another challenge facing SEAs is acquiring funds to support gifted and talented education. The cuts to funding under the provisions of Title V not only decreased the fiscal support provided to implement innovative programs but also diminished the SEA's role in guiding, monitoring, and evaluating such innovation. In order to meet the fiscal needs and demands for support, SEAs should become more flexible with funding and in seeking alternative funding sources and partnerships. Consolidation of federal, state, and local funds can help strengthen the LEA's education program by purchasing instructional materials and providing professional development and training for teachers. Such flexibility is permissible at the federal level under the Section 1114(a)(1) of Title I Part A of the Elementary and Secondary Education Act of 1965, which grants the following provision for schools operating a Title I schoolwide program:

> A local educational agency may consolidate and use funds under this part, together with other federal, state, and local funds, in order to upgrade the entire educational program of a school that serves an eligible school attendance area in which not less than 40 percent of the children are from low-income families, or not less than 40 percent of the children enrolled in the school are from such families.

Flexibility in funding will also allow the SEA to establish balance in its role as both a compliance monitor and a technical assistance provider. The SEA will continue to monitor that LEAs meet the intent of all federal, state, and local programming funds consolidated to support the school's education program. The SEA should also provide technical assistance to LEAs on how to structure the strategies and action steps of their school action plans, and to structure accountability systems to verify that the school meets the intent of all consolidating funding sources.

**Gain leverage using the CCSS.** Because the implementation of the Common Core State Standards (CCSS) in 45 states and three territories is increasing the demand for rigorous and relevant instruction that prepares students for college and career, comprehensive changes will need to be made in areas such as curriculum, assessment, professional development, and educator evaluations at all levels within the education system (Kober & Rentner, 2011). The SEA must provide technical assistance and guidance to educators through professional development and on-site visits, not only in understanding the instructional shifts that accompany the adoption of the CCSS, but also how the rigor and college and career readiness expectations of the CCSS provide teachers support in developing students' innate abilities into applicable skills that can be used to demonstrate learning and depth of knowledge.

SEAs historically and traditionally change in response to the social and political needs of their states. Today, the SEA should take the opportunity provided by the transition to the CCSS to shift its focus and priorities in the areas of accountability and compliance and strengthen its role in providing technical assistance, facilitation, and support. The challenge for SEAs is

> to develop a responsive structure around a coherent vision of student achievement with the capacity to support teaching and learning at the local level through technical assistance, leadership development, and alignment of standards, assessments, and curriculum as well as internal and external systems. (IEL, 2001, p. 14)

In order to meet this challenge effectively, the SEA will need to attain balance between monitoring for compliance within the provisions of federal and state education policies and support in implementing the CCSS. With care, it will be possible not only to increase student achievement, but also develop the innate talents, abilities, and skills of the students served by the state.

# Supporting Talent Development:
# The Role of District Leaders

## *Role of the District's Governing Board*

In working within the system to build effective policies and procedures in gifted and talented education for ELLs and other historically underrepresented students, what is the role of the district's board of education and central office administrators, including the superintendent? Because different states have different policies, or no policies at all for serving gifted and talented students, we will share information specific to the state of Arizona, where serving this population of students is a mandate.

Legislative statutes typically inform the policies that are adopted by a district's board of education. In Arizona, because it is in the public interest to support unique opportunities for high achieving and underachieving pupils who are identified as gifted, state statutes mandate that the governing board of each district shall provide gifted education services to qualifying students. More specifically, they require that the governing board shall modify the course of study and adapt teaching methods, materials, and techniques to provide educationally for those pupils who are gifted and possess superior intellect *or advanced learning ability* (i.e., talent), or both, but may have an educational disadvantage resulting from a disability or a difficulty in writing, speaking, or understanding the English language due to environmental background in which a language other than English is primarily or exclusively spoken. Accounting for special populations of gifted and talented students is a proactive measure, as Arizona educates a large number of low-income, culturally and linguistically diverse students, with a large subset of these students identified as ELLs.

Furthermore, the law requires that the governing board of each school district in Arizona shall develop a scope and sequence for the identification process of, and curriculum modification for, gifted students to ensure that they receive services commensurate with their academic ability and potential. Programs and services shall be provided as an integrated, differentiated learning experience during the regular school day. Board members are also required to explain how gifted education differs from regular education in such areas as: (a) content, including a broad-based interdisciplinary curriculum; (b) process, including higher level thinking skills; (c) product, including variety and complexity; and (d) learning environment, including flexibility.

In setting district policies consistent with legislative statutes, the school district's governing board is, in effect, structuring a framework for defining how the policies inform both procedures and practices at the school level. This framework also serves as part of the gifted program's infrastructure that is required in developing the talent and potential of the district's students. Furthermore, policies directed at ELLs serve as an accountability measure, ensuring that their unique talents are also being developed.

## Role of the Superintendent

In the flow chart of the programmatic infrastructure for serving gifted, advanced, and high-ability students, the superintendent finds him- or herself as the intermediary between the district's governing board and the programs implemented at the school level. The superintendent functions as the administrative manager of the district. As such, according to the Arizona School Boards Association's (2012) Department of Leadership Development, superintendents in Arizona districts are expected to lead the district in the following areas: administration, policy-making, hiring and evaluating personnel, program evaluation, planning goals, budget, facilities planning, and community relations. Table 8.1 offers recommendations to superintendents regarding how they can support talent development among the students served by their district.

In the area of *administration,* the superintendent provides the leadership required to manage the district's day-to-day operations. In advocating for their gifted, advanced, and high-ability students, the superintendent must acquire a conceptual understanding of talent development that informs the decisions that he or she makes.

# Table 8.1

## *The Role of the Superintendent in Supporting Talent and Potential*

| Leadership Area | Supporting Talent and Potential |
| --- | --- |
| Administration: provides leadership and manages the district's day-to-day operations. | Has conceptual understanding of talent development and potential<br>Familiar with continuum of services |
| Policymaking: implements procedures to effect the requirements of policy. | Identifies procedures rooted in research and practice that complement policy<br>Identifies key personnel/experts to help make recommendations |
| Hiring and evaluating personnel: recommends hires and dismissals; renewals as per policy. | Recommends highly qualified and highly effective teachers<br>Implements systematic process for teacher recruitment, hiring, and retention |
| Program evaluation: reports progress toward attainment of increased academic achievement. | Disaggregates data by programs serving gifted and talented students<br>Reports data to stakeholder groups |
| Planning goals: provides leadership and makes recommendations on the implementation of and progress toward the educational goals approved by the board. | Meets with program staff as a way to monitor ongoing progress<br>Seeks evidence of program success aligned with policies |
| Budget: prepares the budget; recommends expenditures; makes budget revisions. | Ensures budget equity and accesses federal budgets to supplement local program |
| Facilities planning: leads effort to plan, operate, and evaluate facilities. | Ensures programs serving gifted and talented students have appropriate space, equipment, and access |
| Community relations: keeps the community informed. | Routinely meets with and reports to stakeholder groups on status of programs<br>Reviews and approves accurate verbal and written communication |

Becoming familiar with the continuum of services afforded these students is also part of the management system that informs the programs, products, and services provided at the classroom level. For

ELLs, this can mean providing accommodations based on individual need.

*Policymaking* occurs at the district's governing board level. The role of the superintendent is to implement procedures to carry out the requirements of policy. They do so by identifying procedures rooted in research and practice. In cases where the superintendent does not yet have the knowledge base in how to develop student talent, it is incumbent that he or she identifies key personnel/experts to help make recommendations.

In *hiring and evaluating personnel,* the superintendent recommends hires, dismissals, and renewals as per policy. She is also responsible for performance evaluations. As with any other academic program, the goal is to recommend hiring highly qualified and highly effective teachers who can move students to maximize their talent and potential. To ensure that only the best teachers are hired for advanced academic programs, the superintendent must work with the human resources office to develop a systematic process to recruit, hire, and retain this high caliber of teacher. In culturally and linguistically diverse school districts, hiring those who have experience and/or expertise working with special populations of talented students is an added bonus and therefore it should be a secondary goal within the larger hiring process.

In the area of *program evaluation,* the role of the superintendent is to report to the district's governing board on district progress toward attainment of increased academic achievement among all types of students. This means disaggregating data for programs serving the gifted and talented and reporting results to all stakeholder groups. Working with the program administrators to develop such a report for accountability purposes may be a suitable first step toward this larger goal.

In *goal planning,* the superintendent provides leadership and makes recommendations on the implementation of and progress toward the educational goals approved by the board. The development of a strategic plan allows all stakeholder groups a voice in what the goals should be. Meeting with program staff as a way to monitor ongoing progress allows for conversations to be had specific to ELLs and other special populations of gifted and talented students, as well as providing the superintendent an opportunity to view evidence of program success aligned with district policies and instructional goals.

The superintendent is responsible for preparing the *budget*, recommending expenditures, and making budget revisions. This fiduciary responsibility extends to all facets of the district and superintendents are held accountable for all local, state, and federal monies. In developing the talent of students through advanced academic programs, the superintendent ensures budget equity and accesses federal budgets to support specific course offerings. In Title I schoolwide projects, for example, all students are to benefit from this program and its offerings.

In *facilities planning*, the role of the superintendent is to lead the effort to plan, operate, and evaluate facilities. In districts with older buildings and dwindling resources, this can be a huge challenge. Nonetheless, as the primary leader of the district's educational and instructional programs, superintendents can help ensure that programs serving gifted and talented students and other advanced learners have the appropriate space, equipment, and facilities.

*Community relations* implies keeping the community informed of the overall progress of the district. For the superintendent, this means being well-informed of all programs and services impacting staff and students. It requires the superintendent to be an effective communicator and to be able to tailor his advocacy to the audience addressed. Thus, the superintendent's verbal and written communication skills should be at a very advanced level. In communities in which languages other than English are spoken, the use of interpreters is essential and is a right of the parents and community served.

As the reader can see, the superintendent is in a key position to advocate for developing the talent of the district's gifted, advanced, and high-ability students. This individual can influence and inform policy, procedures, and practices by her actions. Her unique role also gives her the power to advocate for low-income, culturally, and linguistically diverse students who demonstrate talent and/or potential. As we will see next, the superintendent works very closely with other central office administrators to ensure program implementation, equity, and access.

Assisting the superintendent in the oversight of services offered to gifted, advanced, and high-ability students through advanced academic programs are other central office colleagues who monitor and assist with compliance-related expectations. These personnel may include, among others, the district's director/coordinator of gifted education; director of curriculum, instruction, and assessment; and/or director/coordinator of special education. These individuals provide the "on the ground support," working directly with principals and teachers to ensure all program components are being implemented with fidelity.

## *Role of the Principal*

The principal leads the charge as an advocate for talent development at the building level. Principals are the educational and instructional leaders whose support, or lack thereof, make or break programs serving high-ability, advanced students (Hertberg-Davis & Brighton, 2006). In this chapter, we choose to focus on the former. That is, we focus on the positive role of the principal as a manager of talent and potential, empowering teachers with the programs, products, and services needed to be highly effective in the day-to-day operation of their classrooms. Trust, respect, and a commitment to teamwork allow the principal to build a program infrastructure that is both supportive of, and dependent on, open and transparent communication between and among school personnel. By modeling their expectation for the development of student talent, successful principals also send a clear message that they value and understand the impact teachers are making in the classroom through their efforts.

Principals leading a school with a diverse student population may fill a niche by serving historically underrepresented groups, among them ELLs. With the appropriate support and teaching pedagogy these students have the same potential to maximize their talents as anyone else. Planning for personalization is a strategy that details how a given talent will be developed. Two program options for talent development often considered by principals include enrichment and acceleration.

In the school serving Native American students where I was principal for 3 years (2009–2012), we used our 21st century grant to offer one hour of enrichment, Monday–Thursday, after students completed one hour of academic tutoring. During the school day, our allied arts curriculum (Navajo language/culture, art, graphics, and physical education) and athletic programs/sports teams also served as a platform for students to showcase their talents.

For students with expressed talent in the areas of English/language arts (reading) and/or math, we provided content acceleration through a Total School Cluster Group instructional model (Gentry & Mann, 2008). Through this model, gifted, advanced, and high-ability students were clustered together in the same classroom in which pace, complexity, and depth was a routine part of the teaching and learning process. For a smaller number of students, grade skipping was one additional way to further maximize and accelerate their talent. One of the advantages of acceleration is that it does not require any additional budget allocations. And because it is a Title I school, I was able to direct these funds to help supplement its advanced academic program.

The combination of these programmatic options often found on a gifted education continuum of services helped us accommodate the unique, diverse talents of our best and brightest students. Teachers were supported through professional development opportunities and parents were routinely informed of the progress their children were making.

All in all, the principal plays an important role in the talent development flow chart/framework. He or she is in a position to empower, advocate, implement, monitor, and evaluate progress. He or she can allocate funds and resources, promote professional growth opportunities, and invite stakeholders to be part of a team approach in developing the talent of all students served in advanced academic programs.

## *Role of the Teacher*

Schooling clearly has a direct effect on a student's ability to become proficient in literacy and mathematics, and also on his or her socioemotional development. The question is which is more influential—the school itself or the classroom pedagogy of the individual teacher?

**The influence of teachers.** The Coleman report published in 1966 concluded that the vast majority of differences in student achievement are determined by forces external to the school, such as student aptitude, socioeconomic status, and student's home environment (as cited in Marzano, 2003, 2007); since that time, education research and studies have focused on understanding how much of an impact schooling truly has on student achievement. The research following this landmark report not only has concluded that quality schooling has a stronger impact on student achievement than the report had stated, but also that the skill and expertise of the individual teacher also determines the degree of student learning that takes place (Marzano, 2003, 2007; Marzano, Pickering, & Pollock, 2001). An essential finding of Marzano's research on school effectiveness is the large impact an effective teacher has on individual student achievement, relative to the overall quality of the school or its education program. In other research on teacher and classroom context effects on student achievement, Wright, Horn, and Sanders (1997) also confirmed that the impact a teacher has is the strongest contributor, following only classroom size and differences in student abilities, to academic gains in student learning.

The effect and influence of a teacher on talent development is evident not only from the results of scientifically based research, but also based upon the personal experiences of many successful individuals who have become leaders in their field or career. These individuals can trace their influences to a specific instructor or mentor who recognized their strengths and skills and set them on a path to professional and personal success. In his acceptance speech for winning the Oscar for Best Actor in 1993 for his role in the movie *Philadelphia*, actor Tom Hanks thanked his high school drama teacher for inspiring him to become an actor and teaching him how to hone his craft. Former talk show host and media proprietor Oprah Winfrey credited her fourth-grade teacher, who "believed in me, and for the first time, made me embrace the idea of learning" (National Education Association, 2008, p. 1).

In their 2012 publication, "Who Mentored You?" (see http:// www.hsph.harvard.edu/chc/wmy for more), the Harvard School of Public Health collected quotes and impressions from many notable individuals. Senator John McCain spoke about how one of his high school English teachers "used his classroom as not only a way to teach English but also to teach values, and standards, and morals" (Harvard School of Public Health, 2012, p. 1). Former President Bill Clinton acknowledged the influence a high school band teacher has had on his life and his success as a political leader. Microsoft mogul Bill Gates credited his success to both his math and drama teachers growing up, and he and his wife, Melinda, established the Bill & Melinda Gates Foundation to reward and support the continuous influence of teachers.

**Instructional strategies.** The impact of an effective teacher on student learning extends to the essential role the teacher plays in talent development. Wiggins and McTighe (2007) reported on Adler's identification of three instructional roles of teachers: (1) didactic/ direct instruction in which the teacher uses demonstration, modeling, lecture, and questioning to inform students; (2) facilitation of understanding to guide students in constructing meaning and understanding important ideas and concepts through questioning, probing, and processing of information; and (3) coaching students to transfer their learning and depth of knowledge into completing a performance task that measures knowledge and cognition (Wiggins & McTighe, 1998, 2007).

Gagné's (2008) Differentiated Model of Giftedness and Talent (DMGT) focuses solely on the teacher's role in talent development, categorizing educators as an environmental catalyst in the talent development process under the subcomponent of individuals, which also includes parents, siblings, mentors, and peers. According to the DMGT model, the teacher is responsible for designing a program that supports the transformation of students' innate aptitudes, or "gifts" as Gagné calls them, into well-developed skills, or "talent" (Thomson, 2006). The role of the teacher is to establish a program or system that provides appropriate opportunities for the student to develop and hone his or her talent. Such a program should include supports that positively influence intrapersonal catalysts, such as physical and psychological factors, as well as provisions or even protection from environmental catalysts that could negatively influence students' talent development. It is the responsibility of the teacher, coach, trainer, or director to ensure that the individual student is provided every opportunity to develop and apply his or her innate abilities; to create an environment that is supportive, protective, and challenging and in which risk-taking and mistake-making behaviors are acceptable; and to serve as an advocate for the student throughout the talent development process (Thomson, 2006; Winebrenner, 2001).

The qualities and attributes of an effective teacher are interrelated in regard to student learning and talent development. Marzano (2003) identified three factors influencing teacher effectiveness: instructional strategies, classroom management, and classroom curriculum design. Wiggins and McTighe's (1998, 2007) backward design for instructional planning consists of three stages: identifying desired results, determining acceptable evidence, and planning learning experiences and instruction. Schmoker (2011) emphasized "the conscientious effort, throughout the lesson, to ensure that all students are learning each segment of the lesson before moving to the next one" (p. 11). Along with "what we teach" and "how we teach," Schmoker also stressed the value of authentic literacy, which he defines as "purposeful—and usually argumentative—reading, writing, and talking" (p. 11).

**Teacher characteristics.** Winebrenner (2001) clarified that a teacher who teaches gifted and talented students need not be gifted himself but should be enthusiastic about teaching and lifelong learning, be flexible in his teaching style, and be knowledgeable about the diverse characteristics of his students. Rakow (2005) categorized the qualities identified by Winebrenner along with other education researchers and recommendations from national education organizations such as the National Association for Gifted Children under three attributes: professional, personal, and political.

Professionally, effective teachers are skilled and have received training in implementing a variety of best practices and instructional strategies and methods. They also have an expertise in differentiation of curriculum and instruction that continuously challenges students, meets their needs, and guides them in working through the problems and frustrations encountered in their demonstration of learning. Effective teachers also benefit from professional development in effective instructional strategies, especially in the area of developing and applying student talent to learning, and must also be willing and proactive in attaining such training (Rakow, 2005; Tomlinson, 1999; Winebrenner, 2001; Wormeli, 2007).

Personally, effective teachers need to be creative, lifelong learners who model the value and importance of intelligence, high standards and achievements; understand the impact of challenge, success, and failure; encourage the pursuit of continuous intellectual development; and recognize and respect the individual differences in students and their style and methods of learning, with the creativity, flexibility, patience, and open-mindedness to work with students in developing and applying their individual skills and talents.

Politically, effective teachers must be willing to advocate for the need and value of developing and applying talent to demonstrate learning and be able to communicate, collaborate, and cooperate with all stakeholders. They must ensure equity is practiced within the school in regard to identification, service, and support of top-performing and high-potential students.

**Classroom environment.** Teachers must also create a student-centered learning environment in which instruction is differentiated, lifelong learning is modeled and valued, individuality is emphasized, collaboration is promoted and permissible but not mandatory, and students' choice and responsibility for their own learning are fostered.

Wormeli (2007) identified two charges of differentiation: "[do] whatever it takes to maximize students' learning instead of relying on one-size-fits-all, whole-class methods of instruction" and "prepare students . . . to become their own learning advocates" (p. 154). Tomlinson (1999) detailed how the teacher must remember to appreciate each child as an individual, set high expectations, link students and ideas, and help students make sense of their own ideas. The teacher strives for student independence by providing support and guidance to help students move to the next order of thinking or level of learning and also sharing the responsibility for teaching with students, allowing them not only to teach themselves but one another.

Best practices that encourage higher order thinking, such as differentiated instruction, that support student choice, and are founded upon the multiple intelligence, project-based learning, problem-based learning, cooperative learning, and service learning, are considered to be effective instructional strategies that support talent development. The teacher must also establish a nurturing learning environment in which taking risks and making mistakes are expected and encouraged (Winebrenner, 2001). Challenge and choice are also essential in fostering talent development (Rakow, 2005).

In order to meet the needs of all students and support their ability to use their innate strengths, skills, and talents to demonstrate knowledge and cognition of key academic concepts, the teacher must establish a balance between direct instruction and whole-class assignments with problem- and project-based learning consisting of multiple intelligence, authentic literacy, and cooperative activities that measure student knowledge and cognition of key academic concepts, foster student engagement, and promote student choice, collaboration, and responsibility. This balance can be achieved by developing unit- or concept-based lesson plans that guide both the teacher and the student through the process of transitioning from teacher-led instruction to student-centered instruction that supports the student's ability to apply her individual skills and talents to demonstrate learning.

An effective instructional design could follow the concept and framework of the Individual Lesson Plan (ILP) developed by Carolyn Coil (2004, 2011), which is a unit-based lesson plan that includes homogenous teacher-oriented activities consisting of tasks all students are required to complete and student-choice activities consisting of problem- and project-based learning activities categorized under Bloom's taxonomy, Gardner's Multiple Intelligences, learning styles, learning modalities, or subject areas. Student choice activities that support not only talent development but also the development of 21st century skills should consist of project-based learning, collaboration, creativity and innovation, communication of ideas, and initiative and self-direction. Lesson plans are distributed to students to communicate expectations for learning, to provide a menu of choices students may select to demonstrate learning, and to foster students' time management skills. In her most recent version of the ILP, Coil (2011) has also incorporated the Common Core State Standards that will be addressed within each given unit.

**Maintain rigor.** Although project- and problem-based learning supports talent development by providing an opportunity for students to develop their innate abilities, the tasks must be rigorous enough for students to be challenged and engaged, ensuring these tasks do not simply become examples of "educational arts and crafts," a term derived from Calkins and Allington's observations of how activities focusing on creating "stuff" in the name of "creativity" may support talent development but are not rigorous enough to support higher order thinking or demonstration of depth of knowledge (as cited in Schmoker, 2006, pp. 91–92).

The level of rigor of teacher-oriented and student-centered activities is measurable by using the Hess Cognitive Rigor Matrix, which aligns Bloom's revised taxonomy and Webb's Depth of Knowledge. As an ERIC publication (ED517804), the Hess Matrix can be downloaded off the Internet at http://eric.ed.gov. The Hess Cognitive Rigor Matrix establishes a correlation and differences between the higher levels of thinking and performance detailed under Bloom's revised taxonomy and the levels of knowledge defined under Webb's Depth of Knowledge, allowing educators to determine the level of complexity in both domains as it relates to both demonstration of learning and depth of knowledge (Hess, Jones, Carlock, & Walkup, 2009).

Teachers can use the Hess Cognitive Rigor Matrix as an evaluation tool to determine the level of knowledge and understanding that is required in order for a student to complete a particular task. The Hess Cognitive Rigor Matrix also allows teachers to realize that the levels of higher order thinking and depth of knowledge are not always correlated. What may require higher levels of thinking according to Bloom's may not necessarily require deeper knowledge in the content according to Webb's. For example, while a timeline rests at the highest level of Bloom's under creation or synthesis of ideas, the depth of knowledge lies at the lowest level of Webb's scale in that all a student needs to do is recall and remember information to successfully demonstrate learning and understanding. Conversely, developing generalizations of the results obtained or strategies used and applying them to new problem situations requires extended thinking, the highest level of knowledge on Webb's scale, but in terms of performance the student must only demonstrate understanding and application of the results and strategies, which lies at the lower level of Bloom's.

Authentic literacy, which Schmoker (2011) described as "purposeful—and usually argumentative—reading, writing, and talking" (p. 11), is also an essential component of not only demonstration of learning and talent development, but also of communication of concepts, process, and self-awareness. Schmoker (2006, 2011) called for not only higher order thinking but higher order literacy that emphasizes close reading and communication of ideas through written expression, which inevitably supports students' ability and opportunity to demonstrate knowledge.

Communication is considered an essential attribute of 21st century skills. Many students struggle with argumentation, which includes the ability to defend or support a claim, to defend conclusions, or to distinguish between facts and opinions (Schmoker, 2006). To increase the complexity of the teacher-oriented and student-centered tasks assigned in the unit, the tasks should be accompanied by authentic literacy activities in which the student documents the ideas and information uncovered through extensive research and the processes through which she synthesized the ideas and information in the completion of the performance task. These content and procedural authentic literacy activities can serve as a self-assessment in which the student communicates her learning and depth of knowledge of a particular concept or subject, not only to demonstrate her individual conceptual understanding but also to extend her thinking by explaining her interpretations and conclusions to others.

Authentic literacy activities may also be used as a peer evaluation tool by having other students communicate the degree to which they can recognize or draw inferences from a classmate's final project or product and the concepts of the unit. Such peer evaluation allows the teacher to not only measure whole class conceptual understanding and depth of knowledge to the key academic concepts, but also to assess the developing ability of the student who created the project to express the ideas and information associated with the concept effectively.

Questioning is another essential part of both the learning process and talent development. Questions should measure thinking and depth of knowledge, and also should serve as a foundation and resource for students in considering how to apply their innate abilities to demonstrate learning and to communicate understanding. One idea for instructional design could be to incorporate Wiggins and McTighe's (1998, 2007) essential questions as a tiered structure of open-ended questions that are factual (Who? What? Where? When?), analytical (How? Why?), hypothetical (What if . . . ? What would happen . . . ? What could happen . . . ?), reflective (What is the effect . . . ? What is the impact . . . ? What is the result . . . ?), and affective (Do you think . . . ? Do you feel . . . ? Do you believe? What is your opinion? How would you . . . ?). Students could also form a personal question related to the unit or concept. Such questions emphasize higher order thinking, measure depth of knowledge, and require students to demonstrate knowledge and cognition of key academic concepts.

The teacher plays a pivotal role in developing the environment and opportunities for students to actualize their innate abilities into effective, applicable skills. The teacher who is most effective in supporting and nurturing talent development is one who establishes a classroom environment that supports risk-taking and permits mistake-making; recognizes the individuality of students; and balances rigorous traditional instruction that is teacher-led with differentiated instruction that is student-centered, each consisting of opportunities for students to develop and apply their skills and talents.

## Conclusion

Supporting talent development of our most able students from diverse backgrounds requires the same fundamental commitment pledged to those special needs students found on the opposite end of the bell curve. Success comes in many forms. When programs, products, and services are part of a programmatic infrastructure designed to meet the individual needs of talented students, opportunities for experiencing success know no boundaries. From the state education agency to the school district's governing board, from the superintendent to other district office administrators, and from the principal to the classroom teacher, where direct services are administered, all levels play an important role in supporting and developing talent and potential. Districts with this degree of accountability maximize equity, access, and opportunity for students. The tiers of support also send a strong message that expectations for high standards, strong leadership, collaborative teams, and clear communication are acknowledged by all school- and district-based stakeholders.

This shared vision ensures the capacity of the school district to support talent development and potential of its most able students. Success breeds success and ensures that our future as a community, state, and nation will be left in good hands. That is our hope as educators.

# References

Arizona School Boards Association. (2012). *Senior leadership team workshop for Ganado Unified School District.* Phoenix, AZ: Author.

Brown, C. G., Hess, F. M., Lautzenheiser, D. K. & Owen, I. (2011). *State education agencies as agents of change: What will it take for the states to step up on education reform?* Washington, DC: Center for American Progress.

Coil, C. (2004). *Standards based activities and assessments for the differentiated classroom.* Marion, IL: Pieces of Learning.

Coil, C. (2011). *Differentiated activities and assessments using the common core standards.* Marion, IL: Pieces of Learning.

Elementary and Secondary Education Act of 1965, §114, 20 U.S.C. 6301.

Gagné, F. (2008, July). *Building gifts into talents: Overview of the DMGT.* Keynote Address at the 10th Asia-Pacific Conference for Giftedness, Asia-Pacific Federation of the World Council for Gifted and Talented Children, Singapore.

Gallagher, J. (2002). *Society's role in educating gifted students: the role of public policy.* Storrs: University of Connecticut, The National Research Center on the Gifted and Talented.

Gentry, M., & Mann, R. L. (2008). *Total school cluster grouping: A comprehensive, research based plan for raising student achievement and improving teacher practices.* Waco, TX: Prufrock Press.

Harvard School of Public Health. (2012). *Who Mentored Senator John McCain?* Retrieved from http://www.hsph.harvard.edu/chc/wmy/Celebrities/john_mccain.html

Hertberg-Davis, H. L., & Brighton, C. (2006). Support and sabotage: Principal's influence on middle school teachers' responses to differentiation. *Journal of Secondary Gifted Education, 17,* 90–102.

Hess, K. K., Jones, B. S., Carlock, D., & Walkup, J. R. (2009). *Cognitive rigor: Blending the strengths of Bloom's taxonomy and Webb's Depth of Knowledge to enhance classroom level processes.* (ERIC Document Reproduction Service No. ED517804) Retrieved from http://eric.ed.gov/?qED517804&id=ED517804

Institute for Educational Leadership. (2011). *State education agencies as agents of change: What it will take for the states to step up on education reform.* Washington, DC: Author.

Kober, N., & Rentner, D. S. (2011). *States' progress and challenges in implementing Common Core State Standards.* Washington, DC: Center on Education Policy.

Marzano, R. J. (2003). *What works in schools: Translating research into action.* Alexandria, VA: ASCD.

Marzano, R. J. (2007). *The art and science of teaching.* Alexandria, VA: ASCD.

Marzano, R. J., Pickering, D. J., & Pollock, J. E. (2001). *Classroom instruction that works: Research based strategies for increasing student achievement.* Alexandria, VA: ASCD.

Miller, L. S. (2004). *Promoting sustained growth in the representation of African Americans, Latinos, and Native Americans among top students in the United States at all levels of the education system.* (RM04190).

Storrs: University of Connecticut, The National Research Center on the Gifted and Talented.

National Association for Gifted Children, and Council of State Directors of Programs for the Gifted (2011). *State of the nation in gifted education: A lack of commitment to talent development.* Washington, DC: Author.

National Education Association. (2008). *Celebrities, notable public figures reveal their most memorable teachers.* Retrieved from http://www.nea.org/grants/17345.htm

Rakow, S. (2005). *Educating gifted students in middle school: A practical guide.* Waco, TX: Prufrock Press.

Seashore-Louis, K., Leithwood, K., Wahlstrom, K. L., & Anderson, S. E. (2010). *Investigating the links to improved student learning.* Minneapolis: University of Minnesota.

Schmoker, M. (2006). *Results now: How can we achieve unprecedented improvements in teaching and learning?* Alexandria, VA: ASCD.

Schmoker, M. (2011). *Focus: Evaluating the essentials to radically improve student learning.* Alexandria, VA: ASCD.

Slocumb, P. D., & Payne, R. K. (2000). "Identifying and nurturing the gifted poor." *Principal—The New Diversity, 79*(5), 28–32.

Thomson, M. (2006). *Supporting gifted and talented students in the secondary schools.* Thousand Oaks, CA: Sage.

Tomlinson, C. A. (1999). *The differentiated classroom: Responding to the needs of all learners.* Alexandria, VA: ASCD.

Wiggins, G., & McTighe, J. (1998). *Understanding by design.* Alexandria, VA: ASCD.

Wiggins, G., & McTighe, J. (2007). *Schooling by design: mission, action, and achievement.* Alexandria, VA: ASCD.

Winebrenner, S. (2001). *Teaching gifted kids in the regular classroom: Strategies and techniques every teacher can use to meet the academic needs of the gifted and talented.* Minneapolis, MN: Free Spirit.

Wormeli, R. (2007). *Differentiation: From planning to practice: Grades 6–12.* Portland, ME: Stenhouse.

Wright, S. P., Horn, S., & Sanders, W. (1997). Teacher and classroom context effects on student achievement: implications for teacher evaluation. *Journal of Personnel Evaluation in Education, 11,* 57–67.

# Chapter 9

# Thoughts for the Future

*Michael S. Matthews & Jaime A. Castellano*

## Why Investing in Talent Development Is the Smart Thing to Do

It is clear that talents that go unrecognized, or that remain underdeveloped, represent a tremendous waste of human capital for the individual as well as a failure of progress for the society in which he or she lives. The humanistic perspective, whose goal is self-actualization, and the economic or national competitiveness argument (whose goal is development and utilization of mental resources for the benefit of the country and for humanity in general), both support investing in talent development. The values and ethics of our society also support achievement, innovation, and the pursuit of personal satisfaction in work and in life.

Although some successful individuals may believe that they have become successful solely due to their own efforts, closer examination usually reveals that their success has depended in various ways on their having received the assistance of others at critical points in their development. Teachers and schools have the potential to provide such help more frequently and to greater numbers of their students, and are particularly well suited to assist in the traditional academic domains of reading, writing, mathematics, science, and social studies. Although less often recognized, schools and teachers also can play a crucial role in the development of students' cultural competence and in the cohesiveness of the larger communities within which they reside. Thus, for a variety of reasons, investing in talent development is the smart thing to do.

## *Local and Regional/State Impact*

Talent developed at the local level often remains in the community, where it can benefit those who live there. Strengthening school/community connections and (in the longer term) building community through talent development are important outcomes that school-based programming can foster.

Perhaps the most visible opportunity schools can provide for local and regional involvement is service learning; as Chapter 7 points out, service learning is a high-impact practice that leads to positive outcomes in areas as diverse as civic responsibility, school climate, leadership development, and academic achievement. Because service learning is flexible, can differentiate learning experiences, and can support bilingual/bicultural development, it is ideally suited for developing the talents of high-ability ELLs.

Successful local programming can provide a model to be applied to similar efforts in other settings across the state. In addition to bringing outside visitors in to view innovative programming, schools should consider supporting student travel to other locations across the region and state to share their perspectives and solutions with other school systems. Although some ELL children may have traveled extensively to arrive at their current place of residence, others may never have left the local area; this may be particularly the case for children from low-income households. School-supported travel, whether for program dissemination, extracurricular academic competitions, athletics, or other reasons, can make an important contribution to these learners' perspectives on their world and to the development of their aspirations and life goals.

### National and International Impact

National and international impact is less visible because it is more diffuse, and impact at these levels can only occur if many local efforts are working simultaneously toward shared goals for their students. We suggest that one appropriate goal might be for teachers and schools in the U.S. to develop a better understanding of the educational systems of other countries, of their citizens' attitudes toward these systems, and of the effects these understandings have on the interactions of immigrant families with teachers and schools in the U.S.

Another long-term goal should be to increase the performance of U.S. learners, especially those of high ability, in comparison to their peers in other countries. Attention to the knowledge, attitudes, and practices that we suggest in this book can and will make a difference. These will involve some relatively minor yet fundamental changes in what happens in the day-to-day education of academically capable students who are ELLs.

## Inclusive Settings as a Means to an End

Inclusion of ELLs in the regular classroom is a means to an end, that is, the goal of high proficiency in academic English for all learners. Not all learners will achieve this goal, for a variety of reasons, just as not all native speakers of English will make As in their English coursework or score highly on the AP English examination. The important point to keep in mind is that many more learners can achieve high performance than currently are achieving it. By using the strategies and approaches in this book, more students of high potential will be able to develop correspondingly high achievement.

### The Economics of Inclusive Settings

The relevance of understanding the economics of inclusive settings extends beyond school and district budgets, their fiduciary responsibility to the communities they serve, or the sources from which the funding is acquired. This is not to say that these issues are not important considerations for school principals and district officials. They are, especially in the light of continued budget cuts, federal mandates, and parental pressure. However, the economics of inclusive settings must also consider the benefits of a classroom made up of a diverse cross-section of students and the added educational value associated with their interaction (Chapter 6).

For ELLs, the benefits of exposure to and interacting with their English-speaking peers cannot easily be measured in dollars and cents. For students identified as gifted or talented, focusing on their strengths and interests to provide the intellectual stimulation necessary for them to achieve or reach their potential makes it difficult to apply any type of cost analysis. And for those students who are identified as twice exceptional or gifted and as English learners, and who are present in an inclusive setting with a highly effective teacher, the psychological benefits cannot be expressed in monetary form. When a supportive family also encourages success, add the collective impact on student motivation, self-esteem, and level of confidence and one would be hard pressed to confine such a conversation to strictly economics. Inclusive settings that are student centered provide opportunities and different ways for all learners to demonstrate what they know and are able to do. Education is the key to opportunity and social mobility.

Inclusive settings vary in size, features, costs, and expectations. However, despite differing models of inclusive settings, the desired outcome is always increased academic achievement by the participating students. For those learners who demonstrate interest and commitment to their education, the possibilities for their future are endless. In this regard, the economics of inclusive settings, or any school setting for that matter, make education a valued investment for families, their community, and our nation. Advantages include promoting a sense of lifelong learning for self and others, the benefits that a diverse and inclusive setting bring to a school community, and the preparation of students to be contributing members of our society for the remainder of their lives.

### *Communication, Collaboration, & Collegiality*

Key to the process of developing more effective educational systems are the attributes of communication, collaboration, and collegiality. These are necessary in order to secure for each and every learner an appropriate, individualized education, and they also are important skills for students themselves to see modeled in the course of their own development as learners. Systematic communication and effective collaboration ensure that all of those involved in the child's education and development remain in a position to urge the student toward shared goals.

## Recommendations: Moving Forward

The alert reader likely has noticed a number of similar or even overlapping recommendations that the contributors to this book, coming from different positions, have offered. Based on the preceding eight chapters, below we offer some specific, common, and overarching suggestions that teachers and schools should follow in order to move forward in improving the opportunities available to their high-ability ELLs. By happy coincidence, most of these recommendations also can improve the education that all students receive, so there is little or no downside to their implementation, apart from perhaps the usual reluctance to change "the way we've always done things." Our conclusions and recommendations are summarized for the category of knowledge and attitudes (Sidebar 9.1) and a second category of specific practices (Sidebar 9.2). Sections below describe each recommendation briefly and point the reader back toward the chapter in which more details may be reviewed.

---

# Sidebar 9.1: Six Recommended Areas of Knowledge and Attitudes

1. Second language acquisition proceeds in an orderly fashion, with specific pedagogical goals being appropriate at different stages of the process.
2. Strong language and literacy skills in the students' first language aid in the acquisition and development of English language proficiency.
3. Intelligence is necessary but not sufficient to produce high achievement; motivation also influences achievement, and specific instructional practices can foster motivation.
4. Service learning offers a powerful, research-supported approach to developing individuals' talents while serving the community.
5. Teachers should consciously refocus their attention on students' strengths rather than on their perceived limitations.
6. Cultural competency is a moving target that requires self-reflection to achieve.

---

# Sidebar 9.2: Seven Recommended Practices for Teachers and School Leaders

1. Effective teachers are vital to the success of students and of schools.
2. Students should be taught to understand their own goals, talents, and learning behaviors.
3. Teachers and district leaders alike must actively foster collaborative efforts across programs.
4. Hiring efforts should foster diversity among school personnel whenever possible, and should actively seek teachers who are well qualified to work with high-ability learners.
5. School and district leaders are responsible for securing adequate funding for programming in advanced academics.

6. To truly put the student first, flexibility must be granted precedence over administrative convenience.
7. Formative evaluation of existing programs and services should occur on a regular basis.

## *Recommended Areas of Knowledge and Attitudes*

We offer six recommendations for knowledge and attitude, as follows:

1. **Second language acquisition proceeds in an orderly fashion, with specific pedagogical goals being appropriate at different stages of the process.** Teachers and schools must be aware of these needs, and of how they are similar to (and how they differ from) the needs of high-ability learners who are native English speakers. Specific patterns in students' speech and writing (see Chapter 2) can help the teacher to diagnose each learner's current level of progress. Ongoing, focused professional development should be provided to help all teachers further their knowledge and skills in these areas.

2. **Strong language and literacy skills in the students' first language aid in the acquisition and development of English language proficiency.** Programming that recognizes and utilizes students' skills in their home language may be more successful in developing students' English skills, in comparison with programming that fails to acknowledge these learners' additional competencies (Chapter 7). Awareness of positive and negative transfer from the first language (Chapter 2) can foster more effective English language instruction. Bilingualism is a valuable skill! Full proficiency in English is a vital goal, but instructional climates should be designed to consciously support bilingualism and students' development of a bicultural identity, rather than focusing solely on assimilation within an English-only environment.

3. **Intelligence is necessary but not sufficient to produce high achievement; motivation also influences achievement, and specific instructional practices can foster motivation.** Because teachers and schools can influence motivation more than they can influence ability, it makes sense to focus on instructional practices and attitudes that foster high motivation among ELLs as well as among all students (see Chapter 5). Instruction should target attitudes (e.g., mindset) as well as the structure of assignments (allowing student-chosen products, using curriculum compacting or other forms of academic acceleration, and providing real-world problems that are meaningful in students' lives). Flexible grouping by ability or achievement, as determined by regular preassessment of content knowledge and skills, helps to ensure that students are not bored because it allows instruction to be provided for each learner at an appropriate pace and level of complexity.

4. **Service learning offers a powerful, research-supported approach to developing individuals' talents while serving the community.** Service learning encompasses both the service activity itself, and participants' reflections on the process (see Chapter 7). Activities must be selected both for their inherent value and for their connections to specific student learning outcomes; the school's role in providing these opportunities is especially important for students from low-income households.

5. **Teachers should consciously refocus their attention on students' strengths rather than on their perceived limitations.** Teachers in general education settings, and those who work with ELLs, tend to focus first on areas for remediation rather than on how to develop learners' areas of strength (Chapter 6). By refocusing on student strengths, more transnational children will gain access to advanced academics and to the opportunities that they represent within U.S. schools (see Chapter 4).

6. **Cultural competency is a moving target that requires self-reflection to achieve.** Educators who work with stu-

dents from diverse cultures should strive to understand the prior learning experiences these students and their families have encountered, and should be aware of the structure and philosophy underlying education and schooling in their culture of origin (see Chapter 3). Teachers and schools should be aware that even families who share a common cultural origin may have widely differing perceptions and prior experiences. This individualized understanding and awareness helps U.S. teachers and schools to scaffold their work with ELL students and their families in developing appropriate curricula, in increasing participation by diverse individuals in programming for high-ability and gifted learners, and in fostering collaboration between schools, communities, and the home. Guide 6.1: Teacher-Held Beliefs is also a helpful resource during this process.

## Recommended Practices for Teachers and School Leaders

We offer seven recommended practices for teachers and school leaders, as follows:

1. **Effective teachers are vital to the success of students and of schools.** Effective teachers form the backbone of the approaches emphasized in every chapter of this book. Some of the observable characteristics of effective teachers (see Chapter 8) include enthusiasm for teaching and for modeling lifelong learning; flexibility and patience in teaching style; familiarity with their students as individuals (including their linguistic and cultural backgrounds), and knowledge of the corresponding pedagogical approaches that are effective based on this familiarity; expertise in the content they teach; expectations for learning that are rigorous for all of their students; and a collaborative and advocacy-based focus on the needs of high-ability learners.

2. **Students should be taught to understand their own goals, talents, and learning behaviors.** Students who do not have any idea of their own learning goals or learning styles are not

likely to be motivated to achieve (see Chapter 5). Knowing one's own learning preferences helps in advocating for more appropriate activities. Learning how to manage one's own learning processes, including the ability to deal with failure in a constructive manner (see Chapter 2), is vital to maintaining high achievement over the long term.

3. **Teachers and district leaders alike must actively foster collaborative efforts across programs.** Collaboration is a learned skill, one whose development requires practice as well as active support from school and district administrators (Chapter 8). A formal plan for collaboration should include the setting of personal goals and the outlining of resources and responsibilities for promoting talent development. Collaboration should occur not only across levels within the school system, but also between teachers, schools, parents, and community members. Forming a Comprehensive Resource Collaboration Team (see Chapter 6) can help schools to formalize the collaborative service delivery process for their ELL students. Guide 6.3 and the other discussion questions in Chapter 6 offer a formal approach to help begin discussion of collaborative efforts within the school.

4. **Hiring efforts should foster diversity among school personnel whenever possible, and should actively seek teachers who are well qualified to work with high-ability learners.** When school staff members mirror the diversity of the school population, in terms of cultural origin and skin color, diverse learners more readily can identify and emulate appropriate authority figures as salient models for their own lives. Diverse staff members also may be in a unique position to understand the challenges that some of their students may face as a result of language, culture, or ethnic background. Hiring decisions also should take into account the characteristics that make teachers effective in working with high-ability learners.

5. **School and district leaders are responsible for securing adequate funding for programming in advanced academics.** Flexible yet conscientious allocation of existing funding

streams is necessary in order to support programming for gifted and academically advanced learners, particularly when such funding is not allocated at the state level. Local and state school boards can assist these efforts by creating policies that support the creation and availability of advanced programming for students from all backgrounds, particularly those traditionally underrepresented in such settings.

6. **To truly put the student first, flexibility must be granted precedence over administrative convenience.** Meeting student needs, both individually and collectively, should be the primary goal of schools and teachers. Academic acceleration should be not only allowed, but promoted (when appropriate) through permissive and flexible policies. Policies should address routine objections (e.g., "If we allow X for this child, then everyone will want to do it") with equally routine answers ("X is appropriate under the following circumstances: . . ."). Objections that are founded solely on convenience for the school ("Allowing that would make our scheduling more difficult") should not be allowed to carry the decision. Structural barriers to participation in advanced academics (see Chapter 3) should be reduced whenever possible, perhaps by using the strategies we have detailed in Chapter 8.

7. **Formative evaluation of existing programs and services should occur on a regular basis.** The Coaching Tool worksheet (see Table 2.2) is designed to make this process faster and easier to complete. The Classroom Practices Inventory (Guide 6.2) and Structured Immersion Observation Protocol (discussed in Chapter 7) also can provide helpful starting points for this process. Data collection systems must include reporting on the progress of students with gifts and talents, and school leaders should examine their monitoring efforts to be sure these also include students in advanced academic programming (see Chapter 8). Of course, once evaluation results are in, teachers and schools must engage in active efforts to improve programming and services based on these findings.

# Conclusions

Improving our educational system is a daunting process that is not always successful. However, we concur with the sentiment expressed by the famous anthropologist Margaret Mead, who said, "Never depend upon institutions or government to solve any problem. All social movements are founded by, guided by, motivated and seen through by the passion of individuals." It is up to each of us, following our own beliefs and passions, to work collaboratively with others to improve the world in which we live. The wondrous thing about education is that our efforts in this area can have a tremendous multiplying effect, leading in the long term to a far greater impact than we may ever imagine. All of us who have contributed to this book have set our ideas in motion; now it's your turn!

# About the Editors

**Michael S. Matthews. Ph.D.,** is associate professor of gifted education and graduate coordinator for the Academically & Intellectually Gifted program at the University of North Carolina at Charlotte. He is widely published in gifted education; this is his fourth book. Dr. Matthews is coeditor of the *Journal of Advanced Academics*, and has been an active member of the Research & Evaluation network of the National Association for Gifted Children; treasurer of the SIG-Research on Giftedness, Creativity, & Talent of the American Educational Research Association; and vice president of the North Carolina Association for the Gifted & Talented. In 2010, he was awarded the NAGC Early Scholar Award, and in 2012, he and his coauthors received the Michael Pyryt Collaboration Award for their 2010 article, *Parental Influences on the Academic Motivation of Gifted Students: A Self-Determination Theory Perspective.* Dr. Matthews' research focuses on the areas of gifted education policy; gifted education in science and mathematics; motivation and underachievement; the role of parents in the development of their children's abilities; and the assessment and identification of learners from diverse backgrounds, especially those who are ELLs.

**Jaime A. Castellano, Ed.D.**, is one of the nation's leading authorities on the identification, recruitment, and retention of low-income, culturally, and linguistically diverse gifted students. Dr. Castellano has particular expertise and success in working with school districts across the nation to increase the number of Hispanic/Latino students, as well as English language learners, in gifted education programs. With more than 20 years in the field, he has served as a teacher of the gifted, school-based assistant principal and principal supervising gifted education programs; district-level administrator, coordinator, specialist, and director; state department of education specialist; and adjunct and/or visiting graduate school professor in gifted education, educational leadership, English to speakers of other languages (ESOL), and special education. Castellano has edited three books on understanding our most able students from diverse backgrounds; written and/or edited multiple chapters, articles, and monographs in the field; and serves on the editorial boards of the *Journal of Advanced Academics* (JoAA), *Journal for the Education of the Gifted* (JEG), and *Roeper Review*. He also has served as principal investigator and professional development consultant on a number of Javits grants. Castellano continues to consult with school districts across the county on the inclusion of low-income, culturally, and linguistically diverse students in gifted education programming. He currently resides in Gettysburg, PA, where he serves as the Executive Director of Vida Charter School, a K–6 dual-language Spanish/English immersion program with a significant gifted student population.

# About the Contributors

**Erik M. Francis, M.Ed., M.S.,** has been an educator for more than 15 years, working as a middle and high school English teacher, a site administrator, and an education program specialist in the Title I unit of the Arizona Department of Education, where he trained school leaders in developing Title I schoolwide and targeted assistance programs. He is the owner of Maverik Education LLC, providing consultation to K–12 district and charter schools in the development of Title I programs and professional development focusing on implementing the Common Core State Standards, balancing traditional and differentiated instruction, and teaching literacy across the curriculum. His professional development trainings have been featured at regional, state, and national education conferences. He lives in Phoenix with his wife, who is a third-grade teacher, and has three daughters.

**Bryn Harris, Ph.D.,** is an assistant professor at the University of Colorado at Denver in the School Psychology program. She is also a bilingual licensed psychologist in the state of Colorado and a Nationally Certified School Psychologist. Dr. Harris received her doctorate in school psychology from Indiana University where she conducted research with the Center for Evaluation and Education Policy on underrepresented gifted populations. Her current research interests include investigating identification practices that improve ELL entrance and success in gifted programming, culturally and linguistically responsive bilingual assessment practices, and strategies for increasing school practitioner's multicultural compentencies.

**Linda Iza, M.A.,** is an independent consultant and a Certified Trainer with the WIDA Consortium. She works with educators across the nation focusing on best practices and differentiation for English learners. Prior to working as an independent consultant, Linda taught in the mainstream and ESL classrooms working with students who were oftentimes both English learners and gifted students and as an ESL school support specialist conducting professional development for educators and coaching teachers in planning, assessing, and reflecting on instruction.

**Vicki K. Krugman, M.Ed.,** is a consultant focusing on gifted education and special populations. She supports districts with implementing and problem solving related to support services for gifted and highly able students. During her career, she taught in classrooms and provided resource services for gifted and highly able students in kindergarten through high school. Additionally, she was an instructional lead teacher in middle school, instructional specialist in high school, and recently retired as Director of Gifted, ESOL, and Migrant Services for Clarke County School District. As Director, Ms. Krugman focused on inclusion in classrooms and identifying strengths of all children followed by seamless services. She has presented at numerous gifted and ESOL conferences, sharing models and strategies for resource services. Ms. Krugman's work includes leading the implementation of a Schoolwide Enrichment Model, a partial dual-language program of Spanish, and other innovative programs to build on the strengths of all students. She has received an award for Teaching with Technology from Georgia Centers for Advanced Telecommunications Technology, and been selected as a Teacher of

Excellence and as Teacher of the Year in the Clarke County School District.

**Paul Matthews, Ph.D.,** is the Assistant Director of the University of Georgia Office of Service-Learning (OSL), where he helps support faculty members, students, and community partners in applying academic skills and knowledge to address community needs and enhance student learning. He holds a Ph.D. in language education, an M.A. in Latin American Studies, and an A.B. in Area Studies and was also a Fulbright Fellow to the University of Passau (Germany). He was previously a faculty member in the University of Georgia's departments of Romance Languages and Language Education, and was Co-Director of the Center for Latino Achievement & Success in Education (CLASE) in the College of Education. He was a Service-Learning Fellow in 2006 and the Office of Service-Learning's Senior Scholar for Faculty Development from 2007–2010, and received Georgia TESOL's professional service award in 2009.

**Bernadette Musetti, Ph.D.,** earned her doctorate from the University of California at Davis and is an associate professor and Director of the Liberal Studies Teacher Preparation Program at Loyola Marymount University in Los Angeles, where she teaches and advises both future and current educators and is involved with curriculum development and innovation. Her professional life has been devoted in large part to the equitable and effective education of English learners.

**Michelle Plaisance, M.Ed.,** holds a master's degree in Teaching English as a Second Language (TESL) from the University of North Carolina in Charlotte. She is currently pursuing her doctorate in urban education, specializing in TESL. Ms. Plaisance has experience as an ESL teacher of elementary-aged English learners and as an instructor for an intensive English program for adults. Her research interests include curriculum differentiation and stratification for young English learners.

**Rob Robertson** is a career educator specializing in second language acquisition, writing development, and ELLs. With more than 20 years of experience, Rob has taught students from kindergarten to college. He has worked both in the United States and Europe as a teacher, program coordinator, educational programs director, adjunct professor, and professional development coordinator. He has also worked extensively with the Arizona Department of Education both as a program specialist and committee lead for the Arizona English Language Learner Assessment. He holds a bachelor's degree in French and English and a master's degree in bilingual and multicultural education. He is currently completing his doctorate in curriculum and instruction with a focus on second language acquisition and writing. Rob resides in Flagstaff, AZ, with his wife and two children.

**Spencer Salas, Ph.D.,** is an assistant professor in TESL in the Department of Middle, Secondary, and K–12 Education at the University of North Carolina at Charlotte. His scholarship has appeared in *The Journal of Basic Writing, TESOL Journal, Bilingual Research Journal, Action in Teacher Education,* and *Community College Review.* In 2008, he was named a New Voice Among Scholars of Color by the National Council of Teachers of English. His most recent work is as coeditor of *Vygotsky in 21st Century Society: Advances in Cultural Historical Theory and Praxis With Non-Dominant Communities,* published by Peter Lang.